Heritage Film Audiences

Heritage Film Audiences

Period Films and Contemporary Audiences in the UK

Claire Monk

Edinburgh University Press

Edinburgh University Press Ltd
22 George Square, Edinburgh

www.euppublishing.com

Typeset in Monotype Ehrhardt
by Servis Filmsetting Ltd, Stockport, Cheshire, and
printed and bound in Great Britain by
CPI Antony Rowe, Chippenham and Eastbourne

A CIP record for this book is available from the British Library

ISBN 978 0 7486 3824 6 (hardback)

Contents

List of Appendices

Acknowledgements

This book has had a protracted genesis by any standards, due to some circumstances too mundane, and others too personal, to impose on readers here. The development of the Heritage Audience Survey which forms its primary source, and the inspiration and completion of the book itself, would not have been possible without the help and support of many individuals and several institutions in many ways. If I have forgotten to thank anyone, please consider yourself included in my general acknowledgement here.

Thanks are due first to Middlesex University for their studentship in 'Middlebrow Culture, Audiences and Taste', without which the intensive work needed to develop and complete the survey, and to input and analyse its results, would have been near-impossible to undertake. I must express special thanks and appreciation to Francis Mulhern for his patient and civilised supervision of this work, and for his unauthoritarian yet insightful guidance in tutorials which proved to be an enjoyable escape from the pressures of teaching.

At Edinburgh University Press, I would like to thank Sarah Edwards for commissioning this book, and Vicki Donald and colleagues for steering it towards publication. Particular thanks are due to my current employers, the Faculty of Humanities at De Montfort University, for the research-leave award which has greatly eased the process of bringing the manuscript to completion, and to Donatella Spinelli Coleman, Barry Jordan and Alex Rock for their various roles in covering my teaching.

I would like to extend my thanks to the many scholars who have taken an interest in my work on British heritage cinema since my 1994 MA dissertation at the British Film Institute/University of London – in which I rashly argued for the need for this audience study – or whose work has provided inspiration, or who have simply offered kind encouragement. These include Pam Cook and John O. Thompson as my MA supervisors; John Hill and Sarah Street for their longstanding support, not least as external examiners of the epic PhD thesis now streamlined into this book; and Amy Sargeant, Sue Harper, Pamela Church Gibson, Ginette Vincendeau, Richard Dyer, Jeffrey Richards, James Chapman, Margherita Sprio, and friends beyond, for their encouragement at various stages. A particular debt of acknowledgement is owed to Andrew Higson for his extensive contribution to developing the field of scholarship on British heritage cinema, his critical dialogue, and his tolerance in providing an adversarial focus for the working through of my own arguments. I must also thank Martin Barker for his retrospective advice on methodology – hindsight is a wonderful thing – and my colleagues at De Montfort University (you know who you are).

My most substantial thanks and gratitude, however, go to those who made the Heritage Audience Survey possible: above all, the National Trust members and *Time Out* readers who gave up their time to participate in the survey – and have thus become the subjects of this book – and the earlier volunteers who tested the pilot. I would like to thank Tom Wengraf for his excellent module in research methods at Middlesex University, and all those individuals whose practical help made it possible to publicise, and find suitable respondents for, the pilot study and the main survey: John Pym, Mary Wood, Nigel Kendall at *Time Out*, Tom Burr and Sue Lewis at the National Trust, and all the National Trust local association secretaries who distributed leaflets about the study to their members.

Last but far from least, I must thank James Bainbridge's team of exceptional vitreo–retinal surgeons at Moorfields Eye Hospital in London, who saved my sight not once but twice during this book's journey from research project to publication.

This book is dedicated with love to Brian Watson, to all the friends I have neglected during the *Heritage Film Audiences* years – and to the memory of my parents, who I hope would have been (as my Dad used to say) 'pleased as punch' with the result.

Introduction

Films (and, in latter decades, television dramas/serials) set in the past have formed a prominent, both economically and culturally important, strand within British moving-image culture since at least the transatlantic success of Alexander Korda's *The Private Life of Henry VIII* in 1933. Indeed, the longstanding visibility of culturally (if not always financially) 'British' period films in the global image market – subsequently joined by the BBC-TV Classic Serial format, which transferred from radio to television as early as the 1950s[1] – has generated a perception of these genres as not merely one of British cinema and television's most reliably popular and exportable strands, but as in some sense *essentially* 'British'.

The history packed into the useful shorthand 'British period screen fictions' is, however, a history of complexities. Its sub-categories encompass not merely the distinction between feature films and TV dramas/serials, but literary adaptations – whether from older novels and plays with once-contemporary settings, including those regarded as 'classics', or from contemporary novels or plays set in the past; narratives based on real historical figures or events, well-known or not; films or dramas which reconstruct a distant historical past versus those set within living memory; productions which claim fidelity to fact, the material culture of the past or the source text versus those which foreground expressive and imaginative licence.

Crosscutting all these subdivisions are complex questions of genre, and the further, vexed, question of the films' 'Britishness' or 'Englishness' – which (in the light of the long-established tension in British film culture between subordination to Hollywood and the desire for cultural self-affirmation) is never a straightforward matter. Since at least the 1930s, we might say that 'British' period-film successes have been framed in critical discourse as projections of 'national' identity; valued in terms of their reception and commercial performance abroad; and often made by non-British personnel with non-British money. This venerable transnational history can be traced through the Hungarian Korda brothers' 1930s–1940s productions at Denham; the European influences shaping Gainsborough Studios' costume melodramas of the 1940s; the decades of BBC and independent television costume dramas co-funded by the US public-service consortium Public Broadcasting Service (PBS) and re-broadcast transatlantically as *Masterpiece Theatre*; the 'English' literary adaptations of the highly international self-styled 'wandering company' Merchant Ivory Productions; and the list of 'British' period-film hits since the 1990s backed by Miramax and other US studios.[2]

The history of British period films can also be mapped, cyclically, in terms of moments or flashpoints of intense vilification (such as the opprobrium directed at the flamboyant, 'unauthentic', Gainsborough melodramas by 1940s critics) as often as triumphalist praise. It is the most recent of these critical flashpoints that forms the starting point for this book, and prompted the audience study presented within it.

The cusp of the 1980s and 1990s saw the crystallisation in the UK of a debate – or, more precisely, a critique – which rapidly came to dominate academic discussion of recent cinematic representations of the past, particularly but not solely in the British context: the critique of so-called 'heritage films' or 'heritage cinema'. As I discuss in Chapter 1, this critique was powerfully shaped by the polarised and combative cultural and political mood fostered in Britain by Margaret Thatcher's Conservative government of the 1980s; and one its key features (particularly in its nascent early 1990s manifestations) was that it was at once highly generalised and explicitly dismissive towards 'heritage films' and their audiences. A varying – and, in many ways, varied – list of critically and commercially successful post-1980 British period films (ranging from the patriotic drama of British 1924 Olympic achievement *Chariots of Fire* to Merchant Ivory Productions' E. M. Forster adaptations *A Room with a View*, *Maurice* and *Howards End*) were cast in this new critical discourse as a unified entity – even a genre – about which monolithic ideological and aesthetic claims could be made. Centrally, the early 1990s critique of 'heritage cinema' took issue with the films' (perceived) preoccupation with bourgeois or upper-class subjects and their meticulous recreation and 'spectacular' display of period settings – particularly the iconography of a property-owning, highly class-specific pastoral 'Englishness' – to argue that such films operated textually–aesthetically in ways that served and naturalised conservative ideologies (and, ultimately, the Thatcherite political 'project').

The negative original intent of the 'heritage film' label can be seen clearly from the various synonyms that preceded it from the late 1980s: 'white-flannel' films, 'MFI films' (an acronym for Merchant–Forster–Ivory, implying formulaic mass-production), and the British director Alan Parker's famous dismissal of 'the Laura Ashley school of filmmaking'.[3] Thus the same critical operation that proposed heritage films as a putative 'new genre' immediately denounced them – in advance of more detailed investigation – as the 'far from imaginary work' of 'directors who know perhaps too well their audiences' expectations' (to quote Cairns Craig, one of the heritage film's most hostile detractors).[4]

Despite the heritage-film critique's highly specific historical, cultural and political – and evidently dismissive – origins, and the unresolved definitional issues these raise around the concept itself, the 1990s and 2000s have seen the term 'heritage cinema' applied ever more widely in the discussion of period films. Indeed, as Andrew Higson notes, it 'seems to have become part of the common sense of film culture'.[5] This disciplinary institutionalisation and wide usage give a superficial impression that the heritage film is a clearly defined, agreed and unproblematic category – even genre. The starting point of this book (as in my earlier textual and contextual work on the heritage film, and debate, since the mid 1990s) is to suggest the opposite.[6] Rather, the popularisation of the term 'heritage film' has been made possible, precisely, via a shift in usage – from an explicitly critical term to a widely accepted, if problematic, genre label applied more neutrally to an ever-widening range of films.

Central to these problems – and the central subject of this book – is the heritage-film debate's neglect of the question of *audiences* and their relationship(s) with period films. The very notion – and certainly the critique – of heritage cinema have depended upon a range of spoken and unspoken (and, as we have seen, largely negative) conjectures about period-film audiences and their political–cultural orientation towards 'heritage films'. Yet concrete consideration of these audiences and their tastes and attitudes – particularly, but not only, in the form of qualitative empirical study – has until now been absent.

This absence is, of course, not unconnected with the unavoidable limitations of textual methodologies. Moreover, the heritage-film critique's initial dependence on these is unremarkable, given the history of Film Studies as a discipline which, in contrast with British Cultural Studies and Media Studies (both of which began to engage in empirical audience studies early in their development), had, until the mid-1990s, concerned itself centrally with the workings of texts and left the study of 'real' audiences to its sister disciplines – not solely because of the practical and methodological difficulties of empirical approaches.[7] Against this background, work engaging empirically with audiences from within Film Studies has been a relatively recent phenomenon, much of it spurred by the discipline's wider methodological reappraisals since the 1990s. The body of work in film-audience studies remains small, and much of it post-dates the beginnings of the heritage-film debate – and, indeed, the research design for this study.

However, heritage-film criticism's neglect of audiences and their perspectives is also a symptom and product of the particular genesis and top-down perspective of the critique itself. 'Heritage films' were established from the outset as a 'genre' defined by those who expressly sought to distance themselves from both the films and their audiences – both of which were viewed with political and cultural disapprobation at best. Paradoxically, one of the critique's declared aims was to offer insights into 'how [the films'] representation [of the national past] works for contemporary spectators'.[8] But in practice this 'reception perspective' was constructed from textual generalisations, supplemented in some later work by analysis of media reception discourses.

Heritage-film scholarship's assumptions about the nature and tastes of the heritage-film audience are succinctly summarised by Andrew Higson as follows:

> Heritage films operate very much at the culturally respectable, quality end of the market, and are key players in the new British art cinema . . . Their audience is primarily middle-class, and significantly older than the mainstream film audience, and they appeal to a film culture closely allied to English literary culture and to the canons of good taste.[9]

Possible complexities or differentiations within this projected audience, however, were not explored; and the perspectives of the audiences who paid to see 'heritage films', and presumably enjoyed them, were simply not canvassed. Heritage-film scholarship has, thus – until now – remained largely untouched by the growing interest in audiences and audience perspectives gaining force within academic Film Studies since the mid-1990s.

The goal of this book is to address, by empirical means, this scholarly lacuna around the audiences who watch and enjoy so-called 'heritage films'. In doing so, *Heritage Film Audiences* seeks to offer a corrective to the top-down, textually derived projection of the films' spectators, and to consider and test the heritage-film critique's core claims about the ideological nature and textual workings of 'heritage' period films with reference to the identities, viewing habits, tastes, perspectives and testimonies of their actual audiences. At the very least, it presents forms of empirical substantiation and counter-evidence that introduce new complexities into the debate.

My core primary source for this purpose is the Heritage Audience Survey: a questionnaire-based study, custom-designed and conducted in the late 1990s (as I discuss in Chapter 2, a crucial juncture in the evolution of both the heritage film and the surrounding debate) to generate an analysis of the demographic characteristics and social identities, film-viewing habitus, film tastes and wider attitudes of 92 members of the UK audience(s) for period films. Survey participants were drawn from two highly contrasting sections of this audience: the predominantly young readership of the (sexually liberal and, traditionally, left-leaning) London listings magazine *Time Out*, and the older membership of the National Trust's UK local Associations and Centres. The detailed findings of this survey form the core of the analysis presented in this book.

As we will see in later chapters, these two groups of respondents differed radically in numerous ways; but they nevertheless shared a common enjoyment of many of the British period films regarded as core 'heritage films' by most scholars and critics. As the aim was to access audience members with a strong enthusiasm for – or other strong views about – period films, the participants were, unavoidably, self-selecting. The resulting study therefore has the status of a snapshot – albeit a very detailed one – of identities, tastes and attitudes among those respondents who volunteered from the targeted sections of the period-film audience. It does not claim to present a statistically or sociologically 'representative' sampling of 'the' UK audience for heritage films – but, indeed, one of the questions this book pursues is that of whether a cohesive 'heritage-film audience' can be said to exist.

Chapter 1 sets out the detail of the key arguments around 'heritage cinema' – particularly in the British cinematic and critical context – to which the audience study that forms the remainder of the book responds. It begins by situating the heritage-film critique historically, charting its origins and emergence in relation to the context and mood of late-1980s Thatcherite Britain – origins which raise questions about the critique's continuing applicability to a constantly evolving field of period films and the profoundly changed political, cultural, and globalised industrial conditions in which they are produced and circulated in the 1990s and 2000s. The chapter then explores in some detail the central claims, arguments and assumptions which solidified in the early 1990s into what has become the dominant academic critique of heritage cinema. I identify and discuss the problems of this critique – with particular reference to the question of audiences, and related questions of gender and identity politics – and explore the criticisms and responses it prompted from a broad range of critics and scholars, generating a body of – often – revisionist critical work on heritage films which has pluralised the field as well as expanding it. In closing, the chapter summarises the main lines of development in the broader heritage-film debate in Britain since the mid-1990s.

As Chapter 1 will show, while critical interpretations of, and approaches to, heritage films have multiplied, the bulk of this work remains, to date, predominantly text- (and, more recently, context-)focused in its methodologies – making this book the first study to engage directly, empirically and in detail with 'real' heritage film audiences. Chapters 2 to 8 respond to this task by investigating the contemporary UK audiences for period films – and, specifically, the Heritage Audience Survey participants – from a range of perspectives and using a mix of approaches. Chapter 2 describes the development, design, methodological rationale and practicalities (and limitations) of the

Heritage Audience Survey itself, including an account of my research hypotheses and the ways in which these informed considerations such as the sourcing of survey respondents and the information sought via the questionnaire.

As the Cultural Studies scholar Tony Bennett observed many years ago, 'the process of reading is not one in which reader and text meet as abstractions, but rather one in which an intertextually organised reader meets an intertextually organised text.'[10] In view of the centrality of class ideologies and matters of class culture, the wider components of identity and the formation of middlebrow 'good taste' to the heritage-film debate and its assumptions about audiences, a defining feature of *Heritage Film Audiences* is that it is as interested in the 'intertextual organisation' of the audience members it studies as it is in their readings and uses of heritage films. In accordance with this, the analysis of the survey findings presented in Chapters 3 to 7 – on which conclusions are drawn in Chapter 8 – addresses four broad areas.

Chapter 3 analyses in detail the demographic backgrounds of respondents and a wider range of indicators of identity, with some comparative reference to the demographics of the wider 1990s UK cinema audience (and the thinner existing evidence on the demographics of UK audiences for specific period films) as established in the limited publicly available industry sources. The chapter identifies the distinguishing features of the two sub-samples, highlighting those most resonant in relation to the heritage-film debate, and those of likely relevance in interpreting and understanding respondents' particular tastes, orientations and attitudes in relation to period films. Mindful of the very specific links between class fraction, class identity and educational capital on the one hand, and 'cultural capital', cultural preferences and taste formations on the other, as suggested and demonstrated in Pierre Bourdieu's work on the sociology of taste,[11] my analysis in this chapter takes an interest in a varied range of indicators of respondents' identities – from self-reported sexual orientation to minutiae of schooling, university types, qualifications in fields possible relevance to an interest in literary adaptations and heritage films, and occupational cultures.

Chapter 4 considers the general contours of respondents' cinemagoing and film-viewing habits – or more precisely, to borrow Bourdieu's term, as I shall do in this analysis, their film habitus: their defining sets of cultural practices in relation to the cinematic and domestic viewing and consumption of films. The interests of this chapter include respondents' frequency of cinemagoing and viewing of films in other media, the relative place of commercial and art-cinema venues within their habitus – and, indeed, whether they saw films at the cinema at all (which a significant contingent of older respondents in the National Trust sub-sample did not).

Chapter 5 follows this with an exploration of the specifics of respondents' tastes in films: both in general and – in more detail – with reference to period films. This exploration establishes profoundly contrasting patterns between the *Time Out* and National Trust sub-samples in terms of their breadth of film familiarity, adventurousness of viewing, and the specifics of their tastes. One interest of this analysis is to establish the extent to which specific sections of the 'heritage-film audience' are, or are not, keyed into the wider film culture. Notwithstanding their ostensibly 'uncinematic' characteristics, were heritage films enjoyed in the context of popular cinema tastes by some respondents, or as part of a more informed, cinephilic habitus by others? Or were they indeed a niche taste, enjoyed in isolation from the wider cinema?

Chapters 6 and 7 turn to respondents' self-worded testimonies to explore what these – and wider survey evidence – revealed about their viewing positions, attitudes and expectations in relation to period films (including heritage films), and their dispositions and orientations in relation to a variety of critical questions around the 'heritage film'. Respondents were invited to express their views in their own words in response to open questions asking *what* they most enjoyed, or did not enjoy, about the period films they watched. This analysis also draws upon two multiple-choice elements in the survey questionnaire: a list of twenty-eight pre-suggested 'pleasures' which respondents might hypothetically find in period films, and a list of seventy-four attitude statements, expressing a range of views, opinions or positions in relation to period films, 'quality' literary adaptations, and the suppositions of existing discourses around these – both the promotional, pro-heritage-film discourses of conservative 1980s media coverage, and the critical discourses of academic heritage-film criticism. The listed 'pleasures' and the attitude statements were formulated with direct reference to the ideologies, arguments, counter-arguments and hypotheses in circulation in these pre-existing discourses, and tested and refined during piloting.

Chapter 8 draws together the most significant points to emerge from the preceding analysis of the 'heritage film audience(s)' and considers their implications – not least, but also not solely, for the debate around heritage cinema. Its discussion of these implications is focused around questions of the coherence and distinct(ive)ness of the 'heritage film audience' (or audiences); the related question of how far respondents exhibited a *self*-identity as period-film viewers; third, the question of respondents' levels of consciousness or self-consciousness in relation to the heritage-film debate itself; and, last, the question of audience autonomy: how far were respondents able to produce their own distinct audience discourses around period films?

The progression of the analysis presented in *Heritage Film Audiences* can be summarised, very broadly, in terms of a movement from a sociological focus on the composition and identities of period-film audiences; via questions of cultural (pre-)disposition, film consumption practices and film tastes; to a more interpretative reading of the 'texts' presented by respondents' views and attitudes – and the forms of words in which they expressed these – and, ultimately, their cultural–political positioning in relation to period films. My methodologies move, in other words, between the quantitative and the qualitative, between the analysis of statistical patterns (whether in the specifics of educational capital or respondents' film tastes) and the textual interpretation of respondents' own statements about what they enjoyed, or disliked, in the period films they watched.

Given the small, self-selecting sample studied, it would be imprudent for *Heritage Film Audiences* to claim to be anything other than a 'qualitative' study. Its approach is nevertheless more eclectic – and its interests, at times, more 'social-scientific' – than this label might suggest. In a further disclaimer, I should stress that it is a study whose primary interest is in the place of audiences in relation to the heritage-film debate. My motivating interest has been in what empirical audience-investigation methods might bring to an existing – and, hitherto, far from audience-centred – critical debate rather than in audience-study methodology itself. This study differs, however, from some of the recent British work in film-audience studies in that it takes an interest in statistical patterns and sociological traits as well as in the discourses respondents articulate or reproduce in their self-worded testimony.[12]

While this eclecticism of interests and methods may at times strike the reader as overambitious or unwise, my aim has been, precisely, to bring a variety of forms of evidence and analysis to bear on the investigation of a stereotyped and denigrated, yet hitherto unstudied, audience (or, more accurately, as we shall see, audiences). One of the study's most striking insights is that both the National Trust and *Time Out* 'audiences' for heritage films were drawn from similar strata of the middle classes; and both exhibit taste formations which can persuasively be interpreted in relation to these origins. Yet, as the reader will discover, these taste formations, and the cultural–political logic underlying them, were profoundly different. A recurrent phrase across many respondents' replies was that period films bring history – or, for some, a favourite book – 'to life'; but, in writing this, they often meant very different things. My hope is that this book likewise succeeds in 'bringing to life' the diversity and complexities of the audiences who watch heritage films.

NOTES

1. The term 'serial' (as opposed to series) denotes a multi-episode television drama in which a single narrative is dramatised (or a single novel adapted) across a finite number of episodes. For sources on the genesis of the BBC 'Classic Serial', see Chapter 2, Note 8.
2. For a case study of the US distribution and reception of *The Private Life of Henry VIII*, see Street, 'Stepping westward', and (on a wider range of case studies) Street,

Transatlantic Crossings. On Gainsborough's period melodramas, see Harper, 'Historical pleasures', and (on their European influences) Cook, *Fashioning the Nation*, pp. 80–91.

3. The label 'white-flannel films' has been credited to the *New York Times* critic Janet Maslin (see Kerr, 'Janet Maslin'). For an example of wider (and UK) adoption, see Lyttle, 'Knights in white flannel'. 'The Laura Ashley school of filmmaking' originated in a caption to one of Alan Parker's cartoons, reproduced in Parker, *Making Movies*, and also in Higson, *English Heritage, English Cinema*, p. 68.

4. Craig, 'Rooms without a view', p. 3.

5. Higson, 'The heritage film and British cinema', p. 232.

6. For details of this earlier work, see Chapter 1 and the Bibliography. My involvement in the heritage-film debate began in 1994 with Monk, *Sex, Politics and the Past* [unpublished MA dissertation]. My methodologies in this were textual and critical; but my conclusion rashly called for the study of actual period-film audiences – hence the project summarised in this book. As textual analyses of exemplary 'heritage films', and contextual analysis of the UK journalistic/media discourses surrounding them, can be found in the copious existing literature (including my own earlier publications), *Heritage Film Audiences* does not replicate these methods.

7. Film Studies, initially defined as a discipline by the particular theoretical mix of 1970s Screen Theory, was founded on a deep mistrust of empirical approaches, resulting in a notoriously abstract theoretical approach to the film 'spectator'.

8. Higson, 'Re-presenting the national past', p. 109.

9. Ibid., p. 110.

10. Bennett, 'The Bond phenomenon', quoted in Jenkins, 'Reception theory and audience research', p.166.

11. Bourdieu, *Distinction*.

12. For some examples of such work, see Chapter 2, Note 5.

CHAPTER I

The Heritage Film Debate: From Textual Critique to Audience

HERITAGE FILM CRITICISM AND THE CULTURAL POLITICS OF THE THATCHER ERA

To understand the particularities of the heritage-film critique in relation to its speculative projection of the films' audiences and its problematic conception of the film–audience relationship – and the consequent issues which a study of the actual audiences for period films should explore – it is necessary to understand something of the specific British cultural–political climate from which the debate – and the concept of the 'heritage film' itself – emerged in the late 1980s to early 1990s. As my detailed work 'historicising' the heritage-film idea in relation to this context is presented in earlier publications, this chapter limits itself to a selective digest.[1]

Of particular significance is the tension between (on the one hand) the use of the term 'heritage film' as a quasi-genre label following its academic institutionalisation; and (on the other) the specific, polarised 1980s British cultural–political climate (overwhelmingly coloured by Thatcherite Conservatism and vehement left and liberal opposition to it) which forged the *critique* of heritage cinema. As noted in my earlier work, this critique first emerged 'as a deferred [rather than immediate or spontaneous] response from the academic/intellectual left to certain British period films produced or released since the early 1980s – at the height of Thatcherism – and argued to be ideologically complicit with it'; and its mobilisation of the term 'heritage film' – or contemporary synonyms – was 'openly pejorative and dismissive'.[2] Although the anti-heritage-film stance was, from the outset, a top-down position – defined by self-distanciation from both the films and their audiences – it was not an exclusively left-wing one. It first emerged journalistically, from 1987–8 onwards, in periodicals addressing cinephiles, cultured intellectuals and/or the left (particularly the *New Statesman* and the late London listings magazine *City*

Limits); but a very similar discourse was evident among some critics writing for publications (such as the *Spectator*) associated with the Conservative right, and others aligned with culturally elitist, even aristocratic, perspectives.[3]

The *term* 'heritage film' had in fact been coined by the British cinema historian Charles Barr in 1986, with reference not to the 1980s but to patriotic British films of the 1940s – not all set in past historical periods – which had drawn upon aspects of the 'national heritage', such as Laurence Olivier's *Henry V* (intriguingly, a very popular film among some of the older participants in my own Heritage Audience Survey). Barr's coinage was, moreover, more descriptive than denunciatory, despite the fact that some of his named 1940s 'heritage films' were state-sponsored propaganda, which the 1980s and 1990s heritage films were not.[4]

The emergence of anti-heritage-film criticism in the UK was doubtless, in part, a reaction against the media saturation surrounding the transatlantic success of *A Room with a View* and its jingoistic coverage in mid-market Conservative newspapers such as the *Daily Mail*.[5] In its more developed and academic manifestations, it was also strongly influenced by a then-recent cluster of much-debated books and articles – centrally, those of Patrick Wright and Robert Hewison – criticising the philistine cultural (non-)policy of the Thatcher government and particularly the National Heritage Acts of 1980 and 1983. The Acts legislatively formalised Thatcherism's official promotion of a heritage industry, defined in terms that commodified and commercially exploited the landscapes and private built properties of the past.[6] For Wright and his contemporaries, the activities of the conservation lobby and bodies like the National Trust in preserving the *private* property of the *upper* classes had the hegemonic effect of constructing and maintaining a particular dominant conception of the national past – or national heritage – which, it was argued, worked to naturalise public acceptance of the values and interests of the propertied classes as *national* values and the *national* interest.[7] Hewison echoed these concerns, but also explicitly linked the official promotion of commodified heritage to the Thatcher government's aversion to public funding for the contemporary arts (particularly, he suggested, work which engaged critically with the present).

As argued in my earlier work, however, one of the most decisive contextual influences on the formation of the heritage-film critique was the political viciousness of 1980s Britain and the extent to which this permeated the cultural sphere.[8] By the late 1980s, the Thatcher government's friends in the media had defined both the British political landscape and the field of British cultural production – including film – in highly combative terms. The critic Graham Fuller went so far as to suggest that a 'climate of censorship [was] stifling the basic democratic of thought and information'.[9]

In January 1988, British films joined 'the chattering classes' (liberal intelligentsia) and any 'luminaries of [the] intellectual and cultural establishment' who had the nerve to voice opposition to government policies as the latest target of orchestrated attack from the New Right media.[10] The *Sunday Times* published 'Through a lens darkly': a lengthy – and clearly strategically commissioned – essay by the right-wing Oxford historian Norman Stone in which he attacked six recent (and very varied) low-budget British films set in the present, all of which he condemned as 'worthless and insulting' and 'riddled with left-wing bias'.[11] As Fuller rightly noted, Stone's attack 'reeked of provocation' – and the British media duly gave extensive coverage to the inevitable acrimony it provoked. But, more than this, 'Through a lens darkly' was only one of a series of 'sustained attempts to marginalise the Left' by the 1980s pro-Thatcher British press, in which 'far more was clearly at stake than the critical fate of six British movies.'[12]

The films that would shortly be denounced as 'heritage films' were barely mentioned by Stone, but his penultimate paragraph briefly praised three recent 'very good films of a traditional kind' which 'show what can be done': John Boorman's *Hope and Glory*, Lean's *A Passage to India* and Ivory's *A Room with a View*.[13] The targets of Stone's attack and their supporters were not slow to link these choices with his political agenda – nor to find it significant that all three were set in the past. Hanif Kureishi (the author–screenwriter of *My Beautiful Laundrette* and *Sammy and Rosie Get Laid*), writing in fury, drew no distinction between the three films, nor between Lean's and Ivory's Forster adaptations (which on their release had been perceived very differently by critics),[14] denouncing both as 'stories of the overdressed English abroad . . . glamourised [sic] travesties of novels by the great E. M. Forster'.[15]

As such comments illustrate, much of the left's reaction to Stone's fell into the trap of inverting the right's binary and reductive generalisations rather than dismantling them. The response of the director Derek Jarman, whose despairing, Blakean apocalyptic vision in *The Last of England* was a core target of Stone's diatribe (the article's main illustration was a full-page-width still from the film captioned 'Sick scenes from English life'), presents a rare exception to this pattern. Jarman's comments remain highly pertinent – not least to the project of rethinking the debates around heritage and post-heritage cinema – for his challenge to Stone's and the Conservatives' right to appropriate the values of 'tradition' and 'history' in support of their own political agendas. Jarman's response was to reclaim these same values for his own films and cultural lineage – and hence, by implication, for an alternative 'tradition' of dissent and resistance (with authentic roots in English history):

I have been around now [making films] for two decades, so I am part of history . . . hardly an avant-garde filmmaker at the age of 46. I have made six films. Shakespeare has been the inspiration for two of them . . . I have also directed a film on the Baroque painter Caravaggio . . . My cinema has

tradition and history; it is not just a trite reflection of the political divide
. . . I would suggest that I am the traditionalist and the responsible one
and Stone is the yahoo.[16]

Unfortunately it was the binaristic approach, rather than Jarman's, that shaped
the emerging critique of the heritage film. In a political climate in which it had
become necessary to defend films set in the present or featuring working-class
protagonists robustly, a counter-reaction emerged from the left in which films
set in the past – particularly those with a focus on the comfortable middle or
upper classes – were uniformly cast as politically conservative bad objects.
Despite its nominally more sophisticated concerns, the heritage-film critique
internalised this simplistic politics of class representation, generating a reactive, undifferentiated and often reductive analysis.

THE ACADEMIC CRITIQUE

The crystallisation of anti-heritage-film discourse into an academic critique
dates from 1991, the publication year of two articles – by Cairns Craig and
Tana Wollen respectively – both presenting arguments essentially similar to
those which would be developed further by Andrew Higson two years later in
1993.[17] While Higson's article was the first to apply the *term* 'heritage cinema'
to the group of films under discussion, the analysis presented across all three
texts shows close similarities which justify a collective discussion of them here
as the founding texts of 'the heritage-film critique'. There are nevertheless significant distinctions to be drawn between the three texts in terms of their tone,
publication context, breadth of focus, and the depth and care of the analysis
presented.

Craig's 'Rooms without a view' – published as *Sight & Sound*'s cover
feature, with a supporting editorial from its new editor Philip Dodd, shortly
after the magazine's relaunch as a full-colour monthly[18] – was an overtly
polemical attack on just four films: the E. M. Forster adaptation *Where Angels
Fear to Tread* (from Derek Granger and Charles Sturridge, the producer-
director team behind Granada Television's lavish 1981 dramatisation of
Evelyn Waugh's novel *Brideshead Revisited*); Merchant Ivory Productions'
more successful 1980s Forster adaptations *A Room with a View* and *Maurice*;
and Sturridge/Granger's feature film adaptation of Waugh's *A Handful of
Dust*. Craig's piece became a prototype for anti-heritage-film criticism, but its
sneering tone and parodic generalisations made it a highly problematic one.
Indeed, the literary scholar Alison Light was quick to condemn his reading
of the Forster adaptations as puritanical, inaccurate and 'lordly towards their
audiences'.[19]

Wollen's and Higson's articles, by contrast, both presented wider-ranging, more politically contextualised and more developed analyses: Wollen's within a multidisciplinary collection on the dynamics between enterprise, heritage and nation in Thatcherite culture and policy,[20] Higson's in a collection on British cinema and Thatcherism.[21] Wollen's analysis differed further from Craig's and Higson's in that she focused on 'nostalgic screen fictions' – a category that encompassed British prestige period television drama serials, such as *Brideshead Revisited* and *The Jewel in the Crown*, as well as feature films. Both writers nevertheless shared Craig's distaste for, and political suspicion of, heritage 'screen fictions', and their analyses accordingly displayed many of the same assumptions, slippages of argument and reductive binarisms. Of the three, only Higson has continued to engage in the debate throughout its subsequent evolution, including refinements to and revisions of his 1993 position in response to criticisms.[22]

All three critics defined heritage cinema as a distinct field by offering a list of disapproved films (or, for Wollen, 'nostalgic screen fictions'), followed (in Wollen's and Higson's work) by shorter lists of counter-example approved films. The latter choices were either 'set firmly in the present [in a] post-imperialist and/or working-class Britain'[23] and perceived as realist, socially critical and/or politically engaged; or were held to engage more authentically or critically with historical reality, usually because they were set in a regional or working-class past. Thus the heritage film was defined negatively, and in binary terms.

The disapproved 'heritage' films or dramas, in contrast, were typically set in a 'national past' which was English, southern, bourgeois or upper-class, 'essentially pastoral',[24] and relatively recent – usually from the Victorian era to the pre-World War II decades of the twentieth century. Most – but by no means all – were period fictions rather than dramatisations of real historical events, frequently adapted from 'classic' English literary sources, but typically those which were already popular and widely known. Generalisations on this point are, however, problematic given that some of the most widely recognised and exportable British 'heritage' films of the 1980s and 1990s have had biographical and/or historically based narratives, whether original screenplays – from *Chariots of Fire* (script by Colin Welland) to *Mrs Brown* (John Madden, UK/USA/Ireland, 1997, script by Jeremy Brock) – or stage adaptations, as with *Another Country* or *The Madness of King George* (adapted by Julian Mitchell and Alan Bennett respectively from their own plays). As – notably irreverent – royal biopics, *Mrs Brown*, *The Madness of King George* (focusing on Queen Victoria and George III respectively) and Shekhar Kapur's more boldly revisionist 1998 *Elizabeth* also belonged to a period sub-genre established in British cinema since (at least) *The Private Life of Henry VIII* in 1933.[25] They thus stand as one of several such examples which raise unresolved questions about how, and where, the 'heritage film' should be conceived as intersecting with existing (sub-)genres defined by their subject-matter or source material rather than ideology.

Certain core 'heritage' films and television dramas recurred consistently in these lists.[26] In particular, there was unanimity that the core exemplars of heritage filmmaking were the three E. M. Forster adaptations made by the producer-director team Ismail Merchant and James Ivory (Indian Muslim and Californian respectively), usually with their long-term screenwriting collaborator Ruth Prawer Jhabvala (of German and Polish Jewish parentage via north London, and married to an Indian): *A Room with a View*, *Maurice*[27] and *Howards End*. More recent lists of heritage films have, of course, been able to add the trio's later adaptations of *The Remains of the Day* (from Kazuo Ishiguro's 1989 novel set in the 1930s) and *The Golden Bowl* (USA/France/UK, 2000, from Henry James's 1904 novel).

Despite the construction of Merchant–Ivory–Jhabvala as key heritage auteurs, however, their 1979–84 period literary adaptations immediately prior to *A Room* – *The Europeans* and *The Bostonians*, both adapted from Henry James; *Quartet* (adapted from Jean Rhys, a tale of polymorphous manipulation and desire in 1920s Paris); and *Heat and Dust* (from Jhabvala's own novel, intercutting between the British Raj and 1980s contemporary India) – rarely feature in such lists. All four achieved significant success with critics and art-house audiences in the USA and UK. What they lacked, however, was the more pronounced (art-to-mainstream) crossover and (UK-to-USA) transatlantic success of *A Room* (and, subsequently, *Howards End*) – or the triumphalist UK media saturation of the mid-1980s onwards that began to construct Merchant Ivory's English literary adaptations in *heritage* terms as (British) *national* triumphs.

The film most consistently cited by anti-heritage critics as a positive counter-example was *My Beautiful Laundrette*. The counter-example films set in *the past* proposed by Higson, Wollen and others have, by contrast, been inconsistent and even mutually contradictory. Tana Wollen acknowledged no distinction between the pre-World War II, upper-class dramas of *Brideshead Revisited* or *Another Country* and wartime or post-war narratives focusing on upper-working-class or lower-middle-class characters in very ordinary milieux such as *Hope and Glory* or *Dance with a Stranger* (a biopic of Ruth Ellis, the last woman to be hanged in Britain), but singled out Terence Davies's *Distant Voices, Still Lives* as a sole exception which 'interrogates and resists the nostalgia that memory makes too easily of the past'.[28] Higson, conversely, contrasted *Hope and Glory*, *Dance with a Stranger*, *Wish You Were Here* and additionally *Scandal* – as well as *Distant Voices* – with the bourgeois heritage film on the grounds that they 'concentrate on the everyday lives and memories of "ordinary people" . . . to some extent democratizing the genre'.[29] More recently and in contradiction, the American film historian Marcia Landy has classified *Dance with a Stranger* and *Scandal* as heritage films.[30]

Scandal usefully illustrates heritage-film criticism's tendency to generalise rather than attending to the detail of individual cases. A factually scrupulous but tonally irreverent dramatisation of the 1963 'Profumo affair' which brought down the British Conservative government of the day, it was explicitly marketed on its UK release in 1989 (the penultimate year of Margaret Thatcher's final term as Prime Minister, and a period of escalating unpopularity for her government) an anti-Tory film. It was thus neither heritage nostalgia nor concerned with 'everyday lives' and 'ordinary people'. Such inconsistencies of definition reveal persisting unclarities about what a heritage film is – and which films are heritage films – which become acute when the discussion extends into more complex and contested territory.

We can usefully distinguish films (such as *Scandal* or *Dance with a Stranger*) set in, or remembering, the more recent, post-World War II past – broadly speaking, the past of living memory – from period films/genres set in more distant decades or centuries by referring to the former as 'retro films'. The 'retro film' encompasses both biopics – which Sarah Street has identified as the other dominant period genre of 1980s–1990s British cinema alongside the heritage film – and a further closely intersecting category proposed by Phil Powrie, the 'alternative heritage' film.[31] By 'alternative heritage', Powrie broadly means fiction films set in the period during or after World War II – but, most particularly, those that 'focus on and frequently aestheticise the working class or the lower middle class rather than the upper middle class of "bourgeois heritage"'.[32] The 'retro film' classification will be used in later chapters when I discuss the specific patterns of film taste that emerged among participants in the Heritage Audience Survey.

Institutionally and in their audience address and aesthetics, heritage films were said to 'operate primarily as middle-class quality products', made and circulated with an 'emphasis on authorship, craft and artistic value'.[33] Higson later located them (more correctly) as 'crossover' films, circulated and received somewhere between the commercial and art cinema.[34] However, the equation of the heritage film with 'quality' carried a negative force, connoting aesthetic conservatism (and, for some commentators, a punning second connotation, since 'the quality' had once been a common British term for the upper classes). Insofar as directors such as James Ivory favoured techniques that produced a relatively static 'pictorialist' style rather than making the fullest use of the *moving* image – long takes, slow, smooth camera movement, and narratively unmotivated crane and high-angle shots 'divorced from character point of view'[35] – the films were regarded as uncinematic. Their claims to 'quality' therefore rested precisely *not* on their qualities as cinema, but on a second-hand affiliation with 'high' literary and theatrical culture which was presumed to appeal to audiences by flattering their snobberies and sense of cultural distinction.

The heritage film was, however, defined by its critics centrally in terms of a particular aesthetic approach to the visualisation of the past – to be precise, the *material world* of the past – which was implied to distinguish the films clearly from their precursors (in the British context, period films made before the Thatcher era). For Richard Dyer and Ginette Vincendeau, the heritage film was 'characterised above all by a museum look: apparently meticulous period accuracy, but clean, beautifully lit, and clearly on display'.[36] It was held to be characterised, too, by an analogously reverent approach to the adaptation – indeed, the *display* – of 'classic' literary sources. Whether the 'already canonic cultural properties adapted for the screen' were English literary classics or English country houses, heritage films were held to adopt a particular position – and, by implication, promote a particular *viewing* position – in relation to them which Andrew Higson summarised as the 'discourse of authenticity': 'the desire to establish the adaptation . . . as an authentic reproduction of the original'.[37]

Here, Higson articulates the pivotal concepts and claims of the critique: the heritage film was defined, centrally, by its *aesthetic of display* and its mobilisation of the '*discourse of authenticity*' in relation to both the period mise-en-scène and the literary source. But, more than this, the 'museum' aesthetic – produced, as Dyer and Vincendeau's description suggests, by both the meticulously researched and realised period mise-en-scène, and the film techniques (lighting, framing, cinematography) which place this 'on display' – was argued by Higson to have *consequences*: for the films' narrative functionality, for their ideological workings and – crucially – for the spectator positioning of their audiences.

Despite the centrality of international creative inputs to so many key heritage films, their international circulation and their frequently international funding, the critique conceived of them as a 'genre' centrally engaged in the hegemonic construction of *national* identity. The films were argued to construct a vision of the 'national past' that operated ideologically – by implication, on 'national' audiences within the UK – in ways that served the Thatcherite political and economic project. For Tana Wollen, the very fact that 'so many' screen fictions 'deal[ing] with the past' had been produced in the 1980s 'suggests that it has been difficult to make British fictions about the present' (a conclusion that would have surprised Norman Stone). More insidiously, she argued, in the combative decade of the 1982 Falklands/Malvinas war and the 1984 Miners' Strike, these period screen fictions had served a 'wider enterprise': 'the reconstruction of national identity' and a concomitant 'disavowal of the coercion used to forge national unity'.[38]

To understand how the Forster adaptations *A Room with a View* or *Maurice* – notable for their lack of gung-ho nationalism or militarism, adapted from novels renowned for their liberal social and sexual critiques, and likely to be enjoyed by audiences as romance, social comedy and/or melodrama – let alone retro films focusing on 'ordinary people' such as *Wish You Were Here* or *Dance with a Stranger* – could be claimed to contribute to the powerfully hegemonic operation Wollen proposes, we must attend to the detail of the ideological–aesthetic argument asserted by Craig and refined by Higson.

Heritage films were argued by Higson to be 'fascinated by the private property, the culture and values' of the bourgeois and upper classes. The point of core importance, however, is that the *aesthetic of display* – the manner in which the private property of the bourgeois or upper classes was styled and presented – was itself held responsible for the films' ideological workings upon (by implication) their audiences. The 'fascination' thus produced was argued to work to transform this *classed* heritage 'into the national heritage'.[39] (At times, however, the critique went further, seeming to suggest that heritage films were insidious simply because they were set in the past.) Accused of reproducing only the seductive surface 'trappings' of this classed past, the films were attacked by Craig as 'film as conspicuous consumption', 'designed to deny everything beyond the self-contained world the characters inhabit'.[40]

As Higson's writings acknowledge in some detail, the underpinning argument here owed much to Wright's and Hewison's critiques of the heritage industry, which in turn owed much to Fredric Jameson's analysis of the commodification of history as 'a characteristic feature of postmodern culture'. For Jameson, postmodernity reduces the past to 'a vast collection of images': a 'version of history [in which] critical perspective is displaced by decoration and display, a fascination with surfaces . . . in which a fascination with style displaces the material dimensions of historical context'.[41] In the context of 1980s concerns about the place of the heritage–enterprise couplet in Thatcherite policy, Hewison was able to argue with some credibility that, by rendering the past as 'an attractively packaged consumer item',[42] the heritage industry promoted false notions of historical reality, substituting surface spectacle for historical understanding. But, given that film is innately a visual – and spectacular – medium, this argument becomes less persuasive when applied without translation to narrative feature films as if they were merely or primarily part of the heritage industry.

The pivotal charge directed at heritage films, however, argued *precisely* that their 'heritage' character overrode any other possible sites of meaning or (by implication) sources of pleasure. Higson fully acknowledged that 'almost all' the story sources adapted in 1980s heritage films 'have some edge to them of satire or ironic social critique' (he meant particularly the Forster and Waugh adaptations denounced by Craig).[43] But the aesthetic of display was argued to work *against* this, 'invit[ing] a nostalgic gaze that resists the ironies and social critiques so often suggested narratively'.[44] The result, Higson argued, was that the films constructed not narrative space but 'heritage space . . . *a space for the display of heritage properties rather than the enactment of dramas*', in which the period spectacle itself became the primary pleasure: in tension with the narrative at best; at worst, neutralising satirical, socio-political or moral concerns.[45]

The following section considers further the problems raised by this critique, with particular reference to its conception of spectatorship and its projection of the heritage-film audience.

FROM TEXTUAL INTERPRETATION TO AUDIENCES

As I noted in 2002, 'the construction of the idea of the "heritage film" is interesting for its entanglement of political criticisms with a gut-level cultural–aesthetic aversion.'[46] A question prompted by – but not addressed in – the early 1990s critique is why films set in the past rather than present – and moreover, often fiction- rather than fact-based – should have become the particular or sole focus of the anxieties expressed by anti-heritage critics. The critique's binarisms had the effect of implying that films set in the present invariably had a working-class or multicultural focus (an implication visibly belied by the huge international success of the Working Title/Richard Curtis upper-middle-class romantic comedy cycle instigated by *Four Weddings and a Funeral* from the mid 1990s), and that films with a working-class focus were invariably politically 'progressive' and innocent of insidious ideological operations. But, of course, as I have discussed in earlier work, both simplifications are fallacious.[47]

Moreover, as Richard Dyer and Ginette Vincendeau, and others, have noted, heritage films themselves have often played a seemingly progressive role – compared to the male-centred and heterosexist norms of mainstream cinema – by 'represent[ing] the lives of women, lesbians and gay men, ethnic minorities and the disabled in the national past'.[48] Indeed, they have frequently made women or gay characters their central protagonists, and are one of the few film genres with a record of giving substantial screen time, character complexity and agency to older women.[49]

The critique's selectivity in these respects, coupled with its negativity towards the pleasures of period mise-en-scène, has led some scholars, including John Hill, to suggest that 'dislike of the heritage film may be linked to a traditional suspicion of texts which primarily appeal to women (or gay men).'[50] The critique's preoccupation with the heritage mise-en-scène solely as a conduit for the workings of ideology disregards the wider range of pleasures and meanings it may hold for the films' actual audiences through its 'sensuousness and . . . iconographic expressivity' – the latter, Richard Dyer has suggested, 'typically requiring the skilled reading of a female spectator'.[51] As John Hill points out, however, there is a risk of such arguments slipping into gender essentialism:

> It is not always evident what follows from [the female appeal of the heritage film]. There is a danger that a conventional (or essentialist) notion of the 'feminine' (an interest in clothes and appearance, for example) is simply validated (or claimed as 'subversive') without a critical inspection of how this 'feminine' appeal is ideologically mobilised.[52]

As Hill also notes – and as Chapter 3 will confirm – the gender balance of UK audiences for period films in fact varies from film to film, and is more strongly female-dominated for some films than others. There is also plentiful evidence for the appeal of some heritage films to gay men, although the extent of this is more difficult to quantify statistically.[53]

A more general and indisputable point to emerge from the debate around the heritage film's gendered pleasures is that the early 1990s critique allowed little space for textual differentiation between individual heritage films, differences of interpretation, or differentiated reception among their audiences. These difficulties can be expressed in terms of three interrelated problems of methodology, which have consequences both for the critique's interpretative construction of the 'heritage film' and for its projection of the heritage-film audience. First, there was the monolithic, generalised nature of the critique itself, which could be achieved only by brushing aside significant textual distinctions between films.[54] Second, the critique's fundamental definition of the heritage 'genre' from a perspective of top-down, self-distancing disapproval (it essentially addressed a community of the likeminded) led it barely to acknowledge the pleasures beyond the heritage mise-en-scène that the films might offer from an audience (or, indeed, popular entertainment) perspective, such as those of narrative, character, performativity, sexuality or humour. Third, there was the critique's dependence on unsubstantiated (and largely inexplicit) conjecture regarding the heritage films' audiences, their cultural–political orientation(s) and their reception of the films.

Some more specific problems arise from these general ones. For example, given the heritage film's international exportability and appeal, it is not self-evident why they would function centrally as vehicles for 'national' messages. The international character of 'British' heritage films (institutionally, financially and – via star casting, for example – even culturally) has, if anything, intensified since the 1990s. But, even in the context of UK reception, this over-privileging of 'the national' – which Alan Lovell has identified as a persistent, yet also 'odd', feature of established critical discourses around British cinema – may tell us more about the concerns of critics than those of audiences.[55]

A further difficulty was that the fixation upon the 'fetishisation of period details',[56] combined with the othering of the audience, shaped a critique which seemed to treat visual pleasure itself as politically suspect. As Raimund Borgmeier rightly observes, there are close affinities between 'this line of criticism' and 'the 1970s distrust of cinema as a source of mere [scopophilic] pleasure' – particularly, he suggests, with Laura Mulvey's famous 1975 argument in 'Visual pleasure and narrative cinema'.[57]

Borgmeier's comparison can usefully be pushed further. In Mulvey's account of how mainstream cinema operates to pleasure the 'male gaze', the 'visual presence' of the fetishised figure of the woman 'tends . . . to freeze the flow of action in moments of erotic contemplation'. In the critical account of how heritage films supposedly operate on a (largely female) audience, the display of 'fetishised' period spectacle clearly takes the place Mulvey accorded to 'the woman'. However, where this heritage spectacle was held to *override* 'narrative space' and narrative meanings (and, presumably, pleasures), Mulvey, in acknowledging that 'mainstream film neatly *combines* spectacle and narrative,' proposed a significantly different narrative–spectacle relationship.[58] She did *not* argue that narrative functionality was disabled by the display of 'the woman'. On the contrary, the male protagonist both 'articulates the look and creates the action' – a sense of mastery (over both narrative and 'the woman') shared by the male-identified spectator.[59]

The critique of heritage cinema, by contrast, assigned the central role in the production of pleasure, meaning and ideology to inanimate elements in the mise-en-scène. Performance, human actors and character identification, although hardly absent as potential pleasures, were assigned no place in this account. Moreover, the nature of the ideological critique implied that the spectator's positioning in relation to this non-human period spectacle was passive. Certainly there was no suggestion that the heritage-film spectator might exercise an active gaze, or experience a sense of mastery or agency (however illusory); rather, the period spectacle was conceived of as acting on the spectator. Whether or not the heritage-film's real audiences were predominantly female, this projection of a staggeringly passive, textually determined spectator certainly positioned them as feminised.

As this analysis suggests, the ideological critique of heritage cinema depended on a discredited textual-determinist model of the film–spectator relationship.[60] Like the theoretical spectator of 1970s Lacanian/Althusserian film theory, the 'audience' of the early 1990s heritage-film critique was really no more than a product of the (supposed) textual operations of the heritage-film 'apparatus'.[61] Moreover, through its undifferentiated conception of the films themselves, the critique conceived of this audience as an undifferentiated mass.

Some further assumptions about the heritage-film audience can be inferred from the critique. First, there are the explicit demographic assumptions that the heritage-film audience is composed of viewers who are middle-class, older than the average mainstream cinemagoer, and predominantly female. Beyond this lie less explicit assumptions. Broadly, the critique assumes that the classed iconography of many heritage films and the aesthetic of display *do* operate ideologically on audiences; that audiences respond to heritage films in terms which fit the ideological–aesthetic reading proposed in the critique; and that they do so uniformly, regardless of their pre-established social identities and views. Perhaps most fundamentally, the critique assumes that audiences do enjoy and engage with heritage films centrally through the 'conspicuous consumption' of period spectacle – regardless of the films' other potential pleasures – and that the 'discourse of authenticity' is as central for audiences as it is to the heritage-film critique. Such assumptions exclude from consideration matters such as patterns of sympathy or identification with (or against) characters; the role of human bodies, behaviour or desires; and the possibility that iconography may perform *narrative* functions in support of meanings excluded by the 'heritage' discursive framework.

All these assumptions are, of course, made without reference to the actual audiences who choose – and pay – to watch and enjoy period films. And, in treating the 'heritage film audience' as an undifferentiated mass, they all share a fundamental problem which illustrates why an empirical study engaging directly with these audiences is needed.

THE EVOLVING DEBATE SINCE THE MID 1990S

As will already be evident, the initial critique of heritage cinema was greeted almost immediately by criticisms, calls for a pluralisation of approaches, and revisionist work producing readings of specific films (or groups of films) from alternative perspectives. As Eckart Voigts-Virchow notes, most of this work has contributed to 'a clear paradigm shift . . . [in which] the early critical obsession with issues of national identity gave way to a more pluralistic agenda focusing on questions of sexual politics and audience'.[62] The easing of the 'cultural cringe' around heritage films has, however, owed as much to the conscious strategic efforts of filmmakers and the industry to revise, rebrand, reinvent and 'modernise' heritage film (and, equally, TV) productions in a climate of heightened (self-)consciousness around the politics of period representation. Some of the 'changes in the heritage film' observed by Pamela Church Gibson can be credited to the politics of individual filmmakers (whether those of Sally Potter or Patricia Rozema, or the class politics prompting Michael Winterbottom to film *Jude*).[63] But other changes – calculated to realign critical, public and industry perceptions and attract expanded and diversified audiences – and prompting some revision of critical attitudes (at least among the British media)

– owe their logic to an increasingly commercialised (and globally aware) British film culture. A further significant contextual change occurred in 1997, when the election victory of Tony Blair's New Labour government ended eighteen years of Conservative rule and brought a significant shift in the policies and ideologies surrounding cultural production and the projection of the nation.[64]

In 1995, I proposed the term 'post-heritage' for films which self-consciously seek to distance themselves from the heritage film's negative/conservative associations via varied strategies that may include an overt, foregrounded 'concern with sexuality and gender, particularly non-dominant gender and sexual identities'; aesthetic self-differentiation from the authenticity and 'restraint' of the 1980s heritage film; adjustments to narrative, character or costume to stress resonances with the present; knowing anachronisms of production design or casting; and a generally self-reflexive approach to style, adaptation and/or the treatment of history.[65]

However, my earlier textual/critical work on *A Room with a View* and *Maurice* had taken its cue from Alison Light to argue for the importance of gender and sexuality to the pleasures and meanings of key heritage films, and to question the evasion of these elements by the early 1990s anti-heritage critics.[66] A broader range of work – starting as early as Finch and Kwietniowski's groundbreaking 1988 article 'Melodrama and *Maurice*' – has focused on feminist and gay concerns, both as themes explored directly within many heritage and post-heritage films and as critical frameworks for their interpretation. Richard Dyer challenged the stereotype of British cinema – and, within this, the heritage film – as emotionally repressed in an analysis that placed *Maurice*, *A Room with a View*, *A Handful of Dust* and the C. S. Lewis biopic *Shadowlands* in a tradition of 'typically English [films], awash with feeling' in which 'concentrated feeling [is] expressed very powerfully through understatement'. More polemically, Jeffrey Richards argued that the 'comprehensive critique of the ethic of restraint, repression and the stiff upper lip' offered by some of the key 1980s British heritage films was 'profoundly subversive'.[67] Many of these concerns are synthesised and taken forward in Julianne Pidduck's monograph *Contemporary Costume Film*, which productively draws together the fields of 'heritage', 'post-heritage' and 'alternative heritage' films to argue that they 'use the frame of the past to dramatise postmodern dilemmas' including 'gendered, class, colonial and queer struggles over representations of the past' and 'love, intimacy and deep feeling in (post)modern times'.[68]

In a distinct (and less widely disseminated) development, Dyer and Ginette Vincendeau's mid-1990s European 'Heritage' Film project sought to clarify definitional issues around the heritage film while expressly conceptualising it as a *European* phenomenon, seeking input from scholars across Europe to build a provisional account of how the 'heritage' – or 'quality' – film was defined and understood in different national cinemas.[69] Conversely, a growing body of work on British heritage cinema from Germany (primarily from British Cultural Studies and English Literary Studies departments) treats the heritage film as an expressly British phenomenon.[70]

The continuing trends in textual work on British period films and/or cycles can be divided into two broad areas. First, critical work has continued within the framework of the heritage-film debate, analysing the significant changes in British period films since the mid-1990s, notably their evolution in directions such as the 'post-heritage' film,[71] and refining the available critical vocabulary by proposing further variations such as the 'alternative heritage' film.[72] The second strand of work pays close textual attention to specific period films and/or television dramas, but gives a new centrality to formalist and aesthetic concerns, while bracketing or breaking free of the earlier heritage-film debate to draw upon a wider field of theory. In this second category can be placed Pidduck's essay on spatiality in 1990s Austen adaptations and the expanded charting of 'the spatial imaginary' of contemporary costume film in her later monograph; those parts of Stella Bruzzi's detailed analysis of film costume concerned with period films; and Sarah Cardwell's study of the medium-specific conventions of the classic literary adaptation on British television.[73]

A further emerging strand of work makes a valuable move away from textual methodologies to study British period films as industrial products and cultural commodities. The main example of such work to date – Higson's comparative study of the innovative *Elizabeth* and the more conventional *Howards End* – focuses on the economic logic and funding, distribution and exhibition, marketing strategies and circulation context of these case-study films, drawing on industry and other empirical sources.[74]

But alongside these many developments, the scholarship and critical debate around heritage and post-heritage films has, until now, left audience perspectives almost wholly uninvestigated and unvoiced. As Andrew Higson commented back in 1996, the initial critique of heritage cinema and the many revisionist responses it has prompted – whether taking issue with it or seeking to refine it – 'all suggest different readings of the films'. But without complementary work which engages directly with reception – studying what real audiences have to say about the films; the discourses they produce (or mirror, or reject) around them; and, through this, seeking to understand how they use and receive them – such textual interpretations 'are all at the end of the day no more than readings'.[75] It is this gap in the scholarship that the rest of this book seeks to begin to remedy.

NOTES

1. See, centrally, Monk, 'The British heritage-film debate revisited' (abbreviated hereafter as 'Revisited').

2. Ibid., p. 177.

3. For examples of these various strands, see Forbes, '*Maurice*' [review], *Monthly Film Bulletin*; Ackroyd, 'Pictures from Italy' [on *A Room with a View*], *Spectator*; Mantel, 'Tasteful repro' [on *Maurice*], *Spectator*; Hollinghurst, 'Suppressive nostalgia' [on *Maurice*], *Times Literary Supplement*; and Christiansen, 'Biting the dust' [on *A Handful of Dust*], *Harpers & Queen*.

4. Barr, 'Introduction', p. 12.

5. See especially Usher, 'A breath-taking view. . .!' [review of *A Room with a View*] and 'The gentle English conquering America' [feature].

6. Wright, *On Living in an Old Country*; Hewison, *The Heritage Industry*. See also the analyses in Corner and Harvey (eds), *Enterprise and Heritage*. For criticisms of the 'heritage-baiting' position, see Samuel, *Theatres of Memory*, pp. 259–73.

7. See Higson, *Waving the Flag*, p. 42.

8. Monk, 'Revisited', pp. 188–90.

9. Fuller, 'Battle for Britain', p. 66.

10. Anon., 'From argument to abuse': a 1988 *Sunday Times* editorial whose tone exemplifies these attacks. The term 'New Right' is used here with reference to its meaning in the post-1979 British context – that is, the marked break from paternalistic Old Tory values and post-World War II consensus politics that took place in the UK Conservative Party under Margaret Thatcher's leadership – rather than its differently nuanced usage with reference to US politics (and in some other international contexts).

11. Stone, 'Through a lens darkly'. The films attacked by Stone ranged from the multicultural hit comedy-drama *My Beautiful Laundrette* to its less successful sequel *Sammy and Rosie Get Laid* (Frears, UK, 1987), and from the TV *Comic Strip* team's crude farce *Eat the Rich* (Peter Richardson, UK, 1987) to Derek Jarman's desolate avant-garde response to current social and political oppressions, *The Last of England* (UK, 1987).

12. Fuller, 'Battle for Britain', p. 66.

13. Stone, 'Through a lens darkly', p. C2.

14. See, for example, French, 'The Forster connection' and Clinch's review of *A Room*.

15. Kureishi, 'England, bloody England'.

16. Jarman, 'Freedom fighter for a vision of the truth'.

17. Craig, 'Rooms without a view'; Wollen, 'Over our shoulders'; Higson, 'Re-presenting the national past' (abbreviated hereafter as 'Re-presenting').

18. Dodd, 'An English inheritance' [editorial].

19. Light, 'Englishness' [letter].

20. Corner and Harvey (eds), *Enterprise and Heritage*.

21. Friedman (ed.), *British Cinema and Thatcherism*.

22. Higson's initial 1993 arguments are reworked, with some revision in response to criticisms, in 'The heritage film and British cinema'. Higson, *Waving the Flag* seeks to establish the heritage film's roots in earlier British film culture dating back to the 1920s. Higson, *English Heritage, English Cinema* presents an expanded and updated overview of both the field of films and the debates, with an increased emphasis on the polysemy of the films and 'the richness of the reception process' (cover copy). It also incorporates detailed industrial case studies of heritage films drawing upon empirical sources.

23. Higson, 'Re-presenting', p. 110.

24. 'The pastoral' connotes the idealised, and socially hierarchical, myth of rural England as famously dissected by Raymond Williams in *The Country and the City*.

25. On royal biopics, see Bastin, 'Filming the ineffable' and McKechnie, 'Taking liberties with the monarch'.

26. For a more detailed discussion, see Monk, 'Revisited', pp. 178–9.

27. Jhabvala did not adapt *Maurice*, which was scripted by Ivory and Kit Hesketh-Harvey.

28. Wollen, 'Over our shoulders', p. 179 and p. 193.

29. Higson, 'Re-presenting', p. 128.

30. Landy, 'Introduction' in Landy (ed.), *The Historical Film*, p. 10.

31. Street, *British National Cinema*, pp. 105–6; Powrie, 'On the threshold between past and present'. For a discussion of three 1980s–1990s British retro films (including *Scandal*), see Sargeant, 'The content and the form'.

32. Powrie, 'On the threshold between past and present', p. 317. Powrie conceives the 'alternative heritage' film as 'a third category' in addition to the heritage film and the period biopic. However, his detailed analysis is reserved for three 'rites of passage film set in the past' – *Distant Voices, Still Lives*; its sequel, *The Long Day Closes* (Terence Davies, UK, 1992); and *Small Faces* (Gillies MacKinnon, UK, 1995) – which he finds 'alternative' in a further sense due to their 'self-reflexivity [in encouraging] spectators to question . . . both the status of the films, and the status of the spectators themselves' (ibid., p. 316). The term 'alternative heritage film' is also used by Moya Luckett ('Image and nation in 1990s British cinema'), but with an entirely different force; see also Note 47.

33. Higson, 'The heritage film and British cinema', pp. 232–3; Monk, 'Revisited', p. 178.

34. See Higson, *English Heritage, English Cinema*, Chapter 3, especially pp. 93–101.

35. Higson, 'Re-presenting', p. 117.

36. Dyer and Vincendeau, leaflet publicising *The European 'Heritage' Film: A Workshop Conference*, University of Warwick.

37. Higson, *Waving the Flag*, p. 26.

38. Wollen, 'Over our shoulders', p. 179.

39. Higson, 'Re-presenting', p. 114 (his emphasis). Early-1990s heritage-film criticism typically conflated the bourgeoisie and aristocracy into a single class, in contrast with the clear distinctions crucial to Paul Dave's more recent analysis in *Visions of England*.

40. Craig, 'Rooms without a view', p. 4.

41. Jameson, 'Post-modernism, or the cultural logic of late capitalism', p. 66, cited in Higson, 'Re-presenting', p. 112.

42. Hewison, *The Heritage Industry*, p. 144.

43. Higson, 'Re-presenting', p. 119.

44. Ibid., p. 109.

45. Ibid., p. 117.

46. Monk, 'Revisited', p. 180. See also Monk, 'Heritage films and the British cinema audience in the 1990s'; Higson, 'Re-presenting', p. 110; Higson, *English Heritage, English Cinema*, pp. 101–6.

47. Monk, 'Revisited', pp. 190–1 and p. 195. On the nostalgic and reactionary appropriation of a (masculine/ist, populist) canon of 'alternative heritage' films, see Luckett, 'Image and nation in 1990s British cinema', p. 88. On the ideological workings of 1990s popular British films focusing on a working-class post-industrial present, see Monk, 'Underbelly UK'.

48. Dyer and Vincendeau, leaflet publicising *The European 'Heritage' Film* conference.

49. Consider, for example, *A Room with a View*'s gallery of significant older female characters, or, in a broader European context, the protagonists of *Babette's Feast*. The marketing of the more recent *Tea with Mussolini* (Franco Zeffirelli, Italy/UK, 1999) and *Ladies in Lavender* (Charles Dance, UK, 2004) suggests that the foregrounding of the appeal of older female protagonists – and veteran female actors – is now a conscious strategy.

50. Hill, *British Cinema in the 1980s*, p. 97.

51. Dyer, 'Heritage cinema in Europe', p. 205.

52. Hill, *British Cinema in the 1980s*, p. 97.

53. See Chapter 3. Industry surveys of the UK film audience, centrally *Caviar*, do not collect information on sexual orientation, and refusals to answer such questions present a known difficulty for social researchers.

54. For an indicative discussion of the 'blatant differences' between two of the agreed core 1980s British heritage films, *A Room with a View* and *Chariots of Fire*, see Monk, 'Revisited', pp. 180–1.

55. Lovell, 'The British cinema: the known cinema?', p. 241; see also Monk, 'Revisited', pp. 184–6.

56. Higson, 'Re-presenting', p. 113.

57. Borgmeier, 'Heritage film and the picturesque garden', p. 65; Mulvey, 'Visual pleasure and narrative cinema'.

58. Mulvey, 'Visual pleasure', pp. 62–3 (my emphasis).

59. Ibid., p. 64.

60. 1970s spectatorship theory, its monolithic conception of spectator positioning, and its evacuation of historically and socially situated 'real' audiences had already attracted many criticisms and methodological revisions by the 1980s. For indicative accounts, see Mayne, *Cinema and Spectatorship*; Branston, *Cinema and Cultural Modernity*, Chapter 6; and Stokes, 'Introduction' in Stokes and Maltby (eds), *Hollywood Spectatorship*.

61. 1970s 'apparatus theory' conceived of the cinema itself as an 'apparatus', whose workings – including, centrally, its operations on the spectator – were simultaneously technological, industrial, psychological (unconscious) and ideological (Baudry, 'Ideological effects of the basic cinematic apparatus'). In appropriating the term, I propose that similarly mechanical workings were attributed to the heritage film.

62. Voigts-Virchow, '"Corset wars"', p. 14.

63. Church Gibson, 'Fewer weddings and more funerals'.

64. See Monk, 'Underbelly UK' and 'Projecting a "New Britain"'.

65. Monk, 'Sexuality and heritage'. See, for example, *Orlando*'s casting of 'the stately homo of England' Quentin Crisp as Elizabeth I, the casting of footballer Eric Cantona (among other strategies) in *Elizabeth*, or the dark, expressionist aesthetic of *The Wings of the Dove*. For detailed 'post-heritage' readings of *Elizabeth* and Rozema's *Mansfield Park* respectively, see Church Gibson, 'From dancing queen to plaster virgin' and 'Otherness, transgression and the postcolonial perspective'.

66. Light, 'Englishness' [letter]; Monk, *Sex, Politics and the Past*, 'The British "heritage film" and its critics' and 'The heritage film and gendered spectatorship'.

67. Dyer, 'Feeling English', p. 17 and p. 16; Richards, *Films and British National Identity*, p. 169. Dyer's and Richards' critiques were also reactions against the 'quality film consensus' which had dominated post-war British film-critical culture until it was challenged (and, ultimately, reversed) by the 'new' British film history of the 1980s onwards. See Monk, 'Revisited', pp. 184–5, and also Chapter 7, Note 1.

68. Pidduck, *Contemporary Costume Film*, cover copy.

69. Dyer and Vincendeau, leaflet publicising *The European 'Heritage' Film: A Workshop Conference*; Dyer, 'Heritage cinema in Europe'.

70. See Voigts-Virchow, '"Corset wars"', p. 23, and other German contributions to Voigts-Virchow (ed.), *Janespotting and Beyond*.

71. Monk, 'Sexuality and heritage' and, in particular, Church Gibson's body of work (see Notes 63 and 65).

72. See Note 32.

73. Pidduck, 'Of windows and country walks'; Pidduck, *Contemporary Costume Film*; Bruzzi, *Undressing Cinema*; Cardwell, *Adaptation Revisited*.

74. Higson, *English Heritage, English Cinema*: see especially Chapters 5 and 6. For a more specialised example of industry-focused analysis, see Sargeant, 'Making and selling heritage culture'.

75. Higson, 'The heritage film and British cinema', p. 246.

CHAPTER 2

The Heritage Audience Survey: Methodology and Issues

INTRODUCTION

The analysis presented in Chapter 3 onwards draws centrally on the findings of the Heritage Audience Survey: my detailed questionnaire-based survey of real members of the UK audiences for quality period films – including, specifically, culturally British 'heritage' and 'post-heritage' films – which was undertaken expressly for this study. Chapter 2 describes the development, practicalities and methodologies of the survey – including the sourcing of the survey sample, which comprised two demographically and culturally contrasting sub-samples of period-film viewers drawn from very different 'populations'.

The particular timing of the survey – the questionnaire was completed by respondents between the end of 1997 and mid-1998 – gives the resulting study fortuitous advantages as a portrait of contemporary period-film audiences in relation to the evolution of the heritage-film debate. Crucially, the questionnaire was completed by respondents at a juncture contemporaneous with the innovations and transformations in the heritage 'genre' discussed in Chapter 1 – during the UK cinema release of John Madden's *Mrs Brown* but before the September 1998 Venice Film Festival world premiere of Shekhar Kapur's *Elizabeth* – but also at a time when the key British heritage-film successes of the 1980s to mid 1990s were still frequently screened on British TV and (alongside the TV phenomenon of the BBC's 1995 *Pride and Prejudice*) remained vivid in audiences' minds. This benefit should not be underestimated, given the dependence of a project of this kind on *what* respondents recall seeing and *how* they remember it (and the difficulties this presents for 'memory work' which seeks to retrieve cinemagoing or film memories of much earlier decades) – although (given the advancing ages of many participants: see Chapter 3) the issue of memory was not entirely absent.[1]

Similarly, the survey was designed and completed during a period when the concept of the heritage film remained current but had been joined in critical discourse by new propositions such as the post-heritage film. Last (as I discuss in Chapter 3) it coincided with a pivotal moment of political change (and optimism) in the UK, as eighteen years of Conservative rule gave way to the May 1997 landslide election of Tony Blair's New Labour government. In short, *Heritage Film Audiences* is simultaneously a study of respondents' *current and recent* film-viewing practices, film tastes and attitudes in the late 1990s, but one which is able to situate these historically and contextually in relation to the cinematic and cultural–political context of the 1980s heritage debate, the late 1990s 'present' of the survey, and points in between.

As will be clear from Chapter 1, the decision to undertake an empirical survey of a sample of the real audiences for 'heritage films' was prompted, first and foremost, by shortcomings in the text- and context-centred critique of heritage cinema and the tangible connection between these and the absence of an audience perspective; and, second, by assumptions about the suitability, practicality and likely benefits of empirical (and, predominantly, qualitative) methodologies as a tool for addressing some of these. The survey's methods, the detail of its design and the sourcing of its participants were also shaped by hypotheses – formed in response to the established critique of heritage cinema, but also to test my own counter-theories and a wider range of imagined possible survey outcomes (envisioned as broadly as possible). The core hypotheses motivating the study and feeding into its research design are set out and discussed on pages 33–6. Smaller hypotheses and research expectations following on from these are identified in subsequent chapters as the need arises in the course of analysis and interpretation of the survey findings.

SURVEY DESIGN AND METHODOLOGY

The Heritage Audience Survey was conducted via a postal questionnaire, comprising fifty-eight questions (subdivided into six parts), most of which were later broken down into 503 database fields for purposes of analysis. The questionnaire was designed to collect detailed information on respondents' demographic backgrounds and identities (including questions on areas such as occupation, educational qualifications, newspaper readership and political affiliations); their film-viewing habitus and film tastes, including favourite period films, directors and actors; respondents' own written accounts of what they most enjoyed, or disliked, about the period films they watched; and their opinions, positions and attitudes in relation to period films and on a range of issues salient to the existing debate and literature around heritage cinema.[2] For the text of the questionnaire, see Appendix 2.1.[3] As can be seen, the questionnaire presented a mix of pre-coded multiple-choice questions, and open questions inviting participants to answer in their own words. The questionnaire was structured so that these open questions were presented to respondents earlier than any multiple-choice questions seeking information in related areas (such as period-film tastes and likes), in an effort to minimise the influence of the questionnaire itself on their self-worded replies.

During the period of initial research and questionnaire design for the project, I attended several conferences, public talks and study days on British and European period films, heritage cinema and the films of Merchant Ivory. With one exception, these events were aimed mainly at the 'general public', adult-education users and/or interested cinemagoers rather than professional academics. They thus provided opportunities to observe the discourses, themes, attitudes and concerns which emerged in public/audience – rather than solely academic/critical – discussion around British period films, including films commonly identified as 'heritage films'. These observations informed my research hypotheses and the questionnaire design, and self-selecting volunteers drawn from the audiences at these events tested a pilot version of the questionnaire.[4]

Audience-research methodologies such as interviews, focus groups or non-participatory observation of group discussions, obviously have some methodological benefits that cannot be replicated in a postal questionnaire. I nevertheless opted for a detailed questionnaire as my data-generating source for a combination of practical and methodological reasons. First, as a doctoral student undertaking my own data collection, processing, analysis and interpretation single-handed and unpaid, it was clear that the use of depth interviews or focus groups (requiring transcription and annotation of recorded interviews) would be unworkably labour-intensive – unless confined to a sample considerably smaller than the already modest sample surveyed in this study – while being less effective than a questionnaire for the systematic collection of detailed data. Second, I was interested in collecting detailed data of a variety of kinds: sociological, relating to respondents' identities; broadly statistical (for example, measuring the numbers/range of films respondents had seen in particular categories); and qualitative, soliciting and analysing respondents' own testimony on their reasons for enjoying period films, their tastes in these, and so on. Face-to-face methods such as interviews would have been appropriate for the last of these purposes, but not the first two.

Third, and importantly for this project, a postal questionnaire made it possible to survey a larger sample, to draw respondents from varied regions of the UK, and to ask them a wide range of questions in a variety of ways – both multiple-choice, and open questions seeking self-worded answers – that would not be achieved in interview. A possible downside was that, although a great variety and density of data was collected, only some of this material – centrally, respondents' self-worded written statements – invites the forms of qualitative analysis (those which analyse respondents' testimonies as texts, often in search of recurrent discourses or themes) favoured in much of the foundational empirical film-audience-studies work that has been published in the period of my own work towards this study.[5] More beneficially, readers will find that I bring sociological and (loosely) statistical approaches to bear in my analysis that are made possible by the less 'qualitative' forms of data also collected.

As with all empirical methods, the data collected need also to be interpreted with an awareness of the features and limitations of the chosen methodology. As a postal questionnaire is conducted without face-to-face contact, it provided no opportunity for the researcher to engage personally with respondents (individually or as a group), to probe for elaboration, or to seek immediate clarification of ambiguous answers via follow-up questions as one would in a depth interview. Nor did I feel it would be considerate to contact respondents again *after* analysis of their already detailed original responses to ask for clarifications or additional information (not least in the light of the advanced ages of some participants). One related – if also near-inevitable – limitation is that the study was unable to capture respondents' views on certain significant (and subsequently much-discussed) British period films released in the time between the finalisation of the questionnaire and completion of the data analysis – most prominently and detrimentally, Shekhar Kapur's *Elizabeth* – although some respondents did comment unprompted on another awkwardly timed film omitted from the questionnaire, John Madden's *Mrs Brown*.

At times, such limitations – whether due to accidents of timing or decisions of methodology – impinge on the findings and their interpretation; but, even beyond these, inevitable areas of opaqueness or ambiguity remain. To give one illustration (already touched upon in the Introduction), a postal questionnaire cannot ask respondents who wrote that they enjoy period films because they 'bring history to life' what, precisely, they meant. But would this necessarily have become clearer if these respondents had been asked to elaborate in follow-up interviews? It seems likely that any attempt to explain or theorise the structures of thought and feeling underpinning such statements will remain at least partly speculative and inconclusive.

Such lacunae are, arguably, a hazard of all empirical research dealing with qualitative data and the subjective or experiential testimony of participants – particularly if the research is conducted and interpreted with care and integrity – and, ultimately, the gap must be filled by methodologies of interpretation. And if the interpretation of films by members of their audiences is itself a creative activity – as Henry Jenkins and other contemporary scholars argue[6] – the same is surely true, to a greater or lesser degree, of qualitative academic interpretation of audiences. A duty of the scrupulous researcher is to acknowledge opacities and ambiguities in their findings rather than to mask these in order to give a false impression of authority and finality. Yet, in the face of all these limitations, it remains true that empirical work engaging with actual audiences situated within the 'real' social world is able to present forms of evidence – and therefore insights – that other methodologies cannot, making it a valuable pursuit even though imperfections of design and interpretation may always remain.

RESEARCH HYPOTHESES

From the outset, one of my central hypotheses – and therefore my starting point for both the questionnaire design and the sourcing of survey respondents – was that the real audiences who enjoyed 'heritage films' and other 'quality' period films were more *diverse* – demographically, culturally, politically and in their broader film tastes – than the narrow, bourgeois, 'older' heritage audience projected in the founding critiques of heritage cinema and some sections of the media.

I therefore also expected to find that film (and cultural) tastes among heritage film audiences would be wider and more eclectic – less confined to a heritage monoculture and in every sense less conservative – than the academic critique had implied. More speculatively, I expected to find that the taste for period films would not necessarily be specific to, or dominated by, British or Anglophone period films (that is, these audiences would include people who watched, and were at ease with, subtitled non-Anglophone films); and that, for some, enjoyment of heritage films might be compatible with enjoyment of films or genres that most would regard as their antithesis.

On the other hand, and in keeping with the dominant criticisms directed at British heritage cinema, I expected to find some sections of the audience whose attraction to the films was more conservative and implicitly or explicitly Anglocentric. A further possibility flowing from this was that a taste for British heritage films – closely equated by many commentators with 'Englishness' or Anglocentricity – might be part of a wider preference for British films. Such a preference, however, is open to significantly differing interpretations. Is it an assertion of resistance to the cultural colonialism – or commercialism – of Hollywood? Does it signal a preference for nuanced narrative and characterisation over big-spectacle, CGI (computer-generated imagery)-reliant blockbusters? Is it a symptom of an inward-looking Little England mentality, xenophobia and Europhobia (as the tone of some anti-heritage-film criticism had tended to imply)? Or an assertion of cultural discernment or distinction, expressed (in a continuing echo of the 'art, culture, quality' strand in British film criticism)[7] as a preference for British films over Hollywood?

My hypotheses were also grounded in a conception of post-1979 British period films as belonging to a *continuum* with their relatively critically neglected 1960s and 1970s precursors, both cinematic and televisual. While this approach might seem obvious, one effect of the critical construction of the Thatcher-era heritage film as a 'new genre' was to repress consideration of possible continuities between post-1979 British period films and their precursors – most crucially, the likely place of 1970s and earlier period screen fictions in forming the tastes of the audiences for heritage (and post-heritage) films of the 1980s onwards.

Questions of how and when these audiences became period-film viewers, and of whether specific decades, films or areas of the generic map were especially significant in this, have some importance for a fuller understanding of the place of 'heritage films' within the longer recent history of British period screen fictions, and the cultural politics of their enjoyment by particular audiences. One obvious point is that many members of the UK audiences who enjoyed 1980s heritage films would have acquired their taste for period screen fictions before that decade. Another is that period television dramas/ serials – notably including the British tradition of classic literary adaptations epitomised by the BBC 'Classic Serial' (first established as a television format in the 1950s) – were one likely formative influence.[8] Looking beyond the Classic Serial, some pre-1980s tastes might suggest an enjoyment of period films in a context of popular-genre, or modernist, tastes (for illustrations, see the discussions of films self-named by respondents in Chapter 5 onwards). But, in other cases, films with clear affinities with the (only slightly later) 'heritage film' had been circulated, and received positively – particularly in the 1970s – expressly within the institution and discourses of art cinema. The tone of the contemporary 1979 review and features coverage of James Ivory's *The Europeans* (adapted from Henry James, and starring Lee Remick as the divorced European baroness out of her element in 1850s New England), and its release strategy – a six-month-plus exclusive run at the Curzon Mayfair cinema in London – presents an instructive case study here.[9]

In view of these questions, I was interested in any earlier, pre-1980s period film or television drama tastes that respondents might mention, and to index the earliest decades mentioned – in order to map the approximate longevity of respondents' period-film habitus, but also to map key decades of their earliest evident viewing. Although a full analysis of these patterns was undertaken, due to space limitations Chapter 5 limits itself to noting only the key insights.

To return to a hypothesis rooted more directly in the debates summarised in Chapter 1, I had argued forcefully in my earlier work that the critical denigration of 'heritage films' (and the excessive tone of this among some male critics)[10] had been coupled with a peculiar silence around (or blindness to) the significance of gender and sexuality in, and to, key 'heritage films' such as *A*

Room With A View and *Maurice* – both in terms of their explicit themes and narrative concerns, and the 'feminine' and/or queer pleasures and attractions they potentially offered their audiences.

My account of the films in these terms had direct origins in self-awareness of my personal reasons for enjoying them. To me, these pleasures and attractions were equally evident within the films as texts – indeed, little 'depth' analysis was required to uncover them – and from empirical observation of the composition and responses of their cinema audiences. Both films very evidently departed from the goal-directed individual-heterosexual-male-centred 'classical' (and also 'post-classical') narrative structures of mainstream cinema. For all their 'well-made' qualities, they were narratives organised around the (inner) journeys of a very young female protagonist and a young gay male protagonist respectively. Furthermore, questions of personal identity, sexual expression and socially constrained gender norms – and the relationship of these to personal happiness – were central to both films at an obvious thematic level.[11] As (at the time) a graduate student for whom text-centric film theory was still a novelty, I developed and sought to legitimate this argument by means of a detailed textual analysis of the two films (drawing, with some inevitability, upon Laura Mulvey's agenda-setting 1975 essay).[12] The salience of this analysis for the *Heritage Film Audiences* study was that it proposed that the Merchant Ivory films – and, potentially, a broader range of 'heritage films' – made available a plurality of pleasurable viewing positions somewhat different from, and certainly not confined to, those suggested by the early 1990s heritage-film critique.

My own interests and concerns, then, had led me to argue for the sexual pluralism and plural appeals of many heritage films, and for the particular appeal of some of them to female and gay male audiences. It will be seen in later chapters that the Heritage Audience Survey findings confirm that heritage films do appeal to female audiences and some gay men, with some respondents justifying their enjoyment of the films in feminist terms. But, conversely, many others – most markedly, older female respondents – did *not* conceive of, or describe, their liking for their favoured period films in any such terms; indeed, the views of some were expressly anti-feminist. In view of this, readers will find that the analysis in later chapters is less intensely organised around questions of gender and sexuality than might be expected from the preoccupations of my earlier work.

Last – as will also be evident in the analysis to follow – the study was shaped by an interest in investigating the possible relationships between respondents' class cultures and educational capital, the general disposition to watch and enjoy 'quality' period films, including heritage films, and their specific orientations towards the films. This interest in class had fewer implications for the targeting of an appropriate survey sample than questions of gender, sexuality

– or age – given that (as Chapter 3 discusses) the largest part of the overall UK cinema audience is, broadly, middle-class, and the same would be true of the pool of volunteers – however selected – likely to be interested in participating in this survey. It is important to add, however, that both of the populations from which respondents were drawn, although predominantly middle-class, were composed of a varied range of class *fractions*, with varied implications for respondents' likely class *cultures* and orientations towards heritage films.

Critics of heritage cinema have routinely presented the taste for heritage films as a high-bourgeois/elite one. I speculated, by contrast, that it might be more an aspirational taste, or a marker of a self-asserted 'educated' class identity – both potentially rooted in lower-middle or upper-working-class experiences, mobilities and insecurities rather than secure membership of the upper middle class. This speculation was informed by my personal biography – characterised by a drastic shift in educational opportunity between my parents' generation and myself (a shift exaggerated, in ways illuminating for this project, by my position as a 1960s child of middle-aged parents); by the origins of my own period-drama/period-film habitus in the cultural values instilled via education and parental aspirations; and by the roots of these, in turn, in complexities of family (lower-middle-/upper-working-)class identity.

SAMPLE SELECTION: WHO WAS CONTACTED AND WHO TOOK PART?

My motivating hypotheses indicated that participants for the audience survey should be sought from more than one source, or 'population'; and that, in addition to their interest in period films, each sub-sample should have definable *and contrasting* expected demographic, cultural and political characteristics. Given the need both to test the cliché and to elaborate on the existing evidence that 'heritage films' appeal to 'older', 'middle-class' audiences, it was particularly important that these sub-samples should have contrasting age and (if possible) class profiles; while my concerns with gender and sexuality made it desirable that both sexes, and, ideally, gay men and lesbians, should be represented in the survey. While, given the 'whiteness' and 'Englishness' of the heritage-film 'genre', there was no guarantee that black or ethnic minority respondents would wish to take part, respondents were sought from sources with the potential to yield an ethnically and culturally diverse sample.

I sought to publicise the project, and access likely participants, through various channels which – combined – would yield respondents with a range of age, gender, class, occupational and educational profiles, cultural preferences and political affiliations which might be expected to equate with differing forms, depths and breadths of engagement with current film culture, 'herit-age films' more specifically, and the wider issues salient to the heritage-film debate. In view of my hypotheses, I specifically sought samples which would include women, gay men, and participants with relatively liberal or left poli-tics, all of whom might display different relationships to heritage films from that implied in the early-1990s anti-heritage-film critique – while also seeking respondents whose engagement with heritage films and heritage culture were likely to be of a more traditionalist kind.

Last, in view of the argument that heritage films present a pastoral, south-ern and Anglocentric notion of British national identity, and also mindful of the likely contrast between urban and rural cinemagoing/film-viewing habits, I hoped to attract respondents from more than one region of the UK and from urban, suburban, semi-rural and rural areas (although it was not self-evident that this would be achievable). As already noted, I also sought participants from sources with an ethnically and culturally mixed profile, and in fact two black British respondents (both female and London-based) participated in the survey, as did nine respondents born outside the UK (although all but one of these were white). A further nine were born in Scotland, Wales, the Republic of Ireland or Northern Ireland. Full details of the national, regional and ethnic origins of survey respondents are given in Chapter 3.

In practice, my available sources of participants were, of course, constrained by the willingness of specific publications and organisations to publicise the project or to allow me access to specific audiences or groups of members; and by the responsiveness or otherwise of the 'populations' approached. The pilot survey was publicised to audiences at the various talks and film-education events on period films and heritage cinema that I attended during the develop-ment process, some of which yielded more, and more enthusiastic, volunteers than others.[13] During May and June 1997, a first draft of the survey question-naire was piloted with twenty-four self-selected volunteers from these groups, plus three further volunteers from other sources.

As the main purpose of the pilot was to test the questionnaire – and aspects of its content and design were consequently modified or updated before circu-lation of the final version to the main Heritage Audience Survey samples – the pilot findings were not included in the analysis of the main survey results (nor do they therefore feature in the main analysis in this book). Any significant differences between the pilot findings and those of the later main survey must therefore be noted here. The primary difference was that the pilot sample, although mostly comparable in age and class profile to the National Trust sample in the main survey (see below and Chapter 3), had a far deeper aware-ness of film culture, had typically seen a far wider and more eclectic range of films, were fully immersed in the culture of art cinema, and had developed their heritage-film interests – predominantly in Merchant Ivory's films – within this context. A much smaller sub-group of the pilot sample were predominantly interested in the films because they were avid fans of a particular actor.

The two sub-samples who comprised the participants in the main Heritage Audience Survey – i.e. the main primary source for the findings and analysis presented in the rest of this book – were sought respectively from the readership of the London weekly listings magazine *Time Out* and the memberships of the National Trust's local Associations or Centres, of which there were 193 in England, Wales and Northern Ireland at the survey date. (The National Trust for Scotland is a separate organisation and was not contacted for the survey.) I had hoped to source a third sub-set of respondents via the women's pages of the *Guardian* newspaper – which (in the late 1990s) would have yielded a largely female but predominantly left/liberal sub-sample with a broader age-span than the other two – but this proved impractical.[14]

While it was certain that both the *Time Out* readership and membership of the National Trust's Local Associations/Centres (abbreviated later as TO and NT respectively) would include individuals with an interest in period films, these two sources were known to exhibit very different demographic profiles, patterns of cultural consumption and newspaper readership, and, implicitly, political views and affiliations. Thus two sub-samples were deliberately sought which, it was expected, would exhibit contrasting social attitudes and cultural tastes, and substantially differing relationships to contemporary film culture and heritage culture, which in turn would colour the respondents' attitudes to, relationships with and tastes in period films and, more narrowly, 'heritage films'. For the age, gender and class profiles of the two source populations – represented by the most recent available data provided to me by the National Trust and *Time Out* at the date of the survey – see Appendices 2.2 and 2.3.

Respondents from *Time Out*'s readership were sought via a letter published in the issue dated 21–9 October 1997. The letter attracted forty-one answerphone requests for questionnaires, as a result of which thirty valid questionnaires were completed, returned and analysed. The National Trust's local Associations and Centres were chosen as the route for contacting NT members because it would have been unrealistic to expect the NT to assist with a nationwide mailing to its 1,296,450 membership addresses (equating to 2,478,771 individual members).[15] The other option, an announcement in the sixteen NT regional newsletters, was impractical due to the lengthy production lead time; and (as with a membership mailing) it would misleadingly have implied a formal relationship between the survey and the Trust's activities.

In October 1997, a letter and a supply of leaflets about the project were sent to the chair of each of the National Trust's local Associations/Centres in England, Wales and Northern Ireland, inviting them to publicise the project to their members at their own discretion. As a result of this, questionnaires were requested by ninety-four members from Associations/Centres across all of the

Trust's English and Welsh regions; of these, sixty-two valid questionnaires were completed, returned and analysed.[16]

The local Associations and Centres are 'independent local groups' run by National Trust 'members and volunteers for members and volunteers'.[17] It is important to understand, therefore, that the 'National Trust' survey sample sourced through these will have a profile distinct from that of the broader NT membership. NT Association or Centre members might be viewed as the most committed, participatory core of the NT membership; at the survey date, they were more likely than the broader NT membership to be drawn from social groups strongly disposed to join interest-based social clubs (such as retired couples and widows/widowers). Where a 'typical' NT member may be a casual leisure visitor to Trust properties and landscapes, Association members clearly have a regular stake in local Trust activities, and may be more deeply involved as event organisers or volunteer guides. Thus the 'National Trust' participants in the survey may well represent an exaggeration of, or distinct variations from, the characteristics of 'typical' members and, indeed, this deeper involvement in aspects of heritage interpretation was evident in some responses. One NT respondent 'lecture[d] with slides: costume through the ages', while a (rare) TO respondent who was also an NT volunteer wore 'a copy of an eighteenth-century gown when I am stewarding'.

Questionnaires were requested, completed and returned by respondents in both groups during the period November 1997 to May 1998. The data from the ninety-two valid completed questionnaires was then input into a detailed, 503-field database (FileMaker Pro) for analysis.

WHO WAS INCLUDED IN AND EXCLUDED FROM THE ANALYSIS OF RESULTS?

Any survey of this kind must exclude data gathered from ineligible respondents – for instance, people who enjoy completing questionnaires but, it is clear from their responses, do not watch films (here, specifically, period films) – or which is in some other way invalid (too ambiguous or incomplete to use). The language used in the letters and leaflets inviting participation in the Heritage Audience Survey, including the specific terms used to define the body or genre of 'period films' or 'costume films', and the film examples listed, was carefully chosen to attract participants from the intended 'populations' – that is, film viewers and cinemagoers with a variety of demographic characteristics who watch and, on the whole, enjoy feature films set in the past – including at least some of the British period films of the past two decades which have been desig-nated 'heritage films' or become a focus of discussion in the heritage debate.[18] My choice of words also invited responses from people who disliked period

films – but no completed questionnaires were received which fell unambiguously into this category. As we will see in later chapters, complex and ambiva-
lent responses, or reactions against *certain types* of period films, formed a more
significant strand in the survey findings.

The majority of completed questionnaires received were judged to be valid
and were incorporated into the survey database. Given the length and complexity of the questionnaires, and the sensitivity of some information sought
(e.g. political affiliations and sexual orientation), partially completed questionnaires were accepted and analysed as long as the completed sections provided
clear and unambiguous data, but any non-responses were explicitly recorded
as such.

Participants were explicitly instructed that the questionnaires should be
completed by individuals. This was particularly important given my interest
in gendered differences in response to the films. Despite this, a very small
number of NT respondents returned joint husband-and-wife questionnaires.
These were treated as the response of the partner who had actually completed
the questionnaire (which in all cases was made evident in a covering note).
However, other questionnaires ostensibly completed by one individual had
clearly benefited from some informal input from other members of the household, or from discussion with friends (some of whom were also completing
the survey). It may also be significant to note here that all eleven of the male
NT respondents who completed the questionnaire were married. Only some
of these replies explicitly mentioned such input ('I've chatted to friends about
this questionnaire'); but, given the social nature of all filmgoing and opinion-
forming, it seemed to me that such responses could fruitfully be included in
the survey.

In addition, six of the NT-respondent questionnaires received came from
three households in which the husband and wife had completed a questionnaire each. Given the demographics of the NT sample, these were longstanding marriages, and these couples tended to record similar film-viewing patterns
and tastes. As these paired responses were, technically, legitimate, they were
included in the survey, but it might be argued that they produce small distortions in the findings. All of these complications should be borne in mind when
reading the findings, and my interpretation of them, in the ensuing chapters.

A standard safeguard in film audience surveys is to exclude responses from
very infrequent film-viewers – typically, those who have not seen a feature film
at all in the past twelve months (on domestic media or at the cinema, depending on the nature of the survey). Of the ninety-six completed questionnaires
returned, four (all from NT members) were excluded from analysis because
they indicated that the respondent watched feature films so infrequently in
any medium, *and* had seen or were aware of so few of the named films listed
in the questionnaire, that it was doubtful whether the opinions they expressed

elsewhere were informed by film viewing. This left a working sample of ninety-two respondents (sixty-two from the NT sample, thirty from the TO sample). All findings reported and discussed in the chapters that follow are derived from this smaller working (or purged) sample of ninety-two valid responses.

However, the advanced age of many NT respondents (particularly relative to the core age group for frequent cinemagoers) meant that it would have been inappropriate to exclude respondents from the survey solely on grounds of infrequent *cinemagoing*. Of the ninety-two respondents whose questionnaires were included in the analysis, seventy-two (75%) were aged 45-plus (compared to 28% of UK cinemagoers in 1994);[19] forty-two (43%) were aged 65 to 81; and, moreover, fifty-seven (59%) were women aged 45-plus. Clearly there are a range of reasons why these age and gender groups may not be frequent cinemagoers – or see films at the cinema at all – and some of these were explicitly mentioned by respondents: reluctance to go out, or drive, at night; lack of local access; lack of access to an art cinema showing the kinds of films they wished to see. But it does not follow, of course, that such respondents do not watch films at home, including recent releases once these are broadcast on TV or available on VHS. (For both cohorts, home viewing meant terrestrial television or VHS, bearing in mind that the first DVDs were not test-marketed in Europe, nor digital TV launched in the UK, until late 1998.)

In view of this, questionnaires were excluded from the study only if they combined the following two indicators of negligible recent film-viewing:

(i) The respondent watched a film *two to three times a year or less* across *three or four* of the four modes of viewing listed in the questionnaire (cinema, on TV at time of broadcast, on rental video, or on sell-through/home-taped video) (Question 1); and

(ii) the respondent had also seen *fewer than ten* of the 241 listed films (mostly recent productions of the 1980s and 1990s) with period and contemporary settings (Questions 16 and 17).

All of the ninety-two respondents included in the study watched a film in at least one of the four viewing modes two to three times a year or more; and, in practice, 63% of respondents in the 45-plus age band reported that they saw films at the cinema at this frequency.

HOW ARE RESPONDENTS QUOTED AND IDENTIFIED IN THE BOOK?

Virtually all respondents stated that they were happy to be quoted in published research but a significant number wished to be quoted only anonymously. For consistency, I have extended the principle of anonymity to all quoted replies, and any further references to individual respondents, in this book. Each respondent is identified by their respective sub-sample (NT or TO), a reference number, and (as a minimum), their gender, age (at the date of completing the questionnaire) and occupation or last occupation. More than 90% of respondents described themselves as white, British or English, and/ or heterosexual (see Chapter 3) – particularly in the larger and older National Trust cohort – and 90% of *Time Out* respondents lived in Greater London.

The identification of respondents who were gay, lesbian or bisexual, and those who gave their race/ethnicity as non-white and/or their nationality as non-British, was important to the study, both because of the relevance of such questions to debates around the heritage film's pleasures, ideologies and spectatorship (see Chapter 1), and because knowledge of sexual, racial/ethnic and national identities (including Irish, Scottish and Welsh) is often relevant to our interpretation of respondents' comments. However, given the dominant composition of the sample, to avoid tedious repetition I have adopted the default strategy of adding further details (self-reported nationality, ethnicity and sexual orientation, and the UK region where the respondent lived) only when quoting or citing non-white, non-British or non-heterosexual respondents and the minority of *Time Out*-reading non-Londoners. I must stress that this has been done solely for brevity, certainly not with any normative intent. As Chapter 3 discusses, a contributory difficulty was that some NT respondents declined to answer the questions on sexuality or race/ethnicity.

INFORMATION SOUGHT

The Questionnaire itself (Appendix 2.1) sought information from respondents in the following areas relevant to the wider debate and existing literature around heritage cinema.

1. Respondents' demographic characteristics, last occupation and occupational status, educational qualifications and background, class of origin (based on head-of-household parental occupation during childhood), newspapers read and political affiliations, sexual orientation, region of residence, and other characteristics contributing to their social identity and likely relationship to heritage films. (Newspapers and political affiliations: Part 4; all other information: Part 5.)

    Class of origin and current occupational class (based on last occupation) were classified and analysed using the ABC1 social grade scale; and also the NS-SEC (National Statistics Socio-Economic Class) scale (the new official UK government schema introduced in 2002) in conjunction with its accompanying Standard Occupational Classification (SOC2000) list. For ease of understanding and comparison with other audience-data sources quoted in later chapters, this book presents and analyses findings on socio-economic class using the (more widely known) ABC1 scale.

In addition, the neighbourhood types where respondents lived at the date of survey completion were classified using the postcode-based CACI Acorn (A Classification Of Residential Neighbourhoods) schema (developed by the marketing-data company CACI). The specifics of the Acorn schema, and its related limitations, are explained in Chapter 3 and Appendix 3.7. The 2001 Acorn schema used in this analysis listed 54 neighbourhood 'types' in the UK, each profiled in terms of the demographic, socio-economic and lifestyle/consumption characteristics of the 'typical' inhabitant of the (geographically diverse) postcodes placed within each type. As CACI themselves stress, these profiles cannot be accurate for every individual or household in each postcode. Nevertheless, I found them useful as snapshots of the types of areas where respondents lived – whether rural, urban or suburban, their characteristic class fractions, ethnic composition, and so on.

2. Respondents' general film-viewing habitus (Part 1). Were films viewed mainly in the cinema, or mainly on TV and video? How frequent were cinema visits? At what types of cinema were films seen and did this differ for period films? How frequently were films watched on TV or video?

3. Respondents' tastes in films and awareness of contemporary film culture (Parts 1 and 2). Did they mainly or exclusively watch period films? How broad or narrow were their awareness and viewing of recent mainstream and 'art cinema', English-language and non-Anglophone film releases set in the present as well as the past, and were specific patterns and tastes evident within this? For reasons of space, this book limits itself to summarising key patterns of viewing and tastes in relation to non-period films, rather than presenting the full detail of the analysis conducted.

4. Respondents' detailed tastes in period films and period television dramas/serials (Part 2). Cohort-specific patterns of taste, and breadth or narrowness of viewing, were analysed to draw out possible indicators of the dispositions underlying or shaping these. Did respondents name favourite period films or favourite period TV dramas/serials? What trends or patterns emerged, and how did these relate, or not, to the suppositions of the literature around 'heritage cinema'? Did the replies suggest that respondents had long enjoyed watching period films and period TV dramas (and, if so, of what genres, styles and kinds), or that this was a more recent habit more tangibly related to the emergence of (the idea of) the 'heritage film' and its supporting (or opposing) discourses?

5. Preferred actors (male and female) and directors (Part 2). Were respondents' viewing (and choice) of period films guided or influenced by a liking for specific actors or driven by fandom? How far was respondents' interest in period films (or any films) guided by an awareness of, or preference for, specific directors? Findings in these areas are reported within the analysis of respondents' pleasures in and attitudes to period films presented in Chapters 6 and 7.

6. Factors or ingredients explaining or influencing respondents' enjoyment (or sometimes dislike) of period films. Respondents were asked to self-report on this in their own words (Part 2: Question 22), and later (Part 2: Question 29) to evaluate a list of twenty-eight possible factors on a scale ranging from 'very important' to 'totally irrelevant' to their enjoyment of period films.

7. Respondents' attitudes to period films, literary adaptations and on related issues salient to the heritage-film debate (Part 3). Here, a list of seventy-four attitude statements were formulated which related either to specific claims, discourses or assumptions circulated in the established debates around heritage films (for example, on issues of 'respectful' adaptation or 'authenticity' of period detail) or to my wider hypotheses. Respondents were asked to respond to these on a scale ranging from 'strongly agree' to 'strongly disagree'.

8. A range of contextual information was also sought on respondents' wider cultural and leisure habitus (Part 4), but due to considerations of relevance and word-length, this was not analysed (with the exception of replies on newspaper readership, Question 34, and political affiliations, Question 37).

9. Any other information or comments respondents wished to add (Part 6).

NOTES

1. For examples of this work, see Note 5. In my own study, one NT respondent (a 66-year-old part-time Crown Court judge) wrote: 'If you had been able to interview me, you would have been able to remind me of a much wider range of period films, etc, than I can now readily recall.'

2. Respondents also answered some questions about 'your other cultural and leisure interests' beyond films (Part 4 of the questionnaire), but (for reasons of manageability as much as relevance) only their answers on newspaper readership and political affiliations were systematically analysed.

3. The text-only questionnaire in Appendix 2.1 is abridged to omit tick boxes and other

multiple-choice formatting and general introductory instructions. The full lists of films presented to respondents in Questions 16 and 17 of the questionnaire are given in the Filmography rather than duplicated in Appendix 2.1.

4. The events I attended that were aimed at the 'general' public were: *The Literary Adaptions* [sic] *of Merchant–Ivory Productions,* a talk by veteran former *Sight & Sound* editor John Pym (Stevenage Library, Hertfordshire, 8 November 1995); *Historical Styling in Film and Television* (Birkbeck College Centre for Extra-Mural Studies day school at the National Trust's Sutton House, London E5, 19 October 1996); and *Past Pleasures* (Birkbeck College Extra-Mural Studies and BFI Education study day at the National Film Theatre, London, 15 February 1997). The earlier *European Heritage Cinema: A Workshop Conference* (University of Warwick, 24 June 1995) was aimed at academics; indeed, the audience included figures already active in the debate, including the late historian Raphael Samuel. In practice, however, the division between 'academic' and 'public' audiences was often blurred. While the Warwick conference gained from the participation of a few non-academics with a strong interest in the field, the Merchant Ivory talk was the sole 'public' event that was *not* colonised to some extent by academics already versed, or engaged, in the heritage debate. Levels of interest in my pilot questionnaire mirrored these patterns. *Past Pleasures* – which, despite its title, attracted a 'public' audience hostile to heritage films – yielded no completed questionnaires, the Merchant Ivory talk fourteen, Sutton House four and the Warwick conference one.

5. The following key examples of such work – each focusing on UK audiences – illustrate the breadth of concerns in this emerging field. Barker with Brooks, *Knowing Audiences: Judge Dredd, its Friends, Fans and Foes* is an early exemplar of a wider trend of work centrally interested in fan interpretations, appropriations and participatory activity. Austin, *Hollywood, Hype and Audiences* (and his earlier 'Gendered (dis)pleasures: *Basic Instinct* and female viewers') present studies of the UK circulation and differentiated audience reception of three Hollywood releases of the early 1990s. A third, distinct strand of studies work explicitly with memory, seeking to recuperate and interpret respondents' historical memories of cinemagoing or stars: see Stacey, *Star Gazing*; Lacey, 'Seeing through happiness'; and Kuhn, *An Everyday Magic.*

6. Jenkins, 'Reception theory and audience research'.

7. See Ellis, 'The quality film adventure'.

8. The Classic Serial format was invented by BBC Radio Drama in the 1940s but soon migrated to television, where it has continued to adapt and survive. The format's commercial viability and global exportability – and its perceived cultural prestige – have led to its adoption by commercial as well as public-service broadcasters (notably Granada Television as producer, in 1981, of *Brideshead Revisited*) and to international co-production/distribution deals (centrally via the US Public Broadcasting Service and its constituent broadcasters such as WGBH Boston under the 'Masterpiece Theatre' banner). See Giddings and Selby, *The Classic Serial on Television and Radio*; and Kerr, 'Classic serials: to be continued'. For a history and database of the BBC and ITV productions screened in the USA as 'Masterpiece Theatre' since 1971, see http://www.pbs.org/wgbh/masterpiece/archive/index.html [12 November 2010].

9. See, for example, French '*The Europeans*' [review] and Watts, 'Three's company' [profile of Merchant, Ivory and Jhabvala].

10. See especially Craig, 'Rooms without a view', discussed in Chapter 1.

11. These arguments were developed initially in Monk, *Sex, Politics and the Past.* On the specific arguments referred to here, see Monk, 'Sexuality and heritage' and 'The heritage film and gendered spectatorship'.

12. Mulvey, 'Visual pleasure and narrative cinema'. For my developed argument, see Monk, 'The heritage film and gendered spectatorship'.
13. See Note 4.
14. Over-exploitation by television researchers – usually seeking participants for human interest stories/programming – had led the *Guardian* women's page to adopt a policy of publicising research projects only through (unaffordable) paid advertising.
15. National Trust membership figures at 30 May 1997: see Appendix 2.2.
16. The Trust's regional structure has since been reorganised; at 2010, there were only nine English regions plus Wales and Northern Ireland. The current eleven National Trust regions are: Devon and Cornwall, East Midlands, East of England, Northern Ireland, North West, South East, Thames and Solent (including London), Wales/Cymru, Wessex, West Midlands, Yorkshire and North East. Questionnaire requests were received from all these regions apart from Northern Ireland, and completed questionnaires were received from virtually all.
17. www.nationaltrust.org.uk/main/w-trust/w-support/w-supporter__groups/w--supporter_groups-member_groups/w-member_groups-search.htm [12 November 2010].
18. For example, the flyer mailed to National Trust Local Association and Centre secretaries for distribution among their members read as follows:

> **Survey participants wanted!**
> Do you enjoy watching costume films, period literary adaptations or other kinds of period film at the cinema, on television or on video, or do you dislike them? Have you particularly enjoyed or disliked (or otherwise formed a strong opinion about) any of the period/costume films set in Britain which have been made over the past two decades – from Merchant Ivory's literary adaptations (such as *The Remains of the Day*, *Howards End*, *Maurice* and *A Room With A View*) to 1990s successes such as *Orlando*, *Sense and Sensibility* and *The Madness of King George*? If you have answered 'yes' to these questions, your interest and knowledge could be what is needed to help with research I am undertaking . . . My aim is to learn more about these audiences: who they are, what they have to say about why they enjoy (or dislike) the films, their attitudes to the films, and their wider cultural and leisure tastes. If you would be willing to spend some time completing a questionnaire on these subjects, I would like to hear from you.

19. Measured as the UK population claiming to 'ever go' to the cinema. Source: *Caviar 12*, Volume 1: Table 1/3 and Appendix A.

Demographics and Identities: A Portrait of the Survey Respondents

INTRODUCTION

Chapter 3 begins this book's account of the identities, tastes and attitudes of the contemporary audiences for period films by establishing the age, gender and social-class profiles of the Heritage Audience Survey's two (National Trust and *Time Out*) cohorts of respondents, and a wider range of indicators of identity pertinent to understanding and situating the broader 'heritage film audience'.

Bearing in mind the small size (and uneven cohort sizes) of the Heritage Audience Survey sample, I begin by doing this with comparative reference to the findings of the main (much larger) surveys conducted for the film and cinema-advertising industries.

These comparative data establish both the known characteristics of the UK cinema audience as a 'whole', and the specific profiles of UK cinema audiences for some of the key 'quality' period films of the 1990s. Here – and continuing in Chapter 4 – I draw on the limited industry sources that are (relatively) freely available to academic researchers covering the period most relevant to the heritage debate and closest to the 1998 timing of the survey: primarily, two of the annual *Caviar* (Cinema and Video Industry Advertising Report) surveys conducted in the earlier 1990s (coinciding with the UK release years of films such as *Howards End* and *The Remains of the Day*), supplemented by summaries of equivalent data from the quarterly statistical report *Cultural Trends* and the UK Film Council (UKFC)'s statistical yearbooks (published from 2002 onwards). The *Caviar* data, in particular, were analysed in detail as a prelude to the analysis and interpretation of my own survey data. The full analysis can be accessed as an already-published journal paper, but (due to space constraints) is not reprinted in this book.[1] In addition, this chapter brings into consideration a wider, more nuanced range of indicators not represented in the large industry surveys: in particular, on class fractions and occupational cultures, generationally differing forms of educational capital, and sexual orientation.

HERITAGE FILMS AND UK AUDIENCES: INSIGHTS FROM INDUSTRY RESEARCH

As my earlier paper discussed, a limitation of industry-commissioned surveys such as *Caviar* is that they are most strongly interested in those sections of the cinema audience most attractive to both the entertainment industry and cinema advertisers: namely, 'a "mainstream" in which children, adolescents and young adults – and particularly young males – are constructed as the most important (although not invariably numerically dominant) consumers'. A consequence of this priority (or bias) was that the *Caviar* samples under-represented older age bands relative to their presence in the UK population. *Caviar*'s presentation of its data was equally youth-orientated, presenting data on audiences aged 45-plus as a homogeneous block in contrast with a detailed breakdown for the under-20s (a limitation shared by post-2000 data sources such as the UKFC statistical yearbooks).[2] Yet, paradoxically, audiences aged 45-plus not only formed a demographic *majority* in the UK population, but (my analysis of the *Caviar* data suggested) accounted for an economically significant number of UK cinema visits. I concluded that 'older' audiences (whether defined as 25-plus, 35-plus or 45-plus) were treated as relatively marginal not because they were objectively commercially insignificant, but because they did not fit the (in reality, outdated) archetype of the 'regular' or 'habitual' cinemagoer craved by the industry. This marginalisation was also coloured by a cultural bias which valorised young male audiences and mascu-line genres, while (discursively) exiling 'older' – and especially older female – audiences and their tastes outside the 'mainstream'.[3]

It can be inferred from post-2002 UKFC reports on UK cinemagoing trends by age that the logic of the industry's continuing intense focus on under-25 audiences lies in their relative *predictability* in forming the most prominent section of the audience for the Top 20 UK box-office films (joined increasingly from the 2000s by those over-35s commercially important as the paying and accompanying adults of child consumers in the increasingly lucra-tive 'family film' market).[4] Thus, although 25- to 34-year-olds were frequent cinemagoers, they formed only 17% of the audiences for the Top 20 UK box-office hits of 2005 (whereas under-25s – and, most strongly, 7- to 14-year-olds – formed 47% of this audience, and the 35-plus age band – who contributed to the audiences for both 'family films' and what the UKFC called 'adult-oriented dramas' – formed 37%).[5] This finding has two implications. First, the industry is less interested in those age/gender groups which account for the majority of (or the most frequent) cinema *visits* than in those most prominent in the audiences for the minority of films which monopolise the bulk of box-office revenue. Second, those audience segments (such as the 25 to 34s and 'older' cinemagoers) who are not prominent in this last category presumably have less predictable, 'adult-oriented', even niche, tastes that might plausibly encompass period films.

My earlier analysis of the *Caviar* data established that the UK cinema audience as a 'whole' is (contrary to widespread assumptions) concentrated in the middle to higher social classes. The UK audience for films in the 'period drama' genre (measured via audience profiles for the examples in *Caviar 12*) was, in turn, revealed to be older and more pronouncedly 'middle-class', and more predominantly female, than the UK cinema audience as a whole, in keeping with commonplace assumptions about the audiences for period films.

However, analysis of the 1990s *Caviar* findings also revealed complexities that challenge these assumptions. First, the UK audiences for period films were only 'older' relative to the *extreme* youth of the 'mainstream' audience of frequent (and box-office Top 20) cinemagoers. Second, cinemagoers aged 25 to 34 (the same age group *least* prominent in the mid-2000s audiences for the annual Top 20 UK box-office hits or 'family films') had formed a quarter or more of the audience for most of the period films named in *Caviar 10* and *Caviar 12* – making them the second most prominent group in these audiences after the 45-pluses. And when audiences in adjoining age bands were added to the calculations, younger cinemagoers (whether defined as 20 to 34 or 25 to 44) outnumbered those aged 45-plus for a number of key period films listed by *Caviar*, including *Howards End*; although the audiences for some others – such as *The Remains of the Day* – were genuinely dominated by the 45-plus demographic (see Appendix 3.2). It can be seen here that the appeal of period films – and even of heritage films made by the same producer–director team – varied from film to film.

Third, audiences for *Caviar*'s named period films were in most cases split more evenly by gender than might have been expected. With the exception of *The Piano* (whose UK audience was 65% female), the audience gender split ranged from 60/40 female to male for the films with the strongest female appeal to around 50/50 for the other listed examples. But, fourth, *Caviar 12* also showed that the 45-plus segment of the *overall* UK cinema audience was dominated by women.[6] This suggested that women past child-rearing age were going to the cinema (and presumably watching films in other media) at an age when their male contemporaries were less likely to do so, with demographic trends – divorce, widowhood and higher female life expectancy – contributing to this pattern. Moreover, the prominence of 25- to 34-year-olds in period-film audiences alongside the 45-pluses suggested a possible correlation between the taste for 'quality' period films and lifestyles (free of parenting responsibilities and the related obligation to consume 'family' films) that enabled these sections of the audience to exercise significant autonomy in their film choices. As we shall see, this hypothesis was strongly supported by the composition of the Heritage Audience Survey sample, the vast majority of whom lived in childless households.

INTRODUCING THE HERITAGE AUDIENCE SURVEY RESPONDENTS

How far did the self-selecting (rather than demographically representative) groups of respondents who completed the Heritage Audience Survey questionnaire conform, or not, with the wider audience trends apparent in the more statistically robust *Caviar* data? Appendix 3.1 presents the age and gender composition of the Heritage Audience Survey sample (ninety-two respondents), and the two 'sub-samples', or 'cohorts', who comprised this: thirty respondents who were readers of *Time Out* magazine, and sixty-two members of National Trust local centres in a broad range of locations across England and Wales. In the interests of brevity, the two groups are abbreviated hereafter (collectively and individually) as 'TOs' and 'NTs', 'the TO cohort', 'the NT cohort', and so on. Appendix 3.1 also presents a comparative age and gender breakdown for the UK cinema audience 'as a whole' – using the best comparable *Caviar* data I was able to access.

Appendix 3.2 presents a comparison between summary age and gender data for the Heritage Audience Survey and *Caviar* findings on the age and gender profiles of the UK cinema audiences for *selected named* period films of the 1990s. Most of the latter is 1994 data drawn from *Caviar 12* (1995), with the exception of the statistics on *Howards End*, which are 1992 data from *Caviar 10* (1993). Due to lack of access to later *Caviar* reports; a lack of equivalent detailed data on the 35-plus age bands and relevant film genres in the UKFC's yearbooks published in 2002 onwards; and a consequent lack of available comparable data collected any closer to the 1998 Heritage Audience Survey date, I have retained the 1994 *Caviar 12* survey as my main comparative source.[7]

Appendix 3.3 shows the composition of the Heritage Audience Survey sample and sub-samples by ABC1 social class, and compares this with *Caviar*'s data on the class distribution of the UK cinema audience in 1994. Appendix 3.4 does the same in comparison to the class composition of the UK cinema audiences for *specific named* period films. Despite the small size and self-selecting nature of the Heritage Audience Survey sample, the demographics of the two sub-sets of respondents were, in fact, broadly consistent with those of cinema audiences for the 'period drama' genre as indicated in the much larger *Caviar* surveys. (The *Caviar* reports do not use the term 'heritage film', in keeping with its origins as a critical, not industry, label.) As would be expected, however, the TO and NT cohorts showed distinctive – and, on the whole, strikingly different – age and gender profiles. A total of 80% of TOs were aged 25 to 44, but all the NTs were aged 45-plus – indeed, more than 60% were 65-plus, and 23% of NTs were aged 75 or above. In line with stereotypes of the audiences for period films and costume dramas, around three-quarters of NT respondents were female, but the TO cohort displayed a more even gender split (43% male, 57% female).

The female-dominated composition of the NT cohort deviated significantly from the even gender split within the National Trust's overall membership (51% male, 49% female in 1993: see Appendix 2.2). Similarly, the slightly-more-female gender balance of the TO sub-sample reversed that of *Time Out*'s – slightly male-dominated – overall readership (63% male, 38% female in 1997: see Appendix 2.3). The survey volunteers in both the TO and NT cohorts were also self-selected solely from the older sections of their source populations. Thus although more than a quarter of the Trust's membership were aged under 45, and 35% of *Time Out* readers were aged 15 to 24, no members/readers in these age bands volunteered to participate in the survey.

Differences in terms of (occupation-derived) raw socio-economic class were less marked. Most TO and NT respondents alike were broadly 'middle-class' – and, in both cohorts, proportions of respondents from the 'middle-class' social grades were higher than in than the (already largely middle-class) UK cinemagoing audience, with some bias towards the highest grades. However, more detailed analysis revealed important nuances within this generalisation, to which I shall return.

The survey's findings on socio-economic class are expressed in this chapter in terms of the well-known ABC1 scale (originally developed for the use of advertisers and market researchers). Official UK government surveys such as the Census, and many social scientists, use a more complex, numeric classification schema, NS-SEC (National Statistics Socio-Economic Class), which was introduced in 2002 as the new official UK schema for establishing socio-economic class, and is used in conjunction with SOC2000 (the UK government's Standard Occupational Classification 2000 list, which numerically codes and classifies all occupations).[8] For accessibility and brevity, this book's presentation uses the ABC1 scale – not least because this is used in both the *Caviar* reports and the UKFC's statistical yearbooks.

Crucially for the concerns of this study, the term 'middle class' – as it is commonly, and often contradictorily, used – masks a diversity of class fractions, characterised by differing – and often unstable and historically fluctuating – degrees of wealth, social status, economic power and cultural authority, as well as differing forms and degrees of educational and cultural capital, and variations in subjective class experience, culture, self-perception and self-projection.[9] When the wider range of indicators listed at the start of this chapter (such as educational background) were brought into the analysis, more significant distinctions between, and within, the NT and TO cohorts emerged which it is legitimate to characterise as differences in class *culture* and educational and cultural capital.

In identifying these as areas of importance and interest for an empirical study of heritage-film audiences, I take my lead from the French sociologist Pierre Bourdieu's dictum that 'cultural needs are the product of upbringing and education', and that 'all cultural practices . . . and preferences . . . are closely linked to educational level . . . and secondarily to social origin.'[10] It follows that the educational capital and class identities of NT and TO survey respondents (and the experiential specifics within these) are likely to have considerable importance for our understanding of their respective dispositions, and cultural–political positioning, towards period films. As Bourdieu famously wrote: 'Taste classifies, and it classifies the classifier. Social subjects, classified by their classifications, distinguish themselves by the distinctions they make.'[11] My own interest, however, is less in how a taste for heritage films might socially and culturally 'classify' the films' audiences – for, as we have seen, heritage-film audiences have already been abundantly, if speculatively, classified by the heritage film's critics – than in how an empirical understanding of the cultural and social location of these audiences might contribute to a more nuanced understanding of the taste for heritage films.

Where, for Bourdieu, social 'distinction[s]' are expressed and legitimated through the exercising of 'judgement[s] of taste',[12] and taste formations and 'habitus' (Bourdieu's term for the set of cultural practices defining an individual or group)[13] are themselves class-specific, two more precise insights of his work are of particular interest for this book. The first of these is Bourdieu's demonstration that a variety of differentially calibrated taste formations exist *within* the middle classes (which he explains in terms of the variations in the balance between economic capital, social status and educational/cultural capital characterising different class fractions and occupational groups). The second is his observation that taste and habitus are *not* defined solely by the cultural products chosen or shunned (for instance, opera versus hip-hop) but rather by the *manner* in which they are consumed or used: 'The manner in which culture is acquired lives on in the manner of using it.'[14]

Such a line of analysis anticipates not just that we will find differentiated taste fractions and habituses within the broadly 'middle-class' NT and TO sub-samples, but that distinctions between the two cohorts may reside in their different *uses* of – or dispositions towards – heritage (and other period) films rather than simply in different film preferences. It also suggests that the ambiguous and contested cultural status of heritage films themselves – as established in media, critical and academic discourses – is likely to equate with complexities around the class identities and cultural–political dispositions of their audiences.

The relevance of Bourdieu's ideas to the study of heritage cinema has already been noted and applied by Martin A. Hipsky in his article 'Anglo-fil[m]ia: why does America watch Merchant–Ivory movies?' – although his analysis is theoretical rather than informed by empirical testimony. Hipsky's interest is in the place of 'Anglophilic' heritage films within 'a *specifically American* middle-class "habitus"' (my italics) – and, in view of this, the specifics of my analysis in the *British* context will clearly differ from his. The general connection he draws between the taste for heritage films and a position of (middle-)class *insecurity* is, however, highly pertinent for this study. Hipsky argues that Merchant Ivory's films owe their success with US audiences to their appeal to the economically redundant 'liberal arts training' of America's 'college-educated elite', and that they function to gratify a need for reassurance among the beleaguered 'professional-managerial class and its aspirants', at a time when 'the traditional ends of an expensive [US] college education' – namely, 'upward mobility or the reproduction of one's own comfortable class privilege' – are no longer guaranteed.[15]

The hypothesis that the taste for heritage films may arise from insecure or marginal(ised) class or cultural positions (albeit broadly within the 'middle class'), rather than being a confident expression of the sense of cultural entitlement or elite taste of a 'dominant' class, is taken forward in this chapter in relation to the Heritage Audience Survey evidence. If my findings support Hipsky's analysis, this will have important implications for the argument that British heritage films operate hegemonically on behalf of a high-bourgeois or even aristocratic class perspective and interests, since the meanings and uses of the films for viewers watching from an insecure class or cultural position will be rather different from their meaning for confident members of a 'relatively privileged' audience.[16]

AGE AND GENDER

Three-quarters of the Heritage Audience Survey's participants were aged 45-plus, with the remainder drawn from the 25 to 44 age band, while under-25s – who, in 1994, accounted for more than one-third of the wider UK cinema audience – were absent from the sample (Appendix 3.1). Despite the monolithic appearance of such statistics, however, a wide span of ages was represented: 26 to 61 in the TO group, and 45 to 81 among NTs. In contrast with these age profiles, the earlier *Caviar* data had shown that viewers aged 7 to 25 had formed around 20% of the audience (varying from film to film) for named 1992 and 1994 UK period-film releases (Appendix 3.2), but their numbers may well have been boosted by educational visits.

The survey's dominance by respondents aged 45-plus offers the benefit of detailed insights into the film-viewing habits and tastes, and views, of a usually neglected sector of the film audience. However, the presence of this age group in the Heritage Audience Survey sample was intensified not merely by the demographics of the National Trust's membership (see Appendix 2.2), but also by the strength of response from that source. Significantly, three-quarters of NT respondents were retired, hence more likely than working-age NT members to have the time and motivation to participate in their NT local Centres or in studies like this one. By contrast, the *Caviar* reports showed that only between 30% and 50% of the audiences for *Caviar*'s selected 1992 and 1994 period films were aged 45-plus. Hence this age group was clearly over-represented in my sample relative to their presence in wider UK period-film audiences (and would have remained so *even if* the survey data had been weighted to correct the size imbalance between the NT and TO cohorts); and, more than this, the composition of the NT cohort meant that more than 40% of all Heritage Audience Survey respondents were aged 65-plus.

Thus, while the strong participation of the 45-plus and 65-plus age groups in the survey affirmed the popularity of period films with 'older' audiences, it would be wrong to conclude that these groups dominate the wider audiences for period films to the same extent as they did my sample. On the contrary, larger surveys such as *Caviar* suggest that the latter have a more diverse age profile in which viewers aged 25 to 44 – and particularly those aged 25 to 34 – are equally significant (see Appendix 3.2).

Despite the temptation to homogenise the NT cohort as 'the 45-plus sample' and the TOs as 'the younger sample' for purposes of analysis, it must be noted that TO and NT respondents aged 45-plus did not share the same precise age profile (more than 60% of NTs were aged 65-plus; the oldest TO respondent was 61) – but more crucially, as we shall see, nor did most of them share the same lifestyles, cultural tastes or political affiliations. While four of the six TO respondents aged 45 to 61 lived in urban areas and reported seeing a film at the cinema at least once a week, only two of the twenty-four NTs aged 45 to 64 lived in urban areas or went to the cinema once a month or more. In fact, NT respondents in this age band proved to have more in common with older NTs than with their TO contemporaries.

Caviar's data had shown that relevant UK period-film releases of the 1990s had attracted audiences with a fairly even gender balance – extending upwards to 65% female for films with a very strong female appeal, notably *The Piano* (Appendix 3.2) – but also that cinema audiences in general became increasingly female-dominated in the 45-plus age bands, reversing a male-dominated gender balance in the 35 to 44 age bracket (implying, perhaps, that men of this age remain less constrained by childcare than their female contemporaries). The Heritage Audience Survey data showed some conformity with both trends. The data supported the cliché of the 'older, female' period-film audience (more than 80% of NTs were women aged 45-plus). Because *all* NTs were in this age band, evidence that this pattern signified an older female (post-child-rearing) return to cinemagoing was far from decisive – and, as we shall see in Chapter 4, the film-viewing habitus of many NTs was mainly televisual – but the National Trust's membership profile (at 1993, around 70% of members had children, but fewer than 30% had children living at home: Appendix 2.2) gives credibility to such a reading.

In a further complexity, while the *number* of NT women in each age band increased with advancing age, peaking at 65 to 74 (before a drop in numbers across both genders at age 75-plus), the *proportion* of women relative to men *fell* with advancing age. This pattern reflected the fact that almost two-thirds of male NTs (who formed only 18% of the NT cohort and were all married) were aged 65 to 74, but also fits with the (related) trends of higher female life expectancy and the older female 'return to the cinema'. The NT data suggest a refinement to our understanding of the latter: namely, that the female 'return' to film-viewing (among NTs, not strongly tied to going out to the cinema) starts in *early* middle age (the 40s) – a likely time of reduced parenting responsibilities – followed by a smaller-scale, male 'return' to film-viewing from age 55 onwards.

The TO cohort, with its younger age profile and more even gender balance, was a closer fit for the period-film audience profile indicated by *Caviar*. Moreover, this gender balance extended across virtually all age brackets, the sole exceptions being that 25- to 34-year-old TOs were predominantly (75%) female, while 35- to 44-year-old TOs were predominantly male (but by a smaller majority than the wider norm for this age band indicated in *Caviar*).

SEXUALITY

As discussed in Chapter 1, one important strand of debate around the representational significance and audience appeal of heritage films argues that they have 'provided a space for marginalised social groups, a sense of putting such people back into history, for instance women [and] lesbians and gay men'.[17] Certainly a significant number of British heritage films since the 1980s – and the post-2000 cycle of joyously sapphic period TV literary adaptations ushered in by Andrew Davies's adaptation of Sarah Waters's *Tipping the Velvet* (Geoffrey Sax, BBC-TV, 2002) – have focused on gay male or lesbian protagonists. A further strand of critical work – not least by gay male critics

– has explored the centrality of emotionalism and melodrama to the appeal of certain heritage films: qualities which, historically, are considered to have held a special appeal for both female and gay male film audiences.[18] In addition, anecdotal evidence of the appeal of heritage films to (some) gay men has circulated for almost as long as the 'heritage film' label itself – although, given the diversity of the 'genre', this appeal clearly varies from film to film, peaking in case such as *Maurice* (now viewed by many as a gay classic) .

In this context, it might be expected that the survey would attract some gay and lesbian participants – and indeed both groups were represented, although only within the TO cohort. Some 10% of TOs self-identified as gay men and a further 10% as lesbian or bisexual women – proportions broadly consistent with the gay and lesbian presence in the UK population, higher concentration in large metropolitan cities (especially London), and profile in *Time Out*'s readership. By contrast, none of the (older, and generally more socially and politically conservative) NT respondents identified themselves as homosexual, gay, lesbian or bisexual. Indeed, 21% of NTs (and one TO) declined to answer the question (which, in sensitivity to generational shifts and variations in both terminology and attitude, merely asked respondents to identify the gender, or possible gender(s), of their partner if, or when, in a relationship) – and some expressed objections that it had been asked.[19]

MARITAL STATUS AND HOUSEHOLD TYPES

Although (as we would expect) there was considerable divergence between the NT and TO cohorts in terms of marital or cohabitation status and household arrangements, one strong unifying trend emerged: most respondents across both cohorts lived lifestyles, or were at a life stage, that permitted significant autonomy in their film-viewing choices rather than these being strongly or exclusively led by the preferences of children. A striking 90% of respondents across both cohorts were free of childcare responsibilities – whether due to their youth (among TOs), advancing age (among NTs), single status (50% of TOs were not yet married nor cohabiting with a partner), or other lifestyle choices. Only eight respondents had children still living with them at home (five married NT women, two female TO co-habiters and one married NT man).

Some 95% of NT respondents but only 50% of TOs were owner-occupiers of (or in the process of buying) their homes – a difference that was related to age more than occupation or socio-economic status, and also a by-product of acutely inflated property values in London relative to the rest of the UK, and a reflection of London lifestyles among the younger working population. Thus 30% of TO respondents were single and lived alone, while a further 20% were singles sharing accommodation with friends (10%) or living with their family (10%). A further one-third of TOs were cohabiting with a partner; only 13% were married. By contrast, marriage was the norm among NTs: 56% were currently married (just under 50% of NT women, 100% of NT men); a further quarter were widows; 6% (all female) were divorced; and 13% (all female) were single and lived alone. Given that co-habitation with a partner was more widespread among TO respondents than marriage (even among the few TOs with children), we can conclude that the contrast between TO patterns and the normative status of marriage among NTs signalled a wider contrast in social attitudes rather than merely age differences. The significant presence of widowed, divorced and single women in the NT sample was not typical of the NT's wider membership profile (in 1993, 75% of NT members were married: see Appendix 2.2).

In combination, these trends affirmed that that the audiences for 'quality' period films are drawn strongly from sections of the adult audience able to exercise significant personal autonomy when choosing the films they watch, without their preferences being overridden by 'family' tastes or the demands of children or teenagers for youth-targeted product. This does not mean, of course, that respondents were wholly free of negotiations with partners or friends when choosing a film; nor (as the comments and film familiarities of some NTs made clear) that older respondents who were grandparents wholly shunned school-holiday blockbusters.

OCCUPATIONAL STATUS

In keeping with their contrasting age demographics, occupational patterns within the TO and NT cohorts were highly polarised. More than three-quarters of TO respondents were employed or (more rarely) self-employed, full-time (67%) or part-time (17%). Almost three-quarters of NTs were retired and only a tiny number (5%) were in full-time employment, although a further 16% were employed or self-employed part-time, and four NTs – classified as 'active retired' – were strongly involved in voluntary work or other activities which may, or may not, have generated income.[20] Around three-quarters of NT women and more than 80% of NT men fell into the retired or active retired categories. All three of the NTs working full-time were women (two single, one married), including a (married) 67-year-old solicitor.

Those NTs working part-time fell into three broad categories: four semi-retired professionals, three respondents in intermediate service occupations (two women, widowed or divorced, and one self-employed man, a former software analyst turned taxi-driver whose wife also worked) – work motivated by financial need – and four married women (three of whom were in their

40s, with children still at home) whose husbands were the main breadwinner. This third group mostly listed occupations which were characterised either by service to the community (special needs classroom assistant), or by pleasure and social contacts as much as profit (a 'designer-maker of clothes and theatrical costumes'), while (in common with two further married NTs who did not work) their husbands' occupations placed them in the highest (managerial and professional) socio–economic brackets.

By contrast, it was no surprise that full-time work was the dominant trend among TOs, accounting for more than 70% of TO women and more than 60% of TO men – all employees, apart from one self-employed male magazine journalist. Six (20% of) TO respondents (ranging in age from 32 to 53) worked part-time, of whom all but one were employees; and although three lived with a working partner, the others were single and lived alone, suggesting that part-time working might owe more to job availability than choice. The only self-employed TO part-timer was a male, 53-year-old 'actor and decorator', and (from a middle-class family and living in an affluent area) his socio-economic status was as ambiguous as this self-description suggests. More typically (and in contrast with part-time work trends among NTs), both the TO part-time workers and their partners worked in the 'lower' – and public sector – professions (teaching), intermediate occupations (civil service, market-research interviewer) or creative industries (photography). Only one respondent – a TO woman – was a 'full-time' degree student, but also worked part-time as a secretary. Last, one respondent (TO male, 61, a former credit controller) was a full-time carer for his father, while finding solace in intense and well-informed cinephilia ('I might as well *boast* at this point, I have a list of *cinematically* viewed films which adds up to 5,223').

CLASS, CLASS FRACTIONS AND SOCIAL MOBILITY

As we have already seen, the heritage-film critique's presentation of the films' 'primarily middle class' audiences as *self-evidently* also 'relatively privileged'[21] is something of a fallacy given that the 'mainstream' UK cinema audience of the 1990s and 2000s is, in any case, largely middle-class. If there *are* meaningful class differences between the 'mainstream' cinema audience and the audience for 'quality' period films, these are therefore likely to hinge on whether one audience is *differently* middle-class from the other, with the differentiating factors extending beyond 'raw' socio-economic class to class identities, cultures and attitudes.

But against what criteria should the class positioning of heritage film audience members be defined? Both the ABC1 'social grade' scale and the post-2002 official UK government NS-SEC classification schema derive 'social grade' or 'occupational class' from current, or last pre-retirement, occupation: usually the occupation of the 'Household Reporting Person', the main, or highest-paid, wage earner. However, occupational trends and the subjectively felt and self-reported class affiliations of British citizens have changed significantly since the mid-1990s. Indeed, the new NS-SEC schema was introduced in response to the former – objective – occupational shifts, consisting at macro level of the transition from a manufacturing economy to a service and knowledge economy, and at micro level of the related emergence of 'new' professions. However, a poll by Mori (reported in a *Guardian* leader in 2002) uncovered a paradox at the heart of contemporary British class identities: 'Some 52% of us are ABC1s compared with 36% in 1972 [and] the majority are safely liberated from manual labour', yet 'more people feel "working class and proud of it" today (68%) than did so in 1997 (58%), let alone in 1994 (52%).'[22] In all, the poll found that 55% of Britons with middle-class jobs identified as working-class. Two important implications for this study are that subjective class attitudes or affiliations clearly have a relationship of relative autonomy with 'objective' occupational class, and cannot simply be read off from it; and that patterns of subjective class self-perception may vary historically in response to changing cultural, social and political conditions. A further question to be explored is whether period/heritage films attract specific class *fractions*, or even occupations, that may have particular implications for respondents' subjective class (or occupational) cultures and dispositions towards heritage films.

The ABC1 profile of the Heritage Audience Survey sample did not merely support *Caviar*'s findings (and commonplace assumptions) that the UK audience for period films contains a greater proportion of the higher socio-economic groups than the UK cinema audience overall; it exceeded them (Appendices 3.3 and 3.4). Where 56% of the 1994 *Caviar* sample claiming to visit the cinema twice a year or more belonged to the ABC1 classes, the percentage among Heritage Audience Survey respondents was 93% (and ABC1s formed 96% of the whole sample).[23] These percentages also exceeded the proportions of ABC1s in the 1992 and 1994 audiences for *Caviar*'s named period films (which ranged between 69% and 83%), and the National Trust's and *Time Out*'s overall memberships/readerships (86% and 75% respectively). In short, the survey sample was more ABC1-dominated than *either* its two sources *or* the UK audiences for specific period films when drawn from a more demographically balanced sample. Whatever the explanation, this finding appears to confirm the period-film audience as conclusively 'an ABC1 audience' (even though C2s and DEs had comprised a quarter or more of *Caviar*'s recorded audiences for named period films such as *Howards End*).

On closer examination, however, this audience as represented in my sample was by no means a privileged, wealthy monolith, nor were many of its members drawn from a *cultural* elite. Rather, the 'middle-class' status of some respondents was fragile or marginal, and significant numbers worked – or had worked before retirement – in occupational sectors that offered neither high status nor a high income. Intergenerational upward social mobility since childhood (measured by classifying the occupations of respondents' parents during their childhood as well as current occupational class) was also a common theme in the class experience of more than one-third of respondents. Analysis of occupational data showed that at least 36% (39% of NTs, 30% of TOs) had experienced upward socio-economic mobility since childhood (effected via education, wider post-1945 socio-economic changes, marriage, or a combination of these): either from a childhood in class C1 or below into classes AB (in two-thirds of these cases, class B); or lower-range mobility from the manual classes (C2 and DE) into intermediate classes (C1). These particular social mobilities seem significant if we hypothesise that the taste for period films may be associated with the experience of either bourgeois *arrival* (into the first generation of professionals) or bourgeois *aspiration* (among first-generation white-collar workers); and with notions of social, educational and cultural *self-improvement* rather than with secure inherited membership of the bourgeoisie or its 'educated' and 'cultured' fractions.

As the breakdown in Appendix 3.3 shows, the social grades that dominated the survey sample were not the two highest, but overwhelmingly B (the intermediate – rather than higher – managerial, administrative or professional grade), followed by C1 (intermediate or lower supervisory, clerical or administrative 'white-collar' occupations rather than the professions). The sample was, in short, dominated *not* by respondents (or heads of household) in senior management and the highest-status professions (such as the law), but by members of the 'intermediate' or 'lower' professions (such as teaching), supplemented by lower-middle-class white-collar workers. Moreover, this was true across both the NT and TO sub-samples: 48% of all NTs and 63% of all TOs were from grade B households; just over a quarter of both groups were from C1 households; while 21% of NTs and only two TO respondents were from grade A households. The key difference between the two cohorts, then, was that a higher proportion of NTs came from grade A, and significantly fewer from grade B, than the TO sub-sample. The data also suggested that the NT respondents in classes A and C1 (rather than B) were those most likely to be very infrequent cinemagoers or to watch films predominantly on television (see Chapter 4). By contrast, virtually all TO respondents saw films at the cinema twice a year or more – and, in most cases, at least once a month – regardless of class.

These findings remained broadly consistent when respondents and their households were classified using the NS-SEC (instead of ABC1) scale. The main difference was that – due to SOC2000's classification of some grade B occupations as NS-SEC class 2, and others as NS-SEC class 1.2 – the use of the NS-SEC scale expands the number of 'higher' managerial and professional households. However, the NS-SEC 'class 1' households in the survey sample (mostly among NTs) were concentrated in the higher *professions* (class 1.2) rather than higher *management* (class 1.1).

In all, then, the most prominent occupational groups represented across both cohorts were the professional rather than managerial classes – and predominantly the lower (class B) professions – followed closely by respondents and households in the clerical, administrative, sales and service occupational categories: predominantly 'intermediate', but in one or two cases semi-routine. Respondents and households from the managerial classes, small entrepreneurs/employers and the self-employed were, by contrast, little represented in either the NT or TO cohort.

OCCUPATIONS

Analysis of respondents' *own* occupations (or last occupations if retired) revealed some striking patterns in terms of occupational sectors and cultures which – when interpreted alongside their self-worded statements, and the wider findings on their tastes and attitudes, analysed in later chapters – seem highly salient to understanding respondents' positionings in relation to period films and their discursive hypertexts. A remarkable number of respondents were drawn from a single occupational sector: education, predominantly schools rather than the college or university sectors, and predominantly as teachers. Of the forty-nine respondents in the lower professional class B, fourteen were either current or retired schoolteachers, one was a self-employed tutor and two were teachers of adults (prisoners and English as a Foreign Language learners respectively). Thus 18% of all respondents were current or retired teaching professionals. A further nine (10%) worked in (or had retired from) other educational or related occupations, ranging in rank from a (male) county chief educational psychologist, via two (university or specialist) librarians, to a special needs classroom assistant and four school or college secretaries or clerks (all women).

In all, this meant that 28% of respondents worked (or had worked) in the education sector in some capacity, and around three-quarters of these in schools, whether as teachers or support staff. More strikingly still, twelve (86%) of the schoolteachers and all five of the school support staff (including the special needs assistant) were female NT respondents – accounting between them for one-third of female NTs, and a quarter of all female respondents across both cohorts. Teaching and educational occupations were, by contrast, a less pronounced feature among TOs (accounting for 13% of the cohort): one

TO male was a schoolteacher, one TO female was a teacher of prisoners and two TO females were (university or specialist) librarians.

The occupations of other respondents (and, where known, their partners) varied, but one striking feature was that very few worked in the creative, cultural or literary industries. Beyond those employed in education, most AB class respondents across both cohorts (had) worked in the public services (especially health and social services), the civil service, the traditional professions (the law, medicine), financial services, or the scientific and higher technical sectors. At least 8% of respondents lived in a household where one partner or both were civil servants, although exact occupations or grades were often unstated.[24] Virtually all C1 respondents worked either in the sectors already mentioned or in the retail or service industries. With the exception of one freelance features journalist, most of the few respondents who worked in the cultural or literary sectors did so in a modest capacity (the actor/decorator, arts centre receptionist, bookselling – although one of the booksellers was the public-school-educated son of a publisher).

The survey evidence suggested, then, that enjoyment of period films was widespread among teachers and others in broadly 'educational' occupations, but also among viewers whose *working* lives were sharply divorced from the artistic, creative or literary spheres. And, despite the fact that most respondents were broadly – and would probably claim to be – 'middle-class', the class fractions represented in the survey sample were distinguished by significant variations in social status, income and likely educational capital and cultural confidence. In particular, a substantial number of both NTs and TOs belonged to 'middle-class' occupational groups with limited economic power or precarious social authority (teachers and other public-sector lower professionals); and a further quarter of respondents were drawn from the intermediate white-collar class C1, a group with less educational capital, cultural confidence or economic security. What both groups seem likely to share is an *identification* as middle-class, coupled with an insecure social status – perhaps producing a need to assert and reassert their identity as 'cultured' and/or 'educated' 'middle-class' subjects.

EDUCATIONAL CAPITAL: INTRODUCTION

As later chapters will explore, audiences' attitudes to and expectations of period films are anchored in existing – and often deep-rooted – cultural attitudes and assumptions. Many respondents' self-worded accounts of why they enjoyed – and what they enjoyed in – period films, particularly those of many NTs, shared a striking characteristic. These respondents held, and expressed, extremely strong views – on matters such as the cultural or educational value of 'the right kind' of period film – yet these were often phrased not as personal opinion but as objective fact.

In addition to the role of education in the transmission of cultural capital as proposed by Bourdieu in *Distinction*, schooling – and the broader experience of 'education', in which we could include the influences of family upbringing – was regarded by Althusser as the most significant of the 'ideological state apparatuses' through which such certainties are transmitted, received and internalised.[25] However, educational capital and influences have a further (if less far-reaching) significance for this study, given that there are concrete connections between the heritage film, formal education, and notions of what it is to be 'educated'.

First, the disposition to enjoy heritage films draws upon educational capital in the most literal way. Defining generic features are that the films are often based on literary 'classics' or real historical personae (if not always well-known, or accepted, historical events) which many viewers (certainly of the generations represented in this study) will have first encountered in school English Literature or History lessons, and which some will have studied in greater depth for A Level or at university. Second, the 'discourse of authenticity'[26] which heritage films are said to embrace – whether by '[striving] to respect the "original" text' or through painstakingly researched recreation of 'the surface qualities that define the pastness of the particular period'[27] – is logically derived from a view of the films as *fundamentally secondary* adaptations or reproductions from another, 'primary', medium. Whether the 'primary' medium is literary fiction, historiography or (truly) primary historical artefacts, in all cases the 'discourse of authenticity' sees the 'original' as culturally or academically more legitimate than film. To put this differently, the 'discourse of authenticity' perceives heritage films as a learning aid – as support materials to the novel, or historical period, or events which are the 'real' object of appreciation or study, or as a *means* of access to (re-presented or reconstructed) historical artefacts – rather than predominantly as films/texts in their own right. As we will see in later chapters, some viewers do regard, and critically evaluate, period films from precisely this perspective – as a kind of substitute, or alias, for the primary source or text. The belief that the film's 'authenticity' as a 'reproduction' of its source *matters* is connected unavoidably to the notion that heritage films have a centrally 'educational' function.

Third, we should recall that the responses to 1980s heritage films from pro-heritage critics explicitly praised the films' 'authenticity' of historical detail and 'fidelity' to literary sources as the qualities that differentiated them from the period films and literary adaptations of earlier decades and/or Hollywood.[28] The promotional value of this differentiation was well understood by those marketing the films – but, more than this, some 'heritage' period literary adaptations (for both film and TV), from at least *A Room with a*

View onwards, were marketed expressly to the schools' market via the production of education packs and/or film tie-in editions of the novels.[29] This move was made possible precisely by the circulation and promotion of the 1980s (and, subsequently, 1990s) adaptations as *more* 'true to the book', and/or more historically reliable (and hence *instructive*) in their mise-en-scène, than their 1960s and 1970s precursors.

In summary, heritage films have been one of the genres most likely to be claimed as 'educational' and, simultaneously, to function as a sign that their viewer is 'educated'. Furthermore, the films provide opportunities to exercise particular forms of educational capital, and to reinforce particular sets of internalised beliefs about what is educationally valuable or culturally prestigious, which are themselves contingent on the viewer's particular educational background. While a viewer unaware of the source novel can still enjoy *A Room with a View* the film, they are likely to respond differently to the latter (and have a different perception of its cultural value) from viewers for whom the novel is already positioned as a 'classic', with different frames of response again from those who read it at school or studied literature at university. To find out more about these particularities, this chapter will now look at the educational backgrounds and qualifications of survey respondents.

SCHOOL TYPES

The British secondary education system and its constituent school types have changed considerably during the post-World War II period in ways that were evident in patterns within the two generationally distinct sub-samples.[30] Some 40% of TO respondents had attended state comprehensive schools but (by definition) none of the older NT cohort had done so. Beyond this, the largest single group of respondents consisted of those TOs and NTs educated in two types of academically selective school straddling the state-funded and fee-paying sectors: the grammar and direct grant schools. While post-World War II grammar schools were state-funded/non-fee-paying, the direct grant schools (abolished in 1976 by a Labour government) were, in effect, fee-paying grammar schools: academically selective schools where a proportion of pupils were funded by local authority or other scholarships, while others paid means-tested fees. A total of 56% of NTs had attended one of these two school types (mostly pre-World War II, either via scholarships or as fee-payers); 27% of TOs had attended grammar schools (all but one in the post-World War II non-fee-paying period).

The shared feature of the grammar and direct grant schools, differentiating them from both state comprehensive schools and the private/'public' schools, is that they delivered an academically selective, usually traditionalist, education to pupils from relatively diverse socio-economic backgrounds. While such schools were strongly favoured by middle-class parents, they were also one of the British education system's main mechanisms for producing the upward social mobility and related attitudinal changes that were features of British society between World War II and the 1970s (the other being the expansion of the universities).[31] These were the schools that shaped (some of) the children of skilled working-class or lower-white-collar parents into 'middle-class' subjects – in educational capital and educationally instilled attitudes, if not always in permanent socio-economic fortunes.

While two-thirds of TOs had definitely been schooled within the UK state system, the mixed funding system for pre-war grammar-school pupils precludes presenting an equivalent statistic for NT respondents. What can be stated is that 40% of NTs had attended either private or direct grant schools for part or all of their schooling; one-third had attended pre-war grammar schools; and 16% had attended state (post-war grammar, secondary modern or technical) schools. In summary, the experience of a selective and self-consciously academic education was a significant trend across both cohorts. But while the TO cohort was dominated by respondents who had experienced the post-war state education system, the older NTs had predominantly been schooled in the pre-war private or grammar-schools – with consequences for the two groups' social and cultural formations that will emerge in later chapters.

QUALIFICATIONS

The post-World War II expansion of UK state education was likewise evident in the differing levels and types of qualifications attained by TO and NT respondents. More than 50% of respondents had passed school qualifications at A Level or equivalent – more than double the UK national achievement rate at any date from the mid-1970s to the late 1990s.[32] The percentage of respondents educated to A Level was highest (63%) among the younger TO cohort, but still almost 50% among NTs. For a further 20% of TOs and 29% of NTs, GCSEs, GCE O Levels, CSEs or equivalents were the highest school qualifications attained. A further 17% of TOs (all born overseas) and 8% of NTs had passed unspecified school qualifications. In total, all TOs, and more than 80% of NTs, had attained school qualifications of some kind. The remaining 18% of NTs either reported that they had no school qualifications (eight respondents – 11% of NTs – mostly female and in their 60s or 70s) or did not answer the question. For comparison, around 16% of the 2004 working-age population of Great Britain had no qualifications.[33]

If, at school level, both cohorts were more educated than the national average, this distinction became more pronounced at university level. Almost three-quarters of TOs, compared to one-third of NTs, held a degree as their highest qualification; but (bearing in mind the uneven cohort sizes) this translated into twenty-two TO and twenty NT respondents with undergraduate or higher degrees, while a further eighteen (29% of) NTs held a non-degree professional qualification.[34] Among the former, four TOs and four NTs had gained a postgraduate degree, mostly taught MAs. In all, then, 61% of NTs and 73% of TOs held a degree and/or professional qualification. For comparison, 12.3–15.6% (depending on region) of the UK population in 2001 held a degree or equivalent qualification – making the proportion of both TOs and NTs qualified to degree or professional level far higher than the national average.[35]

Most NTs had attended one of two types of further- or higher-education institution that would have been seen as a 'natural' progression from their typically traditionalist, selective schooling: either the traditional old or redbrick universities other than Oxford or Cambridge, or training establishments such as medical schools or (for seven of the eighteen NTs who had professional qualifications but not degrees) teacher-training colleges. TO respondents, by contrast, had attended a more eclectic range of university types, ranging from Oxbridge, via the new universities founded in the 1960s, to the post-1992 'new' universities (former polytechnics). Some 60% of TOs held a work or professional qualification in addition to a degree, and these too were very diverse, encompassing some of the same fields as NTs (social work, health, teaching, librarianship), plus accountancy, psychology and drama.

EDUCATIONAL CAPITAL IN ENGLISH LITERATURE AND HISTORY

In view of Hipsky's analysis, I was interested in the extent to which an interest in films adapted from literature or with historical settings might correlate with formal qualifications in English Literature or History. It certainly seems credible that forms of cultural capital salient to reading such films, and the disposition to enjoy them, are likely to be acquired in an 'educational' context (whether formal or informal). However, in arguing that 'the proper level of liberal arts training' is 'central to understanding the films' basic themes and character development', Hipsky may well overstate the need for such 'training'.[36] Writing from personal memory, my interest in watching BBC Classic Serials on television developed too young (between the ages of eight and twelve) to be credited to 'liberal arts training'. This interest was prompted more by a generalised awareness that these productions were supposed to be culturally or educationally enriching, in a context in which the enjoyability of reading – not necessarily the same 'classic' novels I saw televised – had been promoted from an early age, not only by (low-income, lower-middle-class) parents but, more indirectly, by a Dickens-fixated working-class grandfather.[37] Interests fostered in formal education also played their part – but my point in this anecdote is that they will not always provide the primary impetus.

Just over a quarter of survey respondents (thirteen, or 43% of, TOs; eleven, or 18% of, NTs) had studied History, English Literature (or, in one case, Drama), or both, at undergraduate and/or postgraduate level. Moreover, 11% of the overall sample *combined* university qualifications in these subjects with a teaching or librarianship qualification. Their training (and past or present occupation) thus permitted or required them to use or display this subject expertise in a pedagogic context.

Among TOs, degrees in (or including) English Literature were more widespread (held by at least 30%) than degrees in History (held by at least 13%). One TO respondent combined a BA in History with an MA in English, and two had supplemented one of these subjects with an MA or Joint BA in Cultural Studies. The NT cohort showed a more even balance between the two subjects, but also included the only respondent with a History (or any) PhD. The prevalence of English Literature qualifications among TOs could be tracked back to A Level, when 43% of TOs (the same proportion holding English or History degrees) had studied the subject; a further 40% had studied it to O Level, GCSE or equivalent. School qualifications in English Literature were also widespread among NTs: 26% had studied it to A Level, and a further 29% to O Level or equivalent.

On this evidence, it is credible that the disposition to watch or enjoy films and TV dramas adapted from literary 'classics' and/or with historical settings will have been acquired by at least some respondents via the study of literature or history at school or university. But conversely, most respondents did not hold *higher*-education qualifications in these subjects, and some might argue that school qualifications in these subjects are too widespread to serve as strong indicators in themselves.

One final factor seemed likely to have exerted a more decisive influence on respondents' cultural orientations and critical attitudes towards literary adaptation and period films. Predominantly drawn from different generations, the NT and TO cohorts had been educated in eras separated by profound disciplinary shifts within literary and historical studies and the wider Humanities. NT respondents had, typically, acquired their educational capital and notions of cultural value via traditionalist schooling and higher education – the certainties of which would have been reinforced, in many cases, by teacher training and a pedagogic occupational culture. The majority of TOs, by contrast, had acquired theirs via degree study in the post-1960 era in which the Humanities had been transformed by the influences of post-structuralism, Marxism, semiotics and critical theory, and by the emergence of new disciplines such as Cultural Studies. More than this, 40% of TOs held degrees in Humanities subjects (including, in two cases, Cultural Studies); and one-third had studied at 1960s or post-1992 'new' universities, the sectors at the forefront of this transformation. It would be surprising if these experiences of contrasting – even opposed – academic cultures did not, at some level, inflect the two audiences' modes of engagement with 'quality' period films, particularly those adapted from literary 'classics'; and, indeed, substantial evidence of such differences is presented in later chapters.

RACE AND NATIONALITY

Given that heritage films have been charged with imagining an *English* – rather than inclusively British – past, not merely from a classed bourgeois or aristocratic perspective but with an almost exclusively white population, they cannot be assumed to have a wide appeal to non-white/ethnic minority audiences. Despite Richard Dyer's (correct) observation that the heritage film has (in some cases) 'provided a space' for putting 'marginalised social groups' 'back into history',[38] it has remained a rarity for British period films of any genre to give centrality to (or even acknowledge) the historical presence of black or other ethnic minority populations in the UK.[39]

There are, nonetheless, complexities within the apparent 'whiteness' and 'Englishness' of British heritage and post-heritage cinema. On the one hand, we could cite the key contributions of the late producer Ismail Merchant (born in Bombay) to the development of the former, or of the director Shekhar Kapur (born in pre-Partition Lahore) to the latter. On the other, there is Patricia Rozema's emphatically postcolonial 1999 reworking of Jane Austen's *Mansfield Park*, which puts black slavery as a source of English country-house wealth 'back into history' but features no (on-screen) black actors.[40] Moreover, given the variety and popularity of the field of period films and TV literary adaptations, it would be strange if the audiences they attracted in multicultural Britain were 100% white. Back in 1996, I was interested to overhear a young Afro-Caribbean woman enthusiastically discussing the then-current ITV adaptation of Daniel Defoe's 1722 novel *Moll Flanders* on a bus travelling from Hackney (a borough with high deprivation indices and a substantial black population) towards central London. It was clear that Moll's narrative had appealed to her and engaged her in ways that were relevant to areas of black female experience without being directly 'about' race.[41]

Appendix 3.5 summarises the self-reported ethnicities and nationalities of respondents. The survey attracted two black Caribbean or African respondents – both TO women, of whom one was Scottish rather than a Londoner by birth (and also one of the few lesbian respondents) – but no British Asians. Although at least 80% of TO respondents were white, their national origins were notably diverse. While 50% of TOs described themselves as British, 10% as English, and a further four as Welsh, Scottish or Irish, the cohort also included US citizens, white Europeans and one young (self-described) 'British-Iranian' woman. By contrast, all NT respondents described their nationality as either British (82%) or English (18%), and only one – Jewish – described their race as anything other than 'white'. Some 24% of NTs – and also 10% of TOs – did not specify their race. All the non-specifiers described their nationality as British, English or part-British, and (from this and some of their wider statements) it seemed probable that the majority were white – including at least some for whom the terms 'English' or 'British' *self-evidently denote* whiteness – rather than ethnic-minority respondents choosing not to declare their origins. Where TOs' self-descriptions tended to stress a distinctive cultural or regional identity, NTs' preference for calling themselves 'British' or 'English' in some cases effaced more specific origins. Three NTs in this category (including two born in 1920s–1930s Germany) were non-British by birth but had subsequently become British citizens.

REGIONS AND NEIGHBOURHOOD TYPES

In view of the claim that heritage films have promoted a 'southern English' and 'pastoral' hegemonic vision of the nation, the UK regions where respondents happened – or had chosen – to live at the survey date (Appendix 3.6), and the possible urban/rural affiliations encoded in such accidents or choices, are of some subsidiary interest. Given the source populations, it was no surprise that 90% of TO respondents were Londoners by birth or migration – from other UK regions, or more occasionally from abroad – while 89% of NTs lived outside Greater London, mostly in less assertively urban areas. Overall, 37% of respondents lived in Greater London and the remaining 63% in other UK regions.

While stereotypes might lead us to expect the NT cohort to show a southern/Home Counties English bias (and almost 40% of the National Trust's membership is concentrated in these areas),[42] the NT volunteers for the survey in fact came from a more diverse spread of regions. Only 37% of NTs lived in South, South-East or South-West England, while 26% lived in the North, including remote counties such as Cumbria – a pattern of participation showing that heritage films are not a uniquely 'southern' taste. The birthplace regions of both cohorts were, similarly, varied, and did not show a strong bias towards the South or South-East. While the core trend among TOs was net migration into London from other regions or countries (although around one-third had been born in London or the South-East), more than 20% of NTs had been born in London but migrated out (mostly to the South or South-East), and only one London-born NT still lived in the capital. The remaining (majority of) NTs had been born, and lived, outside London, but with significant migration between the regions.

An analysis of the neighbourhood types where respondents lived provides a helpful supplementary tool for understanding socio-economic status and 'life-styles' – at least as suggested by composite indices of these for their local areas. Neighbourhood types were analysed (via respondents' home postcodes at the date of survey completion) using the Acorn (A Classification Of Residential Neighbourhoods) schema (developed by the marketing-data firm CACI), which generates neighbourhood classifications from 'more than 250 pieces of information drawn from the Census and various market-research and lifestyle databases'.[43] For a summary of how Acorn was used in my analysis, details of the thirty-five area types from which survey respondents were drawn (out of a total of fifty-four neighbourhood-type classifications presented in the *Acorn User Guide 2001*), and references for more detailed information on the Acorn schema, see Appendix 3.7, which also presents the findings.

Despite Acorn's evident limitations – it conceives and profiles individuals as *consumers* in terms of consumption-based 'lifestyles', and then general-ises these profiles in terms of the lifestyles and consumption patterns most 'typical' of each neighbourhood type – the Acorn classifications provide a snapshot of the 'average' inhabitants of specific postcodes which it would be difficult to glean by other means. As the Acorn schema includes clusters of area types with close similarities – and this was reflected in the patterns found among respondents – my analysis here focuses only on summary trends, as set out in Appendix 3.7.

Unsurprisingly, 83% of TOs lived in 'urban' Acorn neighbourhood types, and the remainder in 'suburban' areas. The key distinction to be drawn was between the 43% of TOs who lived in urban neighbourhoods described in the Acorn schema as 'affluent', 'prosperous', 'gentrified' or 'well-off' – the domains of 'young professionals' and 'highly qualified executives' – and the 40% in urban areas which were more socially and economically mixed: 'par-tially gentrified' at most, usually 'multi-ethnic', and in some cases with 'severe' or 'high' unemployment. By contrast, a mere five (8% of) NTs lived in 'urban' neighbourhoods – mostly in area types characterised by Acorn as 'affluent'. By far the largest group, almost 60% of NTs, lived in suburban areas of varying socio-economic character; a further 21% in 'rural' Acorn area types; and the remaining 13% in regional small-town centres.

Some 48% of NT respondents lived in areas classified by Acorn schema as 'mature' or 'established' home-owning areas (summarised for simplicity in Appendix 3.7 as 'suburban affluent'), but (within this cluster) only one-third of NTs lived in suburbs *explicitly* classified by Acorn as 'wealthy', 'affluent' or 'well-off'. The remaining 14% lived in 'established' but less wealthy suburbs – in a few cases, 'multi-ethnic' or with some 'council tenants' living alongside 'retired people'.[44] A further 10% lived in suburban intermediate/blue-collar areas, where home ownership was the norm, but where the typical inhabitants were clerical or 'skilled' workers rather than middle-class professionals. Of the 21% of NT respondents living in rural areas, around half lived in neigh-bourhoods where retired or home-working incomers and 'holiday retreats' rubbed shoulders with rural poverty and under-employment. The other half lived in a single Acorn area type (Type 2 in the 2001 schema), 'villages with wealthy commuters': rural or once-rural areas with good access to highly paid urban employment which have been colonised by wealthy professionals (for example, much of the Home Counties) – a more privileged variant on the 'affluent' suburbs.

The small/regional town centres where the remaining 13% of NTs lived varied considerably in their affluence, social status and population mix. These were the kinds of places popular as retirement destinations, either because town-centre amenities are within walking distance or because of their pictur-esque, coastal or historic locations. However, only two NTs lived in the 'well-off' town centres or 'academic centres' in this bracket. The remaining 10% lived in lower-status 'multi-occupied town centres' dominated by 'converted flats and bedsits' inhabited by 'single people': places which, since the 1980s, have increasingly housed transient populations alongside the retired. The characteristics of these areas were noticeably less stable than most of the other Acorn area types; indeed, a number of the postcodes concerned have been reclassified by Acorn since 2001 in ways that suggest the areas themselves have changed significantly.

POLITICS AND NEWSPAPER READERSHIP

The Heritage Audience Survey was undertaken at a particular juncture of political transformation in Britain which – viewed from the perspective of the more recent economic and political convulsions of the early twenty-first century – already feels like a different era. This context must be taken into account when interpreting respondents' replies about their political sym-pathies. If late 1980s/early 1990s critical assumptions about the enjoyment of heritage films were well founded, one might expect to find a correlation between enjoyment of certain types of period film and indicators of aesthetic, social and/or political conservatism on the part of respondents. Conversely, if – as I had hoped – the survey found evidence that heritage films were enjoyed also by audiences with less 'conservative' tastes, attitudes and lifestyles, including viewers with left-of-centre politics, this would unsettle some of the founding assumptions of anti-heritage-film criticism.

However, political developments in the UK during the 1990s made the political positions and party affiliations of the population less easy to gauge by the date of the Heritage Audience Survey than they might have been in the more polarised climate of the mid-1980s. Following Margaret Thatcher's resignation as Prime Minister in 1990, and the increasingly unpopular continuation of the Conservative government under John Major's leadership, May 1997 brought a landslide General Election victory for Tony Blair's New Labour government, in which Conservative Party support evaporated across swathes of the political map of Britain, bringing eighteen years of Conservative rule to a decisive end.[45]

Clearly, significant numbers of former Conservative voters must have switched to Labour (or the Liberal Democrats) in the 1997 election, if only temporarily. At the end of the 1990s there seemed to be no prospect of a Conservative return to government in the foreseeable future. In this climate, much of the opposition to New Labour from the right began to express itself outside the Conservative Party, via informal (and often internally self-contradictory) coalitions such as the fuel protest lobby of autumn 2000 or the Countryside Alliance, as well as new parties such as the anti-European, anti-immigration UK Independence Party (UKIP). At the same time, New Labour's attachment to a market-led pro-business agenda was perceived by many on the left as a continuation of 1980s Conservatism rather than a satisfactory break from it. The late 1990s were also characterised by a rise in voter apathy and fall in electoral participation – due in part to swift disillusion with the New Labour 'project' and the lack of a feasible alternative.

These developments have various implications for the interpretation of the political affiliations (or lack of these) expressed by my respondents in questionnaires that were completed between late 1997 and mid 1998. This was a moment at which it seemed possible that only the most loyal diehards might admit to supporting the Conservative Party, but at which the post-election enthusiasm of New Labour's initial supporters had not yet soured. In such a context, the replies of respondents who claim not to support any political party, or refuse to make their sympathies public, need especial care in interpretation. Rather than necessarily signalling political apathy, the former position might be adopted by disillusioned voters on right or left out of despair. And although there will always be respondents who regard party support as a private matter, refusals to reveal political sympathies may sometimes indicate political views that might be deemed too embarrassing or unacceptable to state openly to strangers – whether this means admitting to being a Conservative supporter following a crushing electoral defeat, or expressing support for the British National Party (BNP).

In view of such issues, respondents' likely political affiliations were mapped by cross-referencing their direct replies on political party support (Appendix 2.1: Question 37) with their replies on newspaper (and, where relevant, magazine) readership (Question 34). The findings both illustrated and affirmed the complexities of late-1990s British political affiliation or disaffiliation discussed above. Forty-five respondents across both cohorts – almost half the sample – claimed to support 'no' political party. There was, however, a striking difference between the 40% of TOs and the 53% of the NTs who gave this answer. While most of the TO 'no-party' respondents were readers of politically indeterminate newspapers (or mixes), more than three-quarters of the 'no-party' NTs were readers of right-wing newspapers – implying that the latter (comprising more than 40% of the NT cohort) were unadmitted or disaffected Conservative supporters. A further three NTs said that they supported a political party but declined to say which one; again, all three were readers of right-wing newspapers.

In addition to these possible disillusioned Conservatives and concealed right-wingers, however, around a quarter of NTs were happy to declare themselves as Conservative supporters. By contrast, none of the TO cohort admitted to supporting the Conservatives, and only three of the 'no-party' TOs were readers of right-wing newspapers. The evidence thus suggested that three TO respondents, at most, may have tended towards the right – while at least a quarter of NTs were Conservative Party supporters, and a further 47% of NTs appeared to be either conservatives without a party or supporters of an unnamed party on the right. The magazines read by NTs tended to support this impression. Beyond the National Trust and English Heritage members' magazines, and niche titles (such as *Saga*) aimed at the affluent retired, NT respondents mentioned – unprompted – the heritage titles *In Britain*, *This England* and *Heritage*; *Country Life* and *The Countryman*; the *Church Times*; and the magazine of UKIP.

The TO cohort, by contrast, was predominantly split between the 40% who said they supported no political party and 43% who were self-stated Labour supporters. The remaining five (17% of) TOs supported a spectrum of (mostly minority) centre, ecological or far-left parties: two supported the Liberal Democrats, two the Greens, and one was a member of the Socialist Workers' Party.

The daily and Sunday newspapers read by respondents were loosely consistent with these patterns. Daily newspapers on the right were favoured by more than 70% of NTs (predominantly *The Times* and *Daily Telegraph*, followed by the *Daily Mail*). While 43% of TOs read either the *Guardian* or a mix of left/liberal daily titles, 10% read either *The Times* or a mix of right-wing titles. Fewer than 60% of respondents read a Sunday paper. Among NTs, the *Sunday Telegraph* was the most popular choice (read by 18%), followed by the

Sunday Times and the *Mail on Sunday*. Among TOs, the *Observer* was the most popular choice (read by 17%), followed by the *Independent on Sunday*.

NOTES

1. Monk, 'Heritage films and the British cinema audience in the 1990s'. The central sources analysed were *Caviar 10* (presenting data from the 1992 Caviar survey, published 1993) and *Caviar 12* (presenting data from the 1994 Caviar survey, published 1995).
2. Ibid., p. 25.
3. Ibid., pp. 28–31.
4. UK Film Council, *RSU Statistical Yearbook 2005/06*, p. 55.
5. Ibid., Table 8.5, p. 56 and Table 8.8, p. 57.
6. See Appendix 3.1. See also Monk, 'Heritage films and the British cinema audience in the 1990s', p. 28 and Table 2.2, p. 30.
7. At the completion date of this book, the most recent *Caviar* report held by the BFI National Library remained *Caviar 12* (1995). The BFI's only post-1995 *Caviar* acquisition is a summary of *Caviar*'s 1995–9 key findings, but this lacks the detail of the full reports, particularly on the composition of audiences for specific genres or films. The BFI Library's list of 'Directories and reference works for UK film, television, video and media' makes clear that its *Caviar* holdings have been limited by the extreme cost of the reports, cited as more than £700 per year for *non-current* editions three or more years old. The summary data presented in the UKFC's *Films in the UK 2002* yearbook, and later editions, omit crucial relevant age bands from the breakdown of UK cinema audiences by age and gender, and presents no breakdown by ABC social grade.
8. NS-SEC is a two-tier classification system, comprising eight Analytic Classes (broadly corresponding to the old Social Class scale) and seventeen Operational Categories (some subdivided further) which describe broad employment sectors or types within the Analytic Classes. For simplified summaries of the Analytic Classes, see Brindle, 'Teachers get more class in social shake-up', or Ezard, 'Underclass now knows its place in revised social classification'. For full details of NS-SEC and SOC2000, see Office of National Statistics, *The National Statistics Socio-Economic Classification User Manual* (for a summary, pp. 1–2, p. 8 and pp. 24–6).
9. In this book I conceive of the cultural and experiential facets of class as operating in addition to the Marxist relational model of 'objective' class (which, as will be apparent, my analysis does not adhere to solely, or closely). For a lucid discussion, and argument on behalf, of the latter, see Paul Dave, *Visions of England*, pp. 1–4 and beyond.
10. Bourdieu, *Distinction*, p. 1.
11. Ibid., p. 6.
12. Ibid., title and subtitle.
13. To borrow a summary from Martin Hipsky, 'Bourdieu defines the "habitus" as a set of class-associated cultural practices that are defined over against [sic] those of other classes' ('Anglofil[m]ia', p. 102). A number of sociology scholars define the concept in considerably more complex, even obscure, terms (in which 'habitus' tends to be conceived as the *foundation* for cultural practices rather than the set of practices themselves); and, as some point out, the term has a longer philosophical lineage prior to its adoption by Bourdieu for his particular purposes. This book uses the term 'habitus' in the same, relatively simple, sense as Hipsky.

14. Bourdieu, *Distinction*, p. 2.
15. Hipsky, 'Anglofil[m]ia', p. 102 and p. 103.
16. Higson, 'Re-presenting the national past', p. 114.
17. Dyer, 'Heritage cinema in Europe', p. 205.
18. See particularly Finch and Kwietniowski, 'Melodrama and *Maurice*', and Dyer, 'Feeling English'. In support of *Maurice*'s accumulated status (and fan following) as a gay classic a quarter century after the film's release, see Thomas Waugh, *The Fruit Machine*, pp. 187–90 (especially p. 190) and imDb user discussions of the film at http://www.imdb.com/title/tt0009351/board [28 March 2011].
19. Hensher, 'Only gay in the village? Not quite', reveals that even a large-scale 2010 survey of sexual orientation by the UK's Office of National Statistics was impeded by refusals to answer, and even by 'don't know' replies.
20. The 'active retired' category was introduced into my analysis in response to comments from some NT respondents who felt that the questionnaire should have included a question about voluntary work, and to others who named 'occupations' which they evidently took seriously – 'writer and artist', 'part-time genealogist' – but it was unclear whether (or how far) these were paid. Most 'active retired' respondents were married women, and it was unclear whether they had been in paid work prior to their husbands' retirement.
21. Higson, 'Re-presenting', p. 110 and p. 114.
22. Anon., 'The class war is over'.
23. The UKFC *RSU Statistical Yearbook 2005/06* showed that, by 2005, 57% of the UK audience attending the cinema *once* a month or more were ABC1s (broadly consistent with the 1994 *Caviar* data), with this percentage rising to 64% for the year's UK box-office Top 20 films, and to 66% for the UK box-office Top 20 *British* films (p. 58) – illustrating the continuing importance of the ABC1 audience for box-office success.
24. Respondents or their partners whose occupation was described only as 'civil servant' were classified at a social grade consistent with their educational qualifications (class B if they held a degree, clerical class C1 if they held only lower qualifications).
25. Althusser, 'Ideology and Ideological State Apparatuses'. The extended notion of education I invoke here differs from Bourdieu's usage, which by contrast distinguishes between the roles of 'educational level' and 'social origin' – and varying balances between these – in instilling different forms of cultural capital and habitus (*Distinction*, p. 1).
26. Higson, *Waving the Flag*, p. 26.
27. Higson, 'Re-presenting', p. 116.
28. In illustration, see Montgomery-Massingberd's *Daily Telegraph* review of *A Handful of Dust* – 'There has been a marked change recently in the cinema's approach to the novel, with adaptations becoming much more faithful to the text' – which constructs 'the new Novel-as-Cinema genre' as a welcome corrective to such past heresies (which the author, tellingly, associates with the 1960s).
29. See, for example, the education pack produced by BFI Education in relation to Andrew Davies's high-profile 1994 adaptation of George Eliot's *Middlemarch* for BBC-TV.
30. The gradual introduction of comprehensive schools from the 1950s was supposed to herald the abolition in England and Wales of academically and socially selective state education; but in practice this persisted in a variety of forms, while the (fee-paying) private/public school system has remained untouched. Prior to the comprehensive era, children within the state system who failed the 11-plus (grammar school selection) exam attended 'elementary' schools (pre-World War II) or either 'secondary modern' or 'technical' schools (under the post-World War II tripartite system), all of which were replaced by comprehensives. However, the grammar schools remained in many parts of

the UK: in some cases becoming fee-paying, in some others disguised as comprehensives, with the 'selection' of pupils now determined by catchment area (home address) – in effect, by social capital and class rather than competitive exams.

31. Pro-grammar-school commentators have been keen to establish a causal link between the reversal of upward socio-economic mobility trends in the UK by the late 1990s and the abolition of the grammar schools (see, for example, Cohen, 'How our schools are failing the poor'). A more scrupulous analysis would identify other contributing factors: centrally, the sharp increase in income inequality in the UK since the 1970s – produced by forces such as economic deregulation – which by 1995 was more acute than in any other member country of the Organisation for Economic Co-operation and Development (OECD). See Gottschalk and Smeeding, *Empirical Evidence on Income Inequality in Industrialized Countries*, particularly Figure 4.

32. In 1975–6, 12.1% of all girls and 14.5% of all boys in the UK of A Level age passed two or more A Levels or three or more Scottish Highers. By 1997–8 the percentages were 24.8% and 20.8% (Office of National Statistics, 'Achievement at GCE A Level or equivalent: by gender, 1975/76 to 1997/98').

33. UK Office of National Statistics website: www.statistics.gov.uk/cci/nugget.asp?id=963 [20 August 2006].

34. 'Professional' qualifications were defined as those required for entry into occupations defined as 'professions' in the NS-SEC schema. These included newly designated professions (nursing), intermediate professions (librarianship, teaching) and traditional 'higher' professions (doctor of medicine, law), but not (for example) secretarial work, cookery or bookkeeping.

35. Office of National Statistics, 'Population of working age: by highest qualification' at Spring 2001.

36. Hipsky, 'Anglofil[m]ia', p. 103.

37. For a cultural history of working-class reading and reader response, see Rose, *The Intellectual Life of the British Working Classes*.

38. Dyer, 'Heritage cinema in Europe', p. 205.

39. See Bourne, 'Secrets and lies'.

40. As Church Gibson, 'Otherness, transgression and the postcolonial perspective', discusses, Rozema's *Mansfield Park* conveys the structuring presence of the question of slavery indirectly – via devices such as Tom Bertram's graphic drawings of the abuse of slaves on his father's Antigua plantation, distantly heard African song and glimpses of a passing slave ship (pp. 59–60). In this light, the absence of on-screen black actors can be construed as a refusal of representational strategies that would (literally) re-enact the subjugation of the black body.

41. As discussed in greater detail in Cardwell, *Adaptation Revisited*, *Moll Flanders* belonged to a strand of newly 'self-conscious, more sophisticated' mid-1990s productions 'reflect[ing] a wider generic shift in classic novel adaptations' (p. 161). Cardwell cites the production's emphasis on 'eighteenth-century squalor, degradation and darkness' (p. 161) and its exploitation of bawdiness as its 'key selling point' (p. 164), but also its use of devices such as Moll's direct address to camera (pp. 166–8) and her constant performativity (pp. 175–9). Its appeal for a contemporary black female Londoner may lie in the 'realism' of the earthy subject-matter and setting, the picaresque nature of Moll's upward social trajectory, and/or this unusually direct mode of address.

42. The Trust's survey *National Trust Membership by Region* (30 May 1997) showed that 38% of members lived in the South of England, Thames and Chilterns, and Kent and East Sussex NT regions; 20% in Devon, Cornwall and Wessex; 11% in 'Mercia' (extending

from Shropshire to Cheshire and Greater Manchester); 10% in the North West, Northumbria and Yorkshire; 7% in the 'Severn' region (Herefordshire, Gloucestershire, Worcestershire and Warwickshire); 7% in East Anglia; and only 2.5% in Wales. At 2010, the current (restructured) National Trust regions were: Devon and Cornwall, East Midlands, East of England, Northern Ireland, North West, South East, Thames and Solent (including London), Wales/Cymru, Wessex, West Midlands, Yorkshire and North East.

43. www.upmystreet.com [12 November 2005]. The full Acorn profiles incorporate indicators ranging from favoured leisure activities and preferred alcoholic beverages, via levels of ITV viewing, to conservatory ownership and likely ownership of stocks and shares.

44. The descriptive terms quoted here are drawn from the 54 Acorn neighbourhood profiles in CACI, *Acorn User Guide 2001*, accessed via www.upmystreet.com [12–16 November 2005].

45. New Labour's thirteen years in government were, in turn, terminated by the no-overall-majority outcome of the May 2010 General Election, which – at the date this book went to press – had yielded a Conservative–Liberal Democrat coalition government, headed by Old Etonian David Cameron as (Conservative) Prime Minister.

Respondents' Film Viewing Habit(u)s

INTRODUCTION

Chapter 4 considers the main patterns and cultures of cinemagoing and domestic film viewing characteristic among the two groups who took part in the Heritage Audience Survey. The emphasis is on the general contours of respondents' film-viewing habitus (i.e. their cultural practices in relation to film viewing: for a discussion of the concept of habitus as developed by Pierre Bourdieu, and its application in this study, see Chapter 3). Chapter 5 moves on from this to explore the range, and kinds, of films respondents had seen, and key features of the more detailed patterns of film taste found among the *Time Out* readers ('TO respondents') and committed National Trust members ('NT respondents') respectively, beginning with an overview – including the place of *non-period* films in these tastes – before building a more detailed portrait of respondents' film viewing and patterns of taste and enjoyment with reference to *period* films.

In this and later chapters, I use the term 'period films' as a broad, cross-genre label, encompassing both fictional and fact-based narrative feature films which are set in a specific past period that is clearly indicated (by narrative, visual and/or other means) as historically distinct from 'the present' (regardless of whether this past is several centuries distant or within living memory) at the date of the film's production.[1] Conversely, I use the term 'non-period films' – for brevity, if inelegantly – primarily to mean films set diegetically (i.e. in terms of their narrative) in the contemporary world at the date when they were made.

It will be clear, however, that the dividing line between 'past' and 'present' narratives cannot always be sharply drawn; for example, in films where the action takes place over an extended time span from 'past' to 'present', or alternates between both. Moreover, the classification 'period films' in this study refers *only* to films set in the past, while excluding films set in unspecified spaces/times that are styled as distinct from 'here and now' (as in, for example, Caro and Jeunet's *Delicatessen*), or films and genres set in the future. In view of this book's specific interest in audiences for films that represent the *past*, films and genres with future or fantasy settings (including many science-fiction films) are thus included in the *non-period* films category for its particular purposes of analysis – while acknowledging that this is an imperfect decision, and that a different classificatory logic might apply for scholars with different concerns.

Chapter 4 explores respondents' film-viewing habitus in the following four areas. First, their self-reported frequency of cinemagoing. Second, their practices of film viewing on television and other domestic media. (In the context of available technologies in the UK in the late 1990s when the survey was conducted – as well as the practices of the groups who participated in the study – this meant use of home video but not DVD, which had become available across the USA only in 1997.) Third, the place (or not) of home-video collections in respondents' viewing of films and/or period TV dramas. Last, the types of cinemas where films were seen.

My discussion assumes that the patterns of habitus (and, in later chapters, film tastes) identified are indicative of likely trends among the larger segments of the UK film audience from which the two cohorts of survey respondents were drawn. It should not be assumed, however, that the patterns observed here (nor the patterns of film taste observed in later chapters) form an exhaustive portrait of all possibilities among audiences for quality period (or 'heritage') films.

CRITICAL ASSUMPTIONS VERSUS RESEARCH HYPOTHESES

The critique of heritage cinema has demarcated 'heritage films' as institutionally and culturally distinct from the mainstream in particular ways that mark enjoyment of them as a taste, and a sphere of consumption, characterised by a degree of (self-conscious) separation from commercial popular film/culture. However, although heritage films have often been projected as 'elite' cultural products, they occupy an uneasily hybrid position in relation to notions of art cinema – to the extent that significant parts of the audience for art-house (or, to use today's preferred industry term, 'specialist') films would wish to dissociate themselves from 'heritage cinema'. At the same time, many of the best-known heritage films have been both profitable and popular with crossover – and even fairly mainstream – audiences; and since the 1990s, heritage and post-heritage films are, increasingly, circulated as expressly commercial products. Yet their persistent reputation as 'culturally respectable, quality'[2] films makes them far from *cinematically* prestigious from the perspective of cine-literate cinephiles.

If heritage films are deemed unsatisfactory as either popular entertainment or cinematic art (and, in parallel, unsatisfactory from the critical perspectives of both popular-culturalists *and* aesthetic-formalists seeking to champion 'film as film'), their status as 'impure' or 'mixed' cinema[3] is compounded by their multiple intertextualities: with television, with canonic 'classic' novels, and with the manifestations of the heritage industry. These intertextualities have caused the heritage film to be identified as a manifestation of postmodern culture.[4] But, while these qualities might be accepted or even celebrated in other genres, the critical discourse around heritage films has tended to present them as negatives which (via the relationship to 'conservative' cultural forms – such as literary 'classics' – and practices – such as visiting stately homes) serve only to confirm the films' low cultural status as well as ideological conservatism.

This critical construction projects the taste for heritage films, and the context(s) in which they are viewed and consumed, as not only middlebrow – neither properly 'popular' nor appealing to informed cinephiles – but also in multiple senses 'uncinematic'. The label 'heritage cinema' itself hinges on an insistence that the films are 'just one aspect of the heritage industry as a whole'[5] – more, it is implied, than they are part of the cinema 'as a whole'. They are said to 'appeal to a film culture closely allied to English literary culture and the canons of good taste'[6] rather than a culture fanatical about film *as film*. Moreover, the British heritage-film cycle of the 1980s and 1990s 'depend[ed] on television in a variety of ways'[7] – institutionally, financially and for distribution – which have blurred the films' credentials as cinema. Of course, British cinema since the 1970s has been more widely dependent on TV in precisely the same ways. But the implication has lingered that heritage films *in particular* are watched and enjoyed in a context which is more televisual than cinematic, and which is properly understood more as a continuum with other forms of 'heritage' consumption than as part of film culture.

Chapters 4 and 5 test such insinuations about heritage-film viewing and its contexts by drawing on concrete empirical testimony from the audiences who have hitherto not been brought into the debate (despite being frequently stereotyped by it). If dominant critical assumptions, and some industry beliefs, about heritage films and their audiences are correct, we might expect to find, for example, that the 'typical' viewer of 'quality' period films is an infrequent, 'event' cinemagoer; or that they watch their favoured films mainly or exclusively via TV and other home-entertainment technologies. We might also expect to find that heritage films are enjoyed by this audience as part of a cultural diet in which contemporary popular cinema plays a very small part, but in which TV period dramas/serials are more widely and avidly consumed.

However, the established debate around heritage cinema also raises questions whose implications for the behaviour and tastes we might expect to find among the films' audience(s) are less clear. For example, the uncertain cultural status of heritage films as both art/popular cinema crossovers and 'impure', middlebrow cultural products makes it possible that they are enjoyed as part of a pronounced art-cinema diet by some audiences but as part of a popular-cinema diet by others – and that either sub-group may engage knowledgeably with the wider field of contemporary cinema in ways that challenge stereotypes of the heritage-film audience.

Chapters 4 and 5 will show that the viewing contexts and taste fields within which heritage films are enjoyed vary considerably for different sectors of the audience. These contrasting – and sometimes polarised – patterns can broadly be mapped in terms of contrasts between the *Time Out* and National Trust sub-groups of respondents (and accordingly, future chapters take this approach). But it is vital to add that there were also variations and micro-trends within each group, and some micro-trends that spanned both, signalling that an over-reductive reading of the survey's findings must be resisted.

CINEMAGOING FREQUENCY

As Chapter 3 established, very frequent cinemagoing is no longer the norm among contemporary British audiences, regardless of age; but, at the same time, seeing films at the cinema remains a significant cultural or leisure activity for a wider range of age groups than the under-18s and under-25s – and, increasingly since the late 1990s, the 'family film' market – most coveted by the industry. Moreover, the intersection between these trends and an ageing society (in which the baby-boom generations had reached their 30s, 40s or even early 50s by the late 1990s) makes film audiences and cinemagoers aged 45 and over a force of some commercial as well as cultural significance. We also learned that while the audiences for period films tend to be older than the core mainstream audience, this is not homogeneously true. The Heritage Audience Survey participants, accordingly, straddled one cohort (the TOs) of whom 80% were aged 25 to 44, with an only slightly female-dominated gender split, and another (the NTs) who were all aged 45-plus, and predominantly female.

In keeping with this demographic variety, the Heritage Audience Survey findings showed that audiences for 'quality' period films are drawn from a range of sub-groups characterised by differing patterns of cinemagoing and domestic film-viewing, and contrasting levels of engagement with wider film culture. The TO audience consisted overwhelmingly of people who watched films quite frequently at the cinema *as well as* in other media. The NT audience, by contrast, was characterised by an approximate three-way split: one-third of NTs reported that they saw films at the cinema two to three times a year; just under 30% went more frequently; and more than one-third watched films predominantly or only on TV or (more rarely) home video. As will emerge more fully in later chapters, this pattern had implications for many NT respondents' relationships with the period films they enjoyed – indeed, for their sense of them *as films* rather than television productions – and for their awareness of wider contemporary film culture.

Overall, the Heritage Audience Survey sample contained a significantly higher percentage of frequent cinemagoers (defined as respondents who reported seeing a film at the cinema once a month or more) than the UK cinema audience as a whole (as projected in the 1994 *Caviar* survey), but *also* a slightly higher percentage of less frequent cinemagoers (defined as those attending two to three times a year) than the 'national' audience. Thus 37% of all respondents reported seeing a film at the cinema once a month or more (compared to only 15% of the 1994 *Caviar* sample), but a quarter did so only two to three times a year (compared to 17% in *Caviar* 1994).

This high proportion of frequent cinemagoers was clearly coloured by both the self-selecting nature of the survey sample and its particular composition. It is no surprise that a questionnaire about films attracted a disproportionate number of frequent cinemagoers, nor that a high proportion of the younger and almost exclusively London-based TO cohort – who had the best access to a wide choice of cinemas – fell into this category. Thus 80% of TOs, but only 16% of NTs, saw a film at the cinema once a month or more. But, strikingly – and in the face of this apparent polarisation – some frequent cinemagoers (defined as above) could be found across both cohorts and across all age bands under 75, although the numbers declined as age advanced. More than two-thirds of respondents in the 35 to 44 age band (all TOs), and more than one-fifth aged 45-plus (of whom the majority were NTs), reported that they went to the cinema once a month or more, compared to 9% and 4% for these respective age bands nationally in *Caviar* 1994. And eleven respondents (most aged 35-plus, and more than half aged 45-plus) claimed to visit the cinema once a *week* or more, confirming that age was not necessarily a bar to exceptionally frequent cinemagoing.

Less frequent cinemagoing was, however, the norm – as it is nationally – among the (female-dominated and exclusively 45-plus) NT cohort and also for a minority of 35-plus TOs. In addition to likely age- and gender-related reservations about going out at night among NT respondents (44% of whom were single, widowed or divorced women), it should be recalled that more than one-fifth of NTs lived in rural areas, and only 8% in truly urban areas delivering the kind of easy access to cinemas taken for granted by TOs. Indeed, several

NT respondents explicitly mentioned their lack of access to a cinema in the 'additional comments' section of the questionnaire. Despite such issues, 63% of NTs saw a film at the cinema at least twice a year, with two to three times a year the most common visit frequency (accounting for one-third of NTs). The self-evident corollary, however, was that 37% of NTs saw a film at the cinema *less than* twice a year – or never.

FILM VIEWING AT HOME

Moreover, not all of these infrequent, or non-, cinemagoers among the NTs watched films at home to an extent that served as a domestic equivalent to avid cinemagoing. Around two-thirds watched a feature film on television (at the time of broadcast) once a month or more; but this left eight (13% of) NT respondents who saw a film at the cinema less than twice a year *and also* watched films on TV only occasionally (typically, two to three times a year). In short, some NTs were infrequent, 'event', film viewers on television as well as in their cinemagoing.

Conversely, of the thirty-five (38% of) respondents (split evenly between the two cohorts: 29% of NTs and 57% of TOs) who watched a film on TV once a week or more, almost half *also* saw a film at the cinema once a month or more (although all but four of these were TOs). All the TO respondents who saw a film at the cinema *less* than once a month compensated by watching a film on TV once a month or more; in fact, all but two TOs in this category said that they watched a film on TV at the highest suggested frequency: more than once a week. In summary, every TO respondent saw a film once a month or more in one medium or another – in 80% of cases, at the cinema. By contrast, the NT cohort again showed a three-way split that reaffirmed the division between respondents who watched films relatively frequently in one medium or another, and those who were very infrequent, 'event', film viewers regardless of the viewing medium. Thus one-third of NTs watched a film on TV once a week or more; more than one-third did so less often but at least once a month; and just under one-third less than once a month but at least twice a year.

Some 90% of TO respondents and three-quarters of NTs reported that they watched a feature film (either home-taped, bought or rented) on home video at least twice a year. While 47% of TOs claimed to watch a feature film on video once a week or more, a high percentage relative to national norms, only 8% of NTs did so – low by any standards. To place these findings in a comparative context, *Cultural Trends* had reported in 1991 that 'only 17% of those with access to video recorders watch commercially recorded tapes once a week', while the equivalent figure for 'recordings made from broadcast programmes' was 61%; in other words, 'the majority of VCR usage [was] for playing back broadcast material recorded off-air' rather than 'for playing rented or purchased video-cassettes'.[8] My question to respondents about their use of home video *to watch feature films* cuts across both of *Cultural Trends'* cited categories; but, in most households, many of the 'recordings made from broadcast programmes' would not be recordings of films. Taking these factors into account, if the percentage of Heritage Audience Survey respondents watching a *film* on (self-taped, rented or bought) home video once a week was higher than 17% but considerably lower than 61%, this would be in line with UK norms.

An important explanatory factor here is that a significant number of NT respondents did not own (or rent) a video recorder (whereas the *Cultural Trends* data referred solely to households which did). However, this itself placed the NT cohort at odds with UK-wide trends since the mid 1980s. *Cultural Trends* noted by 1991 that 'for some time now, households which do not have access to videos have been part of a declining minority';[9] and by 2001 there were 'in excess of 18 million VHS recorders in 89% per cent of all British TV households' – a rise from 70% in 1991.[10] The resistance to this trend among NTs is made more surprising – and perhaps culturally revealing – by the fact that most belonged to relatively affluent socio-economic groups who might be expected to invest in home-entertainment technologies during retirement. One possibility is that the limited video usage among NTs might signal their affiliation to a generational, and classed, culture for which home video – and especially rental video – carry connotations that are neither 'cultured' nor morally respectable. As *Cultural Trends* itself noted in 1991,'the rapid growth of the rental market in the first half of the 1980s gave the industry a rather seedy reputation, associated with the large-scale pirating of videos and concern about uncontrolled access to pornography and "video nasties".'[11]

In support of this reading, there was a slight inverse correlation among NT respondents between household ABC1 social class and watching films on home video, but no equivalent pattern among the younger TO cohort. (One-third of NTs in class A households watched a film on home video twice a year or more, rising to 41% in classes C1 and C2.) And although both TO and NT respondents were more likely to watch films on home-recorded or bought – rather than rental – video, the distinction between owned and rented videos was particularly sharp among NTs. Three-quarters of NTs watched a film on bought or home-recorded video at least twice a year, but only a quarter ever used rental video, compared to almost two-thirds of TOs.

The difference in video-rental patterns can also be explained as a function of age. Although three-quarters of the thirty-eight respondents aged 65-plus watched films on home video at least twice a year, *none* of these was a rental film, with the same story among the most frequent film viewers on home video (once a week or more) in the 45 to 64 age band. Video rental was thus mostly the preserve of 'younger' audiences (in the context of this study, the under-45s). However, the NT and TO cohorts' differing relationships to rental video also reflected their significantly different relationships to the wider film culture.

Thirteen of the fifteen respondents who rented a video once a month or more were TOs; but ten of these TOs *also* saw a film at the cinema *at least two to three times a month* – a frequency far exceeding the norm even among regular cinemagoers. By contrast, the two NT respondents who rented videos at this relatively high frequency saw films at the cinema once a month or less. Both were class AB married women, aged 59 and 60; their video-rental habitus was thus untypical for their demographic profile or among NTs. By contrast, all but one of the thirteen TOs renting videos once a month or more were under 40, and drawn from both class AB and class C1. (No TO respondents were C2s.) For comparison, of the twenty-two NT respondents who watched a film on (bought or home-taped) video once a month or more, around one-third lived in class C1 or C2 households – that is, this pattern applied to just over 40% of all C1 and C2 NTs. A more significant finding, however, was that only three of these twenty-two NTs saw a film *at the cinema* once a month or more – while all *except* two watched a film on television at that frequency.

It can be seen that although a loose relationship between social class and home-video use was sometimes discernible, it was not consistent across the two cohorts. But – more importantly for the concerns of this study – where frequent video rental among TOs usually corresponded with frequent cinema-going (with the exception of some C2s), NT respondents' viewing of films on video was typically part of a *predominantly* televisual viewing habitus.

HOME-VIDEO COLLECTIONS

Respondents were also asked questions about home-video collections – to ascertain both the prevalence and size of these, and the place of period films and period television dramas within them. The latter was of particular interest in the light of the affinities between heritage films and the British tradition of 'quality' period TV drama, centrally in the form of classic literary adaptations. For example, if some respondents had accrued collections of period films and/or period TV dramas/serials, this might indicate a committed, informed relationship with the genre(s), or a fan relationship with their stars – forms of investment which have not been explored in text-centred discussions of heritage cinema.

Equally, it would be misguided to draw over-large conclusions from the size and content of respondents' home-video collections – or lack of them – alone.

For some respondents, ownership of a small number of treasured period films on video may be more meaningful, and may signify more intense fandom, than the larger collections of habitual VHS (or, more recently, DVD or Blu-ray) users. And one respondent who had viewed – and could discuss – an extraordinary, almost encyclopaedic, range of films made a point of stating that he had seen them all at the cinema (although he also had a substantial VHS collection) (TO37: man, 61, former credit controller/full-time carer).

Some 35% of NT respondents and 17% of TOs reported that they did not own any films on video, whether bought/pre-recorded or home-taped. Among respondents who did, the most common collection size was between one and thirty films. This was true of half the NT cohort and 40% of TOs (although most NTs within this group – 27% of the cohort – owned only between one and ten films).

A few respondents in both cohorts owned between thirty-one and fifty films, but above this level a polarisation occurred: only 8% of NTs owned a collection of more than fifty films, compared to 30% of TOs – and, within this latter group, 20% of TOs owned more than 100 films. One NT household – a married couple who both completed questionnaires – reported that they owned a collection of around 500 films on VHS, but they were the exception. Very large video collections were, in fact, the exception among TO respondents too, although the two very largest reported collections (of 2,180 and 800 videos) both belonged to TOs (TO9: US-born woman, 60, tour company director; TO39: Dutch-born man, 36, market-research professional).[12]

A breakdown of these findings to differentiate between home-recorded and bought/pre-recorded video showed a slight preference among TOs for the latter which was not shared by NTs; indeed, some TOs had substantial, even large, collections of bought films on video.

I was interested in whether these patterns differed for period films. Did home video play a significant role in respondents' viewing of these? While 70% of TO respondents and 62% of NTs owned some period films on video (whether pre-recorded or home-taped), these collections only rarely exceeded thirty period films. Virtually all the larger collections of 31-plus period films (owned by 20% of TOs and 15% of NTs) were owned as part of the very largest collections of (50-plus, or more usually 100-plus) films across all genres already noted. If more than thirty period films were owned on video, home taping had usually played a significant role, particularly among NTs.

Period films tended to form a larger proportion of NT respondents' (generally smaller) home-video collections than they did among TOs. This was, in part, a reflection of a broader trend: the larger a respondent's overall collection of feature films on video, the less prominent period films tended to be in percentage terms. For 63% of the NTs who owned any films on video at all (or 39% of all NTs), period films formed 41% to 100% of their collection – and

80% to 100% of more than one-third of NT home–video collections (those of 11% of all NTs).

By contrast, period films did not account for more than 80% of any film collection reported by a TO respondent; indeed, two-thirds of the TOs who owned any films on video (or 47% of all TOs) had collections in which period films accounted for 40% or less of the total. These trends remained similar when respondents' pre-recorded and home-taped video collections were analysed as distinct entities, although the tendency for TO respondents to favour pre-recorded video, and for NTs to favour home-taped video slightly, broadly extended to collections of period films.

Respondents were also asked how many television period/costume dramas/ serials they retained on home-taped and/or pre-recorded video. Although made-for-TV period drama formed a significant part of respondents' consumption of 'quality' period screen fictions, particularly among the NT audience – and (as we shall see later) had played a significant role in the development of a period-*film* habitus among both groups – only around half of all respondents (across both cohorts) retained any period TV dramas/serials on video, and few had substantial collections. Across both cohorts, by far the commonest size of collection (accounting for around 80% of those TOs and those NTs who retained any period TV dramas/serials on video at all) consisted of between one and ten dramas/serials.

Two factors here were that, although the period-film viewing habitus of many NT respondents was markedly televisual, they were not great users of home video; while TOs drew a sharper distinction than NTs between their film interests and their TV viewing. It may also be relevant that many respondents had acquired their taste for 'quality' period television drama during the 1950s to 1970s heyday of the BBC-TV Classic Serial (see Chapter 5), when it was common practice to screen each episode of these prestige productions twice weekly on their first broadcast, followed by at least one repeat screening of the whole serial. These practices were revived in the 1990s when the BBC screened its high-profile Jane Austen adaptations *Middlemarch* and *Pride and Prejudice*, although in the commercialised context of 1990s television, they now performed a more self-conscious, hype-heightening, function in positioning these dramas as 'event television'. Moreover, respondents' replies, when asked to estimate how many times they had watched their favourite period television dramas/serials, affirmed that home video was used primarily for repeat viewings of a small core (and hence small collection) of favourite period TV dramas.

To draw some more general conclusions, where both video rental and ownership of a video collection were typically extensions of *cine*philia among the TO cohort, NT respondents showed a preference for investing in the *ownership* of a few favoured films on video which they then watched fairly infrequently. These were – typically – small video collections in which period films and period TV dramas/serials predominated (although extensive period film/drama collections were not the norm in either cohort). In short, NTs' investment in ownership was selective: they tended to retain a small number of period favourites on video, of which a few would be viewed again and again.

This pattern suggests that a defining characteristic of the NT 'audience' was not merely an 'event' cinemagoing habitus – in which films promoted in terms of their 'quality' and/or 'rare' intelligence attract a 'discerning' audience who rarely watch other films – but the migration of this 'event' habitus into the domestic sphere. We can already hypothesise that the wider film diet of these respondents may be dominated by 'quality' period screen fictions; and, more speculatively, that they may prove to be embracers of the discourses that equate heritage cinema and TV period literary adaptations with 'quality' and cultural value (to be explored more fully in Chapters 6 and 7).

CINEMA TYPES VISITED

In view of the hybrid status of 1980s heritage films as art-cinema/commercial crossovers – followed by further hybridisation with the 1990s emergence of 'post-heritage' films consciously produced and marketed to offer multiple appeals to a diversified range of audience sectors – respondents were asked about the kinds of cinema they typically visited to see period and other films (Appendix 2.1: Question 3). For data-analysis purposes, respondents who reported that they 'mostly' attended one cinema type but 'never' the other were classified as 'always' attending the former. A 'sometimes' response for both commercial and art cinemas was treated as denoting an even mix.

Were period films being viewed in a context of mainstream, commercial cinemagoing, within a distinct art-cinema habitus, or as part of a more eclectic, mixed habitus? Analysis of respondents' replies revealed the co-presence of all three tendencies, but strongly inflected by the differing regional and urban/rural profiles of the two cohorts. Thus those NTs who saw films at the cinema at all tended to visit small town-centre cinemas (whether 'commercial' or 'independent' in their programming) or larger chain cinemas in the regions, while the (mostly) London-based TOs clearly had maximal access to a choice of independent/art cinemas in addition to commercial or multiplex options.

While 29% of all respondents (one-third of TOs; just over a quarter of NTs) reported that they saw 'films in general' *mostly or always* at independent/art cinemas, this rose only slightly to 32% for period films. The proportion of respondents – across both cohorts – who routinely saw films at commercial cinemas was, however, higher. Some 40% (37% of TOs and 42% NTs) saw 'films in general' *mostly or always* at commercial cinemas, and for period films this dropped only to 36%. If the respondents who saw films 'sometimes' at *both* broad cinema types are added to these findings, then two-thirds of TOs, and 70% of those NTs who went to the cinema at all (or 61% of all NTs), saw films at commercial cinemas at least half the time. Such findings belie easy assumptions about the elitist cultural and cinematic context of heritage-film viewing.

Respondents' actual practices also belied the common assumption that heritage films are 'viewed in special places'. The agglomerated statistics quoted above showed that respondents were only slightly more likely to see period films at art – rather than commercial – cinemas compared to their usual practices when seeing 'films in general'. The variations in patterns of 'art' versus 'commercial' cinemagoing both within and between the two cohorts – and, within these, patterns in the places where period films were seen – were, however, more complex.

One key finding was that the prominence and place of mainstream cinemas as places of period-film viewing differed significantly between the TO and NT groups of respondents. The 47% of cinemagoing NTs (or 42% of all NTs) who mainly saw films at mainstream cinemas did the same for period films. By contrast, the 37% of TOs who saw 'films in general' mainly at mainstream cinemas fell significantly to 23% for period films. At first sight this might seem to suggest a trend for TOs to gravitate from mainstream to art cinemas when seeing period films – but other indicators suggested, rather, that there was some two-way traffic, with the habitus of some other TOs becoming *less* strongly oriented towards art cinemas when they went to see period films. Overall, almost half the TO cohort reported that they saw period films at a mix of commercial and art cinemas.

As this suggests, the behaviour of the younger (and predominantly urban) TO audience encompassed a greater eclecticism of cinema-type choices and practices – but also, within this, a stronger art-cinema habitus and more pronounced indicators of cinephilia – than the older (and predominantly suburban) NT audience. In illustration of the latter, 53% of TOs (compared to 20% of NTs) were members or mailing-list members of at least one independent or specialist cinema, repertory cinema club (typically London's National Film Theatre, now renamed BFI Southbank), or arts venue with a cinema (such as the Institute of Contemporary Arts); and 60% of TOs had 'ever attended' a film festival, compared to only 3% of NTs.

How to summarise these complex findings, and what core conclusions can be drawn? The TO cohort exhibited a fairly even three-way split: between one cluster who usually saw films (of all kinds) at independent/art cinemas; a slightly higher proportion who saw 'films in general' mainly at commercial cinemas; and those who did so at a mix of cinema types. When the same question was asked for period films, the TOs with a strong art-cinema habitus remained a fairly stable group, but beyond this there was a significant net TO gravitation (mainly, but not wholly, from a commercial cinema habitus) into the 'mix of cinemas' category. The NT cohort was split between a large minority (42%) who saw 'films in general' mainly at commercial cinemas, and continued to do so for period films; just over a quarter who saw films mostly at art cinemas; just under 20% who visited a mix of cinema types; and the 11% of NTs who watched films at home but never went to the cinema. When the question was asked for period films, a small number of NTs gravitated from the 'mix' category into the art–cinema category.

It can be concluded – first, and unsurprisingly – that most TO respondents attended (and, of course, had privileged access to) a greater variety of cinema types and programming than NTs, including membership cinemas and festivals. Second, those NTs who relied on commercial cinemas were (with few exceptions) *equally* reliant on these when seeing period films. It was the NTs who already saw 'films in general' at art cinemas, or a varied mix, who were slightly more likely to make a 'special' trip to an art cinema to see period films.

Importantly, these findings show that there is no simple or universal corollary between period-film viewing and an independent/art, rather than mainstream, cinemagoing habitus and attendant tastes. On the contrary, both the TO and NT case studies show that – and illustrate how – period-film viewing gains its meaning(s) (whether as a signifier of cultural value or as an index of a particular taste formation) *relationally*, from its place within the wider film and cinemagoing habitus (or mesh of practices and tastes) of individuals or groups. They also suggest, already, that the film tastes of many NT respondents – and a significant cluster of TOs – tended towards the mainstream, rather than period-film viewing having a particular affinity with an art-cinema/foreign-language film habitus (although TO respondents were more likely than NTs to fit this latter profile).

NOTES

1. The introductory instructions issued to respondents with the Heritage Audience Survey questionnaire defined period films as 'any film which is set in the past (or was set in the past at the time when it was made). (So older films which were set in the present day at the time when they were made are not . . . period films).'
2. Higson, 'Re-presenting the national past', p. 110.
3. The latter concept is borrowed from the critic André Bazin's famous essay, 'In defence of mixed cinema', in Bazin, *What Is Cinema? Volume 1*.
4. Higson, 'Re-presenting', pp. 112-13. See also Chapter 1.
5. Ibid., p. 112.
6. Ibid., p. 110.
7. Ibid., p. 111.

8. Policy Studies Institute, *Cultural Trends* (1991), 'Cinema, film and home video', p. 49. This was the most recent publicly accessible UK study I was able to locate reporting on home VCR or DVD use from a consumer perspective. The (limited) more recent data released publicly by the British Videogram Association (BVA) are predominantly sales-oriented, and the bulk of their research is available only to BVA members.
9. Ibid.
10. British Videogram Association research findings, cited by Dyja (ed.) in the *BFI Film and Television Handbook 2001*. Summarised as 'UK film, television and video overview' at www.bfi.org.uk/bookvid/handbook/overview2001.html [6 March 2004].
11. Policy Studies Institute, *Cultural Trends* (1991), 'Cinema, film and home video', p. 49.
12. Of course, the practices (and collections) of large-scale video collectors can be studied as a subculture in themselves. For a specialised study, see Dinsmore-Tuli, *The Domestication of Film* [PhD thesis].

Patterns of Film Taste: Period and Non-Period Films

INTRODUCTION AND METHODOLOGY

Chapter 5 shifts focus from the broad viewing context within which period films were consumed by Heritage Audience Survey respondents to an analysis of the breadth, and types, of films they watched and enjoyed or were aware of. My full analysis of the findings encompassed respondents' patterns of awareness and taste in relation to films with non-period as well as period narrative settings: how many films (from lists presented in the questionnaire) they recalled seeing across these two broad categories; the place of films from the USA, Britain, other regions and non-English-language films in this viewing; and, above all, the most significant patterns in the *types* of films respondents watched and enjoyed. Due to limitations of space, however, Chapter 5 reserves its presentation of detailed findings for respondents' tastes in period films, preceding this with – and situating it within – a shorter summary of the key patterns of taste *beyond* period films that emerged from the source analysis.

The questionnaire collected indicators of respondents' film awarenesses and tastes in two ways. First, it presented two extensive lists of pre-suggested films, with contemporary/non-period and period settings respectively (Questions 16 and 17 in Appendix 2.1). For the two full lists of films, in the order and under the headings in which they were presented to respondents, see the Filmography (rather than Appendix 2.1). Respondents were asked to indicate (via multiple-choice tick-boxes) which films they had seen or heard of and – if seen – whether they had liked them 'a lot', 'liked' or 'disliked' them. A second, open, question (Question 18) asked respondents whether they had 'any special favourite period films' and, if so, to name these. Questions 19 and 20 performed an equivalent function in relation to period television dramas/serials (though the list of pre-suggested examples offered here was much shorter and more selective, and limited to the UK).

While I did not want the pre-suggested film lists to direct participants' wider replies, it was unlikely that they would recall a wide range of films seen without prompting of this kind. I also did not want to bias the findings by making narrow assumptions about the range of film types or genres that respondents might watch. With these considerations in mind, the questionnaire listed 145 'non-period' and 97 'period' films (as defined at the start of Chapter 4): 242 in all. The inclusion of more non-period than period films was judged necessary to represent the variety of recent releases and potential patterns of respondent taste adequately. Most of the films listed dated from the late 1980s to 1990s, but key earlier films were included if they had been re-released recently prior to the survey or were felt to have benchmark status. The lists spanned examples from the commercial, art-cinema and independent production sectors, and included British and American cinema's recent top box-office successes at the time of the survey, plus examples that had received high-profile media coverage or notoriety regardless of genre. The films were organised into sub-sections by broad geographical/production origin and, within these, listed alphabetically by title – so that, importantly, no classifications of film genre or 'type' were pre-suggested to respondents.

The majority of listed films were then placed into classificatory groups – not divulged to respondents – for the purpose of analysing film tastes. (For the classifications used in the detailed analysis of period-film tastes presented later in Chapter 5, see Appendix 5.1. Equivalent classifications were used in the full analysis of non-period-film tastes, but are not reproduced here as the detail of this analysis lies beyond the scope of this book.) While the use of such pre-classifications (and the irony of having to decide whether specific films should be classed as 'core', 'borderline' or 'post-'heritage films when I myself had strong reservations about the coherence of such categories) might seem to impose interpretations on respondents' tastes that they might not agree with themselves, I found in practice that this method tended to reveal any classificatory anomalies rather than conceal them. In particular, some 1990s films I classified only as 'borderline' heritage films because critical reception had not (or not yet) firmly identified them as heritage cinema – centrally, *The Madness of King George* and *Sense and Sensibility* – turned out to be 'core' favourites among the cluster of respondents who had very cohesive 'heritage' tastes.

BREADTH OF FILMS SEEN

It would be surprising if many respondents, regardless of age or wider profile, had seen an extremely high proportion of the 242 listed films. Only five respondents, all drawn from the TO (*Time Out*) cohort, had seen more than 60% of the full list, making them, self-evidently, a minority even among TOs.

Three sharp distinctions emerged between the NT (National Trust) and TO cohorts. First, for almost two-thirds of NTs, 60% to 86% of *all* the listed films they had seen were period films – whereas for more than three-quarters of TO respondents, 60% to 73% of all the listed films they had seen were *not*. In short, TOs who predominantly watched period films and NTs who primarily watched non-period films formed only tiny minorities within their respective groups. Second, almost 80% of NT respondents had seen 20% or fewer (fewer than fifty) of the listed films, whereas every TO respondent had seen more than this. The vast majority of TOs (83%) had seen 21% to 60% (50 to 145) of the full list; the remaining 17% had seen still more. Third, a startling 42% of NT respondents (but no TOs) had seen fewer than twenty (i.e. 20% or fewer) of the ninety-seven listed *period* films; indeed, only a few (15% of) NTs had seen more than 40% (forty or more). Thus virtually all the TO respondents – as a group who mainly saw *non*-period films – had seen a wider range of *period* films than most NTs.

It was not merely the case, however, that many NT respondents had limited tastes which were skewed heavily towards period films. A significant number also had quite narrow tastes *in* period films – or certainly were familiar with only a narrow range – despite feeling motivated and qualified to participate in a survey on the subject. Despite this paradox, as we will see in later chapters, a presumption of cultural authority, or authority to comment, was a strong feature of the particular discourse around heritage films produced or reproduced by many NTs.

As a further indicator of the extent to which respondents belonged, or not, to a *self-aware* niche audience whose viewing centred on period films, Question 2 asked them to self-estimate what proportion of the films they watched (in the cinema, on video or on TV) were period films. These impressionistic self-estimates were compared with the (relatively) objective percentage findings derived from the film lists. Respondents' self-estimates were broadly consistent with the 'objective' findings, but with two instructive distortions. First, the (mostly NT) respondents' whose Questions 16 and 17 lists of films seen were dominated by period films understandably tended to *under*estimate the prominence of these in their film diet. Second – in an instructive index of the *attitudes* to period films explored more fully in Chapter 6 onwards – only a handful of the (mostly TO) respondents whose films seen were predominantly set in the present self-estimated that they watched a *higher* proportion of period films than their lists suggested.

TASTES IN NON-PERIOD FILMS: SUMMARY TRENDS

For TO respondents – as for the majority of British cinema audiences – contemporary American cinema formed the dominant context within which

British films and films of other national/regional origins were viewed (although two TOs bucked this trend and had seen only a tiny handful of the listed US choices, suggesting conscious resistance). The TO audience was, however, defined centrally – and distinguished from both the 'mainstream' audience and their NT counterparts – by the breadth, variety and even cinephilia of their tastes, which characteristically encompassed elements of both mainstream and art cinema.

In keeping with this cinephilia, analysis of TOs' most favoured contemporary films showed that their core tastes – the point of reference around which their wider tastes clustered – were dominated not by big-spectacle blockbuster Hollywood cinema (which proved to be a focus of explicit antipathy for some TOs) but by American post-classical[1] and contemporary auteur films, and auteur directors from a wider period. Accordingly, 83% of TO respondents named favourite directors (in reply to Question 28, and in contrast with a mere 10% of NTs), and the most mentioned (in descending order) were Martin Scorsese (named by 30% of TOs), Alfred Hitchcock, Billy Wilder and James Ivory (all named by 17% to 20%), followed by Quentin Tarantino, Stanley Kubrick, Joel and Ethan Coen, and Robert Altman.

We can see here that TOs' film and director tastes embraced notions of the cinematic that at first sight were strongly at odds with the qualities routinely attributed to heritage films (although of course Scorsese himself has made at least one film – the 1993 Edith Wharton adaptation *The Age of Innocence* – with close 'heritage' affiliations; and others, such as 2004's *The Aviator*, deploying a precise nostalgic aesthetic). However, we will see in Chapters 6 and 7 that many TOs explained the merits of the period films they enjoyed in terms of complex, nuanced narrative, script and characterisation – qualities shared by the films of some of their preferred American directors – suggesting an enjoyment of character-driven narrative cinema as opposed to effects-driven big spectacle. On this last point, more than three-quarters of TOs *disagreed* (in response to one of the Question 30 attitude statements) that they enjoyed big-budget Hollywood 'blockbuster films with spectacular special effects'.

By contrast, a more blanket unawareness of, uninterest in, or resistance to most contemporary American non-period cinema was the norm among NTs, in a context in which wider analysis confirmed that the majority of the mature, female-dominated NT audience shared very limited, niche, tastes in – and awareness of – films set in present and past alike. Two-thirds of NTs had seen barely 10% of the sixty listed US non-period films, while 83% of TOs had seen more than 40% of them. NTs' niche tastes, however, generated certain limited (and at times, surprising) exceptions to this pattern, which I discuss below. NTs' viewing of British and Irish non-period films was slightly broader: three-quarters of the cohort had seen 11% to 40% of the forty-five films listed.

In short, when NT respondents watched films with present-day settings, home-grown British films were preferred. However, their tastes were more precise than this. First, popular British genre cinema was strongly preferred to the social-realist strand or its associated auteurs. Some 52% of NTs had seen none of the committed social-realist films listed in the questionnaire (as opposed to feelgood hybrids such as *The Full Monty*), and a mere four had seen Mike Leigh's 1997 multiple Oscar-nominated *Secrets and Lies*. TOs, by contrast were significantly more likely have seen British social-realist films, iconoclastic 1990s British independent films such as *Trainspotting*, or British art films (such as those of Peter Greenaway). Second, two particular British genre hybrids formed the core recurrent theme in NT tastes alongside (predominantly British) period films. On the one hand, NTs favoured upper-middle-class romantic and friendship comedies such as *Four Weddings and a Funeral* and the earlier *Peter's Friends*. On the other, they favoured two of the key British woman's films featured in Justine King (later Ashby)'s ground-breaking 1996 analysis of the genre, *Educating Rita* and *Shirley Valentine*, films sharing uplifting self-liberation and self-improvement themes (a taste of particular interest in the light of Chapter 3's analysis of educational cultures and class mobility among respondents).

The *Four Weddings* strand favoured by NTs are, in effect, contemporary heritage films: set narratively in the present or recent past, but criticised by many commentators for their upper- or upper-middle-class subjects, naturalisation of an accordant worldview, exportable heritage iconography and locations, and overall projection of a highly selective fantasy Britain. Indeed, it might be argued that the fantasy Britain of *Four Weddings* or its successor *Notting Hill* (Roger Michell, UK/USA, 1999) is more ideologically dubious than anything in such films' period counterparts, which at least cannot be mistaken for representations of present-day reality. But, of equal importance for the concerns of this book, King's definition of the field of contemporary British 'woman's films' also draws in a cross-genre range of *period* films that span both the 'heritage' and 'retro' categories (she specifically cites *Dance with a Stranger*, *A Room with a View* and *Scandal*), since both strands 'privileg[e] female point of view structures (both diegetic and spectatorial) and [show a] a preoccupation with thematic concerns designated as "feminine" within a patriarchal culture'.[2]

The NT cohort's British genre tastes were supplemented and reinforced by widespread liking for the major Australian export hits of the 1980s and 1990s: again, with a strong emphasis on romantic/friendship comedies such as the Abba-themed *Muriel's Wedding* and – most pronouncedly – the Paul Hogan comedy vehicle *Crocodile Dundee*. In fact, the latter – one of the most profitable Australian films of all time – was also one of the most popular films in the entire questionnaire, seen by 90% of respondents, and liked or liked a lot by half the TO cohort and three-quarters of NTs. By contrast, and in an instructive irony, the Australian quality biopic *Shine* – a recent multiple Oscar nominee at the survey date, and tailor-made for an older, 'intelligent' demographic – had been seen by fewer than 20% of NTs (and 50% of TOs). In a similar vein, some contemporary Hollywood female-targeted films (*Sleepless in Seattle*, *First Wives' Club*), romances (*Forrest Gump* and, more predictably, Baz Luhrmann's contemporary-set *William Shakespeare's Romeo + Juliet*) and comedies (*Mrs Doubtfire*) proved to have a significant niche following among NTs. By contrast, despite widespread Jane Austen fandom among NTs (see Chapter 7), none had seen *Clueless*, Amy Heckerling's US teenpic interpretation of Austen's *Emma*.

In one surprise finding that bucked all the above trends, 39% of the NT cohort had seen Jonathan Demme's *The Silence of the Lambs* – and more than half (21% of NTs) reported that they had 'liked' the film or liked it 'a lot'. (For comparison, 97% of TOs had seen *Lambs* – in keeping with their post-classical/ auteur tastes – and virtually all had liked it or liked it a lot.) The central attraction of the film for NTs (and also many TOs) will have been the involvement of Anthony Hopkins – but, here, he was cast in his most notorious role, as the cannibalistic serial killer Hannibal Lecter. As I discuss further in Chapter 7, Hopkins emerged as by far the most popular favourite male actor self-named by respondents (ten NTs and five TOs, replies to Question 23), centrally, via his starring roles in the Merchant Ivory heritage films *Howards End* and *The Remains of the Day*, and as the writer C. S. Lewis in Richard Attenborough's *Shadowlands*; and, as we can see, two-thirds of his fans belonged to the NT cohort. The acceptability of *The Silence of the Lambs* to 'quality' audiences was undoubtedly smoothed by its particular promotional strategies on initial release – which, as Mark Jancovich has argued, successfully 'negotiate[d] a special status' for it as a quality drama 'distinct from the "ordinary horror film", capable of appealing to those who identified themselves as far removed from "the horror fan"' – and sealed by its subsequent five Oscar triumphs.[3] It was intriguing to find that this strategy appeared to have worked on the kinds of audiences familiar with Hopkins from *Howards End*, many of whom (as we shall see in Chapter 7) professed a strong aversion to screen violence.

In a more widespread and pronounced trait, most NTs had seen only tiny numbers of European or other non-Anglophone films. However, very wide viewing of non-Anglophone films (defined as extending beyond 40% of those listed in the questionnaire) also proved to be a rarity even among TOs. A more detailed analysis showed that the TO 'audience' was split between respondents whose main points of reference were US and/or British films, and a cluster with more pronounced European/non-Anglophone tastes. Although TOs and NTs alike had typically seen slightly higher percentages of the listed European/non-Anglophone *period* films than they had their non-period equivalents, this non-Anglophone period-film viewing nevertheless remained narrow compared to the significantly wider range of English-language period films seen. Among TOs, this finding accords with the wider drift in the UK away from European and world cinema among younger audiences since the early 1990s, a decline attributable to factors that extend beyond shifts in cultural fashion (such as the significant loss of independent cinema screens and the sharp decline in screenings of non-Anglophone subtitled films on British television, not fully rectified by the choices offered on specialised satellite and cable channels).

However, most NT respondents would have reached young adulthood during the 1950s–1960s heyday of European art cinema and the various New Waves. Their limited acquaintance with (admittedly, recent) non-Anglophone cinema therefore invites other interpretations. Factors might include an age-related drift away from cinemagoing of any kind, or age-related difficulties in reading subtitles, coupled with the limited (and often late-night) TV scheduling of such films, and low home-video usage among NTs. Unsolicited comments from a few NTs – coupled with the indicative finding that almost 40% of them had seen and enjoyed Marcel Carné's 1945 French classic *Les Enfants du paradis* – supported such speculations. One respondent recalled the Italian neo-realist films he had seen in the UK immediately after World War II (NT48, man, 69; retired county council chief educational psychologist, West/ South-West). Another recalled seeing French films at a renowned specialist London cinema – Studio One on Oxford Street – during the war while learning the language (NT35, woman, 79; retired teacher, South/South-East). The current viewing of most NTs, however, emerged as narrowly Anglocentric. For most, viewing even of foreign-language *period* films was either confined the best-known post-1980 crossover hits (such as *Jean de Florette* or *Cyrano de Bergerac*, both seen by around 40% of NTs) or non-existent.

PERIOD FILM TASTES: INTRODUCTION

The remainder of Chapter 5 looks in detail at respondents' period-film tastes, centrally via the classificatory film-type groupings presented in Appendix 5.1. Appendix 5.2, by contrast, focuses centrally on the best-known British 'heritage' films to summarise key findings on *individual* period films (rather than grouped film 'types') in a table that illustrates the contrasting *hierarchies of taste* that characterised the NT and TO cohorts respectively.

In addition to the period films listed in Question 17 of the questionnaire, and the shorter list of indicative period TV dramas/serials in Question 19 (see Appendix 2.1 and Filmography), respondents were invited to name their own favourite period films (Question 18) and television dramas (Question 20). This exercise both supported the patterns already emerging from multiple-choice replies and elicited film choices not listed in Question 17, including some enthusiasms that notably departed from the heritage, costume and historical films at the core of the questionnaire's design. As replies were extremely varied (the favourite period films named by two or more respondents generated a list of around fifty), these will be cited only selectively in illustration of key trends.

The classifications used in the period-film types analysis starts from the assumption that – for the UK audiences associated with heritage cinema – the most familiar, and widely seen, period films would be predominantly British (in cultural appearances, if not always finance). Appendix 5.1 therefore subdivides (culturally) 'British' period films into more precise analytic sub-categories – and discusses respondents' tastes in these more extensively – than it does North American, Australasian (in practice, mainly New Zealand) or continental European period films.

The most significant finding was that *all* the film tastes of most NT respondents – not just their tastes in period films – were strongly clustered in and around the two British period-film 'types' (BH1 and BH2: see Appendix 5.1) where the most conventional heritage films were concentrated. There is, therefore, strong justification for identifying these film types as the core (or even 'mainstream') of the NT audience's tastes across period and non-period films alike. As we have seen, these tastes were supplemented by some limited viewing of particular types of 1980s–1990s popular British genre films set in the present, and comparable examples drawn from Australian and Hollywood mainstream cinema. Nevertheless, only a tiny handful of non-period films (notably *Four Weddings and a Funeral*) matched the levels of awareness or popularity among NTs achieved by the best-known British heritage films. The majority of TO respondents, too, watched and (more variably, and with different preferences) enjoyed films in the core British heritage categories. However, we have already seen that for TOs – in stark contrast with NTs – heritage films were viewed as part of a far wider, more diverse, film diet.

The rich array of *self-named* favourite period films listed by respondents, however, introduced complexities and contradictions (although 42% of NTs and 17% of TOs were disinclined or unable to name any). These favourites suggested that familiarity with the diversity of pre-1980 British and Anglophone period cinema was wider among the (younger) TO audience than among NTs; but also that NT respondents' tastes were less narrowly tied to the post-1980 British heritage-film canon than either their multiple-choice replies (Question 17) or their self-worded opinions (expressed in response to Questions 21 and 22) tended to suggest. Thus the favoured period films and genres named by TOs ranged from renowned revisionist 1960s–1970s examples – *Tom Jones* (Tony Richardson, UK, 1963); *Barry Lyndon* (Stanley Kubrick, UK/US, 1975) – via the overtly political – *Partition* (Ken McMullen, UK, 1987) – to (perhaps consciously category-busting) enthusiasms for Hollywood westerns and sword-and-sandal epics. And, although the self-worded *comments* of many NTs directed opprobrium at 'inauthentic', overblown, 'Hollywood-type' period films (see Chapter 7), their named favourite films often embraced tastes for the epic and spectacular that contradicted this abstract position. Thus the favourite film named unprompted by the largest number of Heritage Audience Survey respondents – but particularly (twelve, or nearly 20% of) NTs – was neither a British, nor heritage, choice, but *Gone With the Wind* (Victor Fleming et al, US, 1939), pushing the predictable choices of *Sense and Sensibility* (seven, or 11% of, NTs) and *The Madness of King George* (five, or 8% of, NTs) into second and third place.[4] Other favourites widely self-named by NTs affirmed the place of the epic in these tastes: *Henry V* (Laurence Olivier, UK, 1944), *A Man for All Seasons* (Fred Zinnemann, UK, 1966), Olivier's *Hamlet* (UK, 1948), *Doctor Zhivago* (David Lean, USA, 1965) – alongside Lean's *Great Expectations* (UK, 1946) and his 1984 swansong *A Passage to India* – and even Luchino Visconti's *Death in Venice* (Italy, 1971). The films of Olivier and Lean thus recurred as favourites of NTs across a range of production decades, but less so among TOs.

As noted in Chapter 2, the question of the place of period films (and TV dramas) from earlier decades in forming the tastes of the audiences for heritage (and post-heritage) films of the 1980s onwards makes the origins and longevity of the disposition to watch and enjoy period films or dramas of some interest. Analysis of replies to Questions 18 to 20 from this perspective found that 80% of respondents across both cohorts had been viewers of period drama on television since either the 1960s or the 1970s (with the latter slightly more common among TOs). A further 23% of NT respondents reported that they had watched their first TV period dramas *before* 1960, and two supported this by naming specific productions (both BBC Classic Serials).[5] And, as the examples cited above illustrate, respondents' self-named period-film favourites across both cohorts likewise stretched back to the 1970s, 1960s or earlier decades.

Around one-third of all respondents named at least one favourite period film produced/released before 1950 – making this the most popular earliest-film period even among TOs. The second and third most popular earliest-period-film decades – across NTs and TOs combined – were the 1960s and 1980s. Interestingly, these patterns mirror the key decades (the 1940s, and to a lesser extent the 1960s and 1980s) in which British cinema's critical reputation for 'realism' was at its highest, yet in which it also produced *period*-film strands that were vilified as offering the opposite: the 1940s Gainsborough melodramas, the post-New Wave Woodhall period romps of the 1960s, and the 1980s heritage films. At the same time, there are appreciable reasons why respondents might be less likely to propose favourite period films from the 1950s (pinpointed by Sue Harper as the decade of the British historical film's decline 'in a minor key')[6] or 1970s. When the two cohorts were considered separately, however, it emerged that the favourites named by TOs were both more eclectic and less strongly concentrated in the 'consensus' decades.

With these patterns of taste formation in mind, this chapter now turns in more detail to the analysis of respondents' tastes in contemporary 1980s–1990s period films by 'type'.

BRITISH AND IRISH PERIOD FILMS

For purposes of analysis, the British and (less widely represented) Irish period films listed in the questionnaire – most of which were post-1980 releases – were categorised into six film 'types' (see Appendix 5.1).

Type BH1 consisted of films generally agreed by critical consensus to be 'core' examples of the British heritage 'genre'.

BH2s were 'borderline' British heritage films (dating, mostly, from the later 1980s and 1990s) which shared at least some of the BH1 films' clear heritage characteristics, but which had not (at the date of the survey) been decisively constructed as 'heritage films' in critical discourse, leaving their heritage status ambiguous or open to debate. As will be evident, some inclusions in this category, notably Ang Lee's *Sense and Sensibility*, had attracted varied critical responses on this question, in part because, by the mid 1990s, the shifting discursive mood around British cinema meant that such films were as likely to be celebrated for their success as pigeonholed in 'heritage' terms.[7] Conversely, if I were redesigning the survey in the late 2000s, a BH2 film such as *Tom & Viv* (set in the 1910s, and adapted from Michael Hastings's biographical stage play about the poet T. S. Eliot's first marriage to the troubled Vivienne Haigh-Wood) could logically be regrouped with the more recent – and prolific – cycle of British prestige adaptations from contemporary literary memoirs, fiction and theatre, from *Iris* (Richard Eyre, UK/USA, 2001) via *The History Boys* (Nicholas Hytner, UK, 2006) to *Atonement* (Joe Wright, UK/Fr, 2007) or *An Education* (Lone Scherfig, UK, 2009).

The third film type, BPH, comprised British post-heritage films, such as Sally Potter's *Orlando* or Michael Winterbottom's *Jude*, which self-consciously seek to distance themselves (aesthetically, politically, and/or in terms of content or its treatment) from heritage filmmaking.

BHYs were British and Irish history films: a grouping clearly distinct from heritage cinema in their genre conventions and in their historical and/or political modes of engagement with the past, usually with some reference to real historical events, phenomena or figures.

BR1 and BR2 both comprised retro films, set in the decades during or after World War II, within the living memory of at least part of the audience. The retro films were subdivided into two types in response to academic debates and the varied critical reception of particular instances since the mid 1980s. Both of these suggested the need to draw a distinction between retro films perceived as conservative – in the sense of presenting a comfortable vision of the recent past that permitted nostalgic viewing (BR1) – and those that appraised the recent British past from a more critical, subversive, counter-hegemonic or revisionist perspective (BR2).

As noted in Chapter 1, however, individual retro films have often attracted diverging views on these questions, resulting in a notable lack of consensus regarding their 'conservative' versus 'critical' status. Moreover, as with early-1990s heritage-film criticism (within which some of these evaluations of retro films took place, and to which others responded), the totalising nature of the critique itself sometimes generated contentious, counter-intuitive judgements. When classifying individual films as BR1s or BR2s for purposes of analysis, I followed the dominant verdicts which emerged from these debates even though these do not always match my own view, but then took particular care in the subsequent analysis.

The BH1 'core' heritage films – which included, for example, *Chariots of Fire* and the Merchant Ivory Forster adaptations such as *Howards End* – had been very widely seen by respondents regardless of age and cohort. Almost all respondents had seen some BH1s, and the proportions of both NT and TO respondents who had seen very high percentages were also high. Thus 83% of TOs had seen more than 40% of the listed BH1 films (giving this type a similar profile to the post-classical and auteur American non-period films that formed the core of TOs' tastes) – but so had two-thirds of NTs. Indeed, a third of NTs had seen more than 60% of BH1s, a breadth that considerably exceeded NTs' viewing of *any* other period or non-period film type. For comparison, fewer than one-third of NTs had seen more than 40% of the listed British popular genre and 'contemporary heritage' films, the *non*-period film types *most* popular with this cohort.

Beyond the fact that most respondents had seen and liked a lot of BH1 films, NTs' and TOs' period-film tastes diverged sharply in three key respects. First, as illustrated in Appendix 5.2, NTs and TOs displayed different *hierarchies* of preferences in their responses to the films *within* the core British heritage categories as well as the broader range of period films beyond. These different patterns are very suggestive about how different segments of the audience (represented here by the TO and NT cohorts) may relate differently to a common field of 'heritage films'. Austen adaptations, David Lean's 1984 treatment of Forster's *A Passage to India* – appraised by critic Chris Peachment as a 'well tailored' film, but one which veered 'very wide of the mark over E. M. Forster's hatred of the British presence in India'[8] – and *Chariots of Fire* occupied prime positions in NTs' tastes, while films readable as liberal or feminist social critiques, and those available for queer readings and/or featuring gay protagonists, featured more strongly in TOs'. NTs' most-favoured heritage films clustered around both more conservative choices and (as later chapters explore) more conservative uses of the same films.

Second, the types of British period films *beyond* BH1s watched and liked by NTs and TOs diverged significantly, as did the breadth or specificity of these wider tastes. Third and last, the tastes of the NT 'audience' were sharply polarised between types of period films that were watched and those that were not – whereas TOs' tastes in period films, and their responses to them, proved heterogeneous enough to present challenges for generalised analysis.

While the findings confirmed the existence of a section of the audience (predominantly NTs) whose viewing and tastes were dominated by a very narrow range of British period films, Merchant Ivory's films were less prominent in this kind of taste than critical and media stereotypes might lead us to expect (see pages 110–15). The wider context, however, was that *almost no* NTs expressed their film preferences in director-centred terms. Only six (10% of) NTs answered 'yes' to the question asking whether they had *any* favourite film directors (compared to 83% of TOs), and only two NTs (and five TOs) named Ivory (or 'Merchant Ivory') as one of these favourites. When favourite 'authors' of period films were mentioned by NTs, they were almost invariably the source novelists – most commonly Shakespeare, Jane Austen or Dickens – a point we will return to in later chapters.

BH2 (borderline heritage) films were almost as popular and widely seen among the NT cohort as BH1s. The BH1 and BH2 films combined formed the NT cohort's main and most comprehensive field of viewing – across films set in either present or past, and of all national origins. In short, NT tastes clustered strongly around two film types that were a close fit for academic and critical notions of heritage cinema; and, in contrast with the distinction between the two implied by the positive critical reception of many BH2 films, the tastes of the NT 'audience' drew no equivalent distinction between the two types. This response did not, however, extend to the TO cohort, among whom BH2s were less universally seen, or widely liked, than BH1s, and whose preferred British period-film types beyond these lay elsewhere.

NT respondents' viewing of British films beyond BH1s and BH2s was, by contrast, typically narrow or, in some cases, non-existent. The percentages of NTs who had seen *no* British (or Irish) period films in the remaining four analytic categories ranged from around one-fifth for the 'conservative' retro films (BR1) and 45% for post-heritage films (BPH) to almost 70% for both the 'critical' retro (BR2) and history films (BHY) – the latter being particularly little seen. Thus only the BR1 films – the 'conservative', less critical, retro category – achieved anything approaching the popularity of BH1s and BH2s among NTs.

Similarly, although 55% of NT respondents had seen some of the listed BPH post-heritage films, only 15% had seen more than one or two. Perhaps more significantly, those NTs who had seen some – perhaps attracted by their literary kudos, or by publicity which stressed the visual and costume pleasures of a film such as *Orlando* as much as its self-conscious post-heritage traits – had not invariably enjoyed them. In the most pronounced examples, almost a quarter of NTs had seen *Orlando* and the Bloomsbury Set biopic *Carrington* (the object of an instructively hyperbolic *Daily Mail* attack at its release),[9] but only 16% of the cohort had enjoyed either film. The significance of these negative responses is clear given that NTs (unlike TOs) only rarely expressed dislike of films they had seen. By contrast, the post-heritage film most widely seen among (34% of) NTs, Richard Loncraine's relocation of Shakespeare's *Richard III* to Nazi Germany, was also widely liked (by 31% of the cohort) – perhaps precisely because it was a Shakespeare film.

Most TOs had seen a wide variety of British period films across almost all the analytic types. Beyond the centrality of the BHI core heritage films for most (apart from a few dissenters), patterns of TO period-film taste were complex, exhibiting both similarities to and differences from the simpler dominant trends among NTs.

Thus although BHYs were the British period films least widely seen by TOs (as with NTs), 63% of TOs had seen at least two, and some referred positively to particular BHY films in their self-worded replies. It should be added that some of the films classified as BHYs had been included in the questionnaire as an index of respondents' interest in films taking a politically engaged approach to history, rather than purely as examples of the histori-cal film as a genre. Consequently, the BHY list included films such as *Anne Devlin*, the Welsh-language *Hedd Wyn* and Bill Douglas's *Comrades*, which – despite their importance to debates around historical representation – had received only a limited UK cinema release. However, it also included bigger-budget, widely released (and more recent) films such as *Rob Roy*, *Michael Collins* and Ken Loach's *Land and Freedom* – and the last two of these, in particular, had been seen (and, in almost all cases, liked) by around half the TO cohort.

The key pattern characterising (most) TOs' British period-film tastes – in so far as this can be pinned down – was a strong liking for certain retro films that spanned both the 'conservative' BR1 and 'critical' BR2 categories, along-side many BHI core heritage films, and supplemented by some BPH post-heritage films (although TOs expressed divergent preferences in, and opinions on, these). In statistical illustration, 77% of TOs had seen more than 40% of BR1s; 60% of TOs had seen more than 40% of the films in the shorter BPH list; and, indeed, a significant contingent had seen more than 60% of the films in these categories.

Although (as with the BHYs) TOs had not typically seen high numbers of the BR2 films, some specific BR2s were prominent among their most strongly liked films. Indeed, the second most widely seen and liked of *all* the listed period films among TOs (both seen, and liked/liked a lot, by more than 80%) was *Prick Up Your Ears*, the Stephen Frears-directed biopic (adapted from John Lahr's eponymous 1978 biography) of the irreverent gay 1960s playwright Joe Orton. *Scandal* was another 'critical' retro film well liked by TOs, seen by 70% and enjoyed by 60%. More popular still, however, was the (ostensibly) 'conservative' *Dance with a Stranger* – a 1950s biopic of Ruth Ellis, the last woman to be hanged in Britain – which (although seen by only a quarter of NTs) had been seen by 87% of TOs and enjoyed by 73%, making it more widely seen among TOs than *A Room with a View* and more popular than *Howards End*.

As these examples demonstrate, retro films were as central as heritage films to TOs' period-film tastes – but (in contrast with the pattern observed among NTs) their most-favoured retro films disregarded the (already untidy) dividing line between those received by critics as 'conservative' or as 'critical'. Fewer than one-third of NTs, by contrast, had seen any of the 'critical' BR2 films (only six had seen *Scandal*, and a mere two had seen – and liked – *Prick Up Your Ears*); whereas almost 80% had seen at least one BR1 film. Their most popular BR1 choice by far was *Shadowlands* (seen by 68% of NTs and liked by 60%), a highly emotional account of the writer C. S. Lewis's romantic friendship with a terminally ill American female fan which also happened to star Anthony Hopkins.

In contrast with their general liking for many of the key British heritage and retro films, TOs' responses to the BPH post-heritage films were notably polarised. Some BPHs had been more widely seen than others, and many attracted divided responses. Where the post-heritage film most seen and most liked by NTs had been *Richard III*, for the TO audience it was *Orlando* (seen by 73%), with *Carrington* in second place (seen by two-thirds), followed by *Richard III* (seen by 60%). However, only around 70% of the TOs who had seen these films reported positively that they liked them and three TOs had actively disliked *Richard III*. The most actively disliked BPH film was *Angels and Insects* – but the mere fact that more than one-third of TOs had seen this very distinctive, but not commercially successful, revisionist Victorian drama (adapted from an A. S. Byatt novella) testifies to their wide viewing.

EUROPEAN AND NON–ANGLOPHONE PERIOD FILMS

Given that European/non-Anglophone films in general were less widely watched than English-language films by most respondents, the former were subdivided into only three relatively broad analytic types. The first, European period art cinema (EPA), included key examples made in the English language or by British directors (Derek Jarman and Peter Greenaway). Despite these Anglophone inclusions, the EPA films were validly defined as European given that they were circulated, appreciated and (particularly in Greenaway's case) funded within a European institutional and cultural context. The other two categories, EH1 and EH2, were approximate European/non-Anglophone equivalents of the core and borderline British heritage-film types. EH1 comprised exportable prestige productions that fitted closely with European notions of the 'quality' film (the most widely used international synonym for the heritage film: see Chapter 1). Although the heritage strands of French and other non-Anglophone national cinemas each have their own distinctive themes and conventions, often markedly different from the British heritage film,[10] the EH1 films equate with the British BH1s insofar as both are regarded as exemplars of their respective national heritage cinemas. EH2 was a more hybrid grouping, bringing together films with borderline heritage traits and others with definite post-heritage or critical retro characteristics.

Of the three types, TO and NT respondents alike were most likely to have seen some of the EH1 films, followed by some of the (mostly English-language) EPAs. Almost one-fifth of NTs had not seen any EH1 films – a percentage that rose to 50% of the cohort for the EPA films and 60% for EH2s. Those NTs who had seen some EH1s had mostly seen fewer than 40% of the list (between one and four films), while the numbers of EPA or EH2 films seen by most NTs were (predictably) lower still. As already noted, NTs' tastes in European period films centred on the best-known European (especially French) heritage-film hits of the 1980s, such as *Jean de Florette*, its companion film *Manon des sources*, the Danish *Babette's Feast* and the Italian *Cinema Paradiso* (less widely seen, but named as a favourite by one NT). As can be seen in Appendix 5.2, the first three of these films were among the period films of any national origin most widely seen by NTs; but even then, *Jean de Florette* had been seen by only 42%, compared to the 95% who had seen NTs' most-favoured English-language choice, *Sense and Sensibility*. In an important exception already noted, *Les Enfants du paradis* (classed as an EH2, and included in the questionnaire both due to a successful recent re-release in London cinemas and as a likely index of respondents' tastes in earlier decades) was one of the favourite films – both pre-suggested and self-named – of respondents in both cohorts, and had been seen and enjoyed by almost as many NTs as *Jean de Florette*.

Of the three European/non-Anglophone types, virtually all TOs had seen at least one of the EH1 films (although fewer than a quarter had seen more than 60% of the list), but were least likely to have seen a wide range of EH2s (17%

of TOs had seen none). The latter was a surprising finding given that the EH2 list included choices such as Patrice Chéreau's *La Reine Margot* – a benchmark hit of 1990s art cinema and cited as a favourite film by one TO respondent – and the 1996 Best Foreign-Language Film Oscar-winner *Antonia's Line*.

By contrast, half the TO cohort had seen between three and five films (of six) in the short EPA list. This implied a stronger interest in the – generally more modernist – EPAs than in more conventional European heritage films; but in practice TOs' responses to EPAs were divided (in a similar pattern to their responses to the British post-heritage films). Of Jarman's and Greenaway's films, only Greenaway's (rather static, but visually striking) breakthrough feature *The Draughtsman's Contract* (UK, 1982) featured among any TOs' self-named favourites. While two-thirds of TOs had seen *Caravaggio* and/ or *Prospero's Books*, only half, or fewer, of these had enjoyed them – and some TOs voluntarily cited both Greenaway and Jarman as indices of the kinds of period film they disliked. These directors were associated, for example, (alongside Ken Loach) with 'a more or less anti-establishment whinging bias' (TO3, Irish-born gay man, 38, civil servant). EPAs had also proved problematic viewing for some of the NTs who had seen them – no surprise, given these films' eschewal of 'authentic' period reconstruction in favour of expressionist or historically anachronistic production design. While NTs had perhaps been drawn to certain EPA films by their positive critical reception or relationship to canonic literature – as with *Edward II* (adapted from Marlowe) or *Prospero's Books* (derived from Shakespeare's *The Tempest*) – they did not always like what they saw. Thus *Prospero's Books* was liked by only half the 16% of NTs who had seen it.

US, AUSTRALIAN AND NEW ZEALAND PERIOD FILMS

The 1990s had seen the release of a significant cluster of high-profile and successful period films from the USA, Australia and New Zealand, many of them either adapted from or (most explicitly in the case of Jane Campion's *The Piano*) drawing upon the traditions of the nineteenth- or turn-of-twentieth-century novel. These films can usefully be discussed with reference to the British or cross-national debates around heritage and retro cinema. It was noticeable, however, that in key cases – centrally, the auteur-directed 'post-modern/self-aware' literary adaptations (coded ANP) – they enjoyed a different critical reception in the UK from contemporaneous British productions set in similar periods or adapted from comparable literary works. *The Age of Innocence*, in particular, was discussed centrally on its release as the work of a leading American auteur, in terms of Scorsese's stylistic and technical choices and his treatment of themes – a critical strategy which implied a clear separation between the film and 'heritage cinema' and suppressed direct dis-cussion of it in those terms.[11] I was interested to establish how far this critical differentiation was mirrored in the taste patterns of survey respondents. In addition, how far did generically distinct areas of US, Australian and New Zealand production – such as US period adaptations from gothic literature, or films dealing with events in distant or recent American history – form part of their viewing?

In order to explore these questions, the questionnaire's listed US and Australasian period films were divided into six categories. The American liter-ary heritage films (ALH) were notable for their close affinities with the core British heritage productions: adaptations of (mostly American or English) literary classics, classically filmed, and often sharing directors (James Ivory) or source authors (Jane Austen) strongly associated with British heritage cinema.[12]

US and New Zealand postmodern heritage films (ANP), comprised the three auteur films referred to at the start of this section, all of which mixed evident heritage characteristics with a conscious distanciation from these, both on the part of their directors and at the site of critical reception. The third category, American gothic literary adaptations (AGL), is self-explanatory. American history films (AHY) were analogous to the BHY British and Irish history category; but the variety of events and periods they engaged with in expressly historical terms was significantly broader (as in Oliver Stone's *JFK* and Spike Lee's *Malcolm X*). Other films by Stone – such as *Born on the Fourth of July* and *Nixon* – could feasibly have been added to this category, and his work alone accounts for a significant part of the 1980s–1990s proliferation of US 'contemporary history' films – a sub-genre which had less prominence in British cinema until the post-2000 emergence of examples such as Ken Loach's *The Wind that Shakes the Barley* (Ire/UK/Ger/It/Sp/Fr, 2006) or the Peter Morgan-scripted biopics *Frost/Nixon* (Ron Howard, USA/UK/Fr, 2008) and *The Queen* (Stephen Frears, UK/Fr/It, 2006).

ANR1 comprised films from the US and New Zealand set in the period during and since World War II (with some overlap with the AHY list), but was defined centrally by this periodisation, rather than with reference to genre, 'retro' styling, or judgements about their conservative or critical perspective on the past. Several inclusions (such as Spielberg's *Schindler's List*) were historical films – a classification that extends to *Evita*, despite its adaptation from a stage musical. The final classification, ANR2, US and New Zealand 'critical period films', was another overlapping category but not a critically neutral one. ANR2s were noteworthy for their challenging, non-consensus (or even experimental) depiction of their chosen period or subject-matter, and included films by two contemporary black American directors, Julie Dash and Spike Lee.

The American literary heritage (ALH) and US and New Zealand postmodern heritage (ANP) films had been widely seen by TO respondents. ALHs were also the Anglophone non-British period-film type NTs were most likely to have seen, although this finding will have been boosted by the inclusion of the Miramax/Gwyneth Paltrow Jane Austen adaptation *Emma*. The two Merchant Ivory adaptations of Henry James in the ALH list, in contrast, had been less widely seen; only 16% of NTs and 23% of TOs had seen *The Europeans*, and only 23% of NTs and 37% of TOs had seen *The Bostonians*.[13] I will return to the place of Ivory's films (and Austen adaptations) in respondents' tastes at the close of this chapter; but it can already be seen that few were Ivory completists, and that the two James adaptations (despite their success at the time of release) were not his most popular films with either cohort.

A quarter of NT respondents (compared to two-thirds of TOs) had seen two or three of the three postmodern heritage films (ANPs); but 40% of NTs (compared to 13% of TOs) had seen none, and the three listed films attracted very varied levels of interest. Just over 60% of NTs had seen *The Piano*, and most had enjoyed it. On the other hand, just under 20% had seen *The Age of Innocence*, and a mere five (8% of NTs) had seen *The Portrait of a Lady*. In a similar pattern, *The Piano* was by far the most popular ANP film among TOs – seen by 83%, and enjoyed by two-thirds, of the cohort – while *The Age of Innocence* and *The Portrait of a Lady* had been considerably less widely seen, and the latter not universally liked (indeed, two TOs actively disliked it). There were similarities here to the polarised responses to British post-heritage (BPH) and European period art (EPA) films.

In a striking contrast with the relative uninterest in the British/Irish history genre among NT and even many TO respondents, the AHY (American history) films were the second most widely seen US or Australasian period-film type among NTs (84% of NTs had seen at least one, and around 50% had seen two or three), followed by the ANR1 films (of which 73% of NTs had seen at least one). Virtually all the TO cohort had seen at least one film in both categories – but, predictably, higher numbers: 80% of TOs had seen four or more AHYs, and 50% of TOs had seen four of more ANR1s.

As noted earlier, some of the films classified as ANR1s were also AHY films; and, as can be seen from Appendix 5.2, the apparent importance of both 'types' was boosted by the great popularity of *Schindler's List* among both cohorts, and by the popularity of *Evita* among NTs. Indeed, for the TO cohort, *Schindler's List* emerged as the most widely seen and widely liked of the pre-suggested listed period films in any category; it had been seen by all but two TOs (93%), and liked by all but four (87%), making it slightly more popular than the Joe Orton biopic (and 'critical' British retro film) *Prick Up Your Ears* and Merchant Ivory's *A Room with a View*. Although *Schindler's List* did not match or exceed the popularity of British heritage choices among NT respondents in the same way, it had nevertheless been seen by two-thirds and liked by 60%, making *Schindler's List* the most favoured non-British period film for the NT cohort (followed by *The Piano*).

TO and NT respondents' tastes in US and Australasian period films emerged as generally less polarised than their tastes in British and Irish period films or most areas of non-period cinema. It was films in the two remaining US and Australasian period-film 'types', however – the gothic AGLs, and (least widely viewed) the critical, non-consensus, ANR2s – that attracted the greatest polarisation. Two-thirds of TOs had seen two or three of the three gothic AGL choices – whereas 84% of NTs had seen none. In a further index of this contrast, Coppola's *Bram Stoker's Dracula* had been seen by almost three-quarters of TOs, and liked by more than half the cohort, but seen by only seven NTs (although most had enjoyed it).

To summarise, while the US and New Zealand period films most likely to have been seen by NTs were mostly in the ALH 'literary heritage' category – and the range they had seen compared favourably with their breadth of viewing of British period films beyond the core heritage categories – NTs had not seen large numbers of these films. By contrast, TO respondents had characteristically seen a modest range of ALHs, but alongside higher proportions of films from other US and New Zealand period-film categories, with the AHY and ANR1 films emerging as the types most widely seen.

To draw a broader conclusion, most TO respondents' viewing of period films across most geographical origins and genres showed a breadth and variety matched by only a minority of NTs. Hierarchies and patterns of preferred film types and nationalities were, however, apparent within this relative breadth, just as they were within the narrower tastes of NT respondents. It is important to keep in mind, too, that a minority of TOs showed relatively limited film tastes, just as a minority of NTs showed more adventurous ones.

HERITAGE MARKET LEADERS? MERCHANT IVORY PRODUCTIONS VERSUS JANE AUSTEN

In closing, this chapter will consider two final indicators of patterns of 'heritage' film taste. The numbers of films directed by James Ivory (JIV) and seen by respondents were analysed – of those listed in the questionnaire, and encompassing present-day and period British and US, Indian and European settings – as were the numbers of listed benchmark 1980s to mid 1990s film and television adaptations from novels by Jane Austen they had seen (JAU) (spanning Questions 17 and 19).

A core assumption of most of the early 1990s critical writings on heritage cinema was that Merchant Ivory's films dominated the heritage 'genre'.

However, this assumption immediately raises the question (and problem) of who defines their centrality. If Ivory's films have 'dominated' British heritage-film production, is this because they have been constructed by critics as forming the core of the genre (generating a circular logic), or because they have a centrality among the heritage films viewed, enjoyed, and/or viewed repeatedly, by audiences?

My prior assumption was that the films seen by viewers with narrow heritage-film-dominated tastes would typically include at least some of Ivory's greatest period-film successes – the E. M. Forster adaptations *A Room With A View* and *Howards End* (if not necessarily *Maurice*), plus *The Remains of the Day* – and that these examples would also be among the 'heritage' films widely seen by respondents with broader tastes. Conversely, a relationship with a wider range of Ivory's (earlier and/or non-period) films might indicate a departure from narrow heritage tastes. Some attention to respondents' viewing and liking of specific Merchant Ivory films is clearly useful here. For example, familiarity with *Quartet* (set in 1920s Paris, with a mostly Anglo-French cast) would suggest consumption of Merchant Ivory's films within a definite art-cinema – and European – context; while familiarity with their Henry James adaptations, *The Europeans* and *The Bostonians*, would indicate a habitus established both within a clear art-cinema context and around a decade before the concept of 'heritage cinema' emerged.

By contrast, tastes which focus too intensely or narrowly around Austen adaptations on film and/or television – particularly to the exclusion of other tastes – would indeed seem to affirm a narrow, heritage-dominated period-film habitus, but of a particular kind, grounded in cultural (and perhaps ideological) attitudes not necessarily shared by all viewers of Ivory's films. The obsessiveness and possessiveness of many Austen fans, their sense of ownership of 'Jane', and their strong views on the 'right' interpretation of her work, have been well documented.[14] Enthusiasm for Austen adaptations is not, of course, evidence in itself of membership of this group. But where it forms the core of very narrow tastes, or accompanies a specific pattern of attitudes to period films and literary adaptation, it may become valid to read it as an index of a hermetic habitus, indifferent or even dismissive towards the wider field of film and screen culture.

Virtually all (95% of) NT respondents and 93% of TOs had seen some of the Merchant Ivory films listed in the questionnaire. However (as illustrated in Appendix 5.2), the range, and specific films, they tended to have seen differed sharply between the two cohorts in a manner that almost parodied the hypothetical patterns proposed above. The TO cohort was split between 37% of TOs who had seen between one and four of the eleven listed Ivory films, and 57% who had seen between five and eleven. Among NTs, the equivalent split was 76% versus 19%. In short, some TOs had seen only the most popular of Ivory's post-1980 period films – centrally, the British Forster adaptations – while others had seen a wider range; but the majority of NTs fell into the first category. Among NTs, the viewing pattern for Ivory's films as a 'type' came close to that for the most mainstream type of European heritage films, the EH1s – that is, significantly less widely seen than films in the core British heritage categories (BH1 and BH2) or the British and Irish popular (BIP) films set in the present.

In a trend distinctive to the TOs cohort, 1983's *Heat and Dust* (adapted by Ruth Prawer Jhabvala from her own novel, in which Anne, a young woman in the present, investigates the life of her aunt in 1920s colonial India) seemed to have marked the entry point into Merchant Ivory viewing for many TOs: it had been seen by 70% and enjoyed by 57%, making it as popular and widely seen among TOs as *Maurice*. By contrast, *Heat and Dust* had been seen by fewer than a quarter of NTs (although liked by most), and *Maurice* by fewer still. By contrast (and as already noted), Ivory's breakthrough US period literary adaptations, *The Europeans* and *The Bostonians*, had been seen by only a minority of TOs, and still smaller minorities of NTs (among whom *The Bostonians* had a similar profile to *Heat and Dust*). To place these patterns in a wider context, most TOs had seen fewer of Ivory's listed films than they had films in the British heritage types BH1 and BH2. But, counter to this, the Ivory films seen by some TOs included examples that had found little critical favour, and only a limited audience, in the USA or UK – notably 1994's *Jefferson in Paris* and 1989's *Slaves of New York* – demonstrating an acquaintance with his work that exceeded the norm.

Of the fifty-eight respondents who had seen only a few (one to four) of the listed Ivory films, only eleven were TO (comprising 37% of all TOs), while forty-seven were NTs (76% of all NTs). Unsurprisingly, the films that had been Ivory's greatest hits with cinema audiences in general – *Howards End, A Room with a View, The Remains of the Day* – were also widely seen and very popular among survey respondents, but with significantly different taste hierarchies emerging among NTs and TOs. Thus, among NTs, the most seen and best liked of Ivory's period films (measured on Question 17 replies) was *Howards End* – seen by 89%, 'liked a lot' by 61% and 'liked' by a further 15%, making it NTs' joint-third most-seen of *all* the listed period films, alongside *The Madness of King George* (Appendix 5.2). It was followed in popularity (below the Austen adaptation *Emma*) by *A Room with a View* and then *The Remains of the Day* (occupying joint eighth place with *The Piano*).

Trends among TOs differed from those outlined above in three main respects. First, five – rather than three – of Ivory's period films stood out as very widely seen, although their popularity varied. In addition to the 'big three' – *Howards End, A Room with a View* and *Remains of the Day* – two films with limited impact on NTs – *Heat and Dust* and *Maurice* – had been very widely seen by (70% of) TOs. Second, where *Howards End* was the key Ivory film for NTs, for TOs it was *Room* (seen by 83%), followed by *Remains* (seen by 80%), with *Howards End* (seen by 77%) in third place. Among the TO respondents who had seen only one to four of the listed Ivory films, however, there was a different hierarchy: 73% of this sub-cohort had seen *Room*, but only 54% had seen *Remains* and 45% had seen *Howards End* – whereas 64% had seen *Maurice*. In short, where NTs with limited Ivory viewing were most likely to have seen *Howards End*, followed by *Room*, TOs with limited Ivory viewing were most likely to have seen *Room*, followed by *Maurice*.

These differing preferences seem to indicate significant differences between the TO and NT cohorts' relationships to Ivory's (and other) period films and the kinds of pleasures they expected and derived from them. The preference for *Room* over *Howards End* among TOs is in itself very suggestive; but the further finding that *Maurice* had been so widely seen by TOs – including those who had seen only a few of Ivory's films – seems still more significant, given that it had been seen by only 13% of NTs.

Maurice's status as a gay love story, and its liberal campaigning dimension (the film accrued extra-textual significance at the time of its 1987–8 UK theatrical release, which coincided with the controversy around the Conservative government's introduction of Section 28 of the Local Government Act, outlawing the 'promotion' of homosexuality as a 'pretended family relationship'), set it apart from Ivory's 'big three' hits, and must have problematised its reception among some sections of the heritage audience. However, it was constructed by the majority of contemporary critics centrally as a quality film rather than as especially controversial, and achieved fair box-office success, remaining on central London release for at least six months.[15] In this context, while I expected *Maurice* to have been seen by fewer NTs than the 'big three' hits – and to have had a mixed reception from them – I did not expect it to have been seen by only 13%. Nor did I expect it to have been the second most-seen film among the sub-group of TOs with only limited wider Ivory viewing. These findings do, however, seem to support the arguments – proposed in my earlier textual work on the Ivory Forster adaptations – that both *Room* and *Maurice* make available a set of pleasures distinct from (or at least supplementary to) those claimed by anti-heritage critics and embodied more conventionally by *Remains* and *Howards End*.[16] I should add that the TO taste hierarchy matches my own preferences among Ivory's films.

Third, where a solid majority of those NTs who had seen the 'big three' Ivory period films had liked them 'a lot' (apart from *Howards End*, which, as the Ivory film most widely seen by NTs, also attracted the most 'no strong opinion' replies), the TO cohort was more evenly split between 'liked a lot' responses and those who had merely 'liked' the Ivory films they had seen – with the levels of liking expressed for *Maurice* and *Heat and Dust* more cautious than for the 'big three'. This trend extended across most of Ivory's period films; a substantial proportion of TOs had seen a fair number of them, yet were reluctant to express more than moderate 'liking'. Of course, TOs may simply have enjoyed these films but not passionately so. But, as we shall see in Chapter 6 onwards, a defining feature of many TOs' self-worded comments was an (often acutely self-conscious) awareness of existing critical discourses and denunciations of heritage cinema to which – by contrast – NT respondents were largely oblivious. This discursive (self-)consciousness raises the possibility that some TO respondents had enjoyed the films more strongly than they admitted.

The NT cohort, conversely, tended to reserve their strongest enthusiasm for a narrow range of films – usually, agreed heritage-film successes likely to be endorsed by their peers. This trend of strong liking for a narrow range of conventional period-film choices was abundantly confirmed by NTs' responses to the Jane Austen adaptations – TV dramas/serials as well as films – listed in the questionnaire. These had been ubiquitously seen – and almost as ubiquitously strongly liked – by NTs to an extent unmatched by the films in any other category. Where no NT respondent had seen more than 80% of the eleven listed Ivory films, and only 15% had seen more than 80% of the core British heritage (BH1) films, 87% of NTs had seen virtually all (five or six) of the six Austen adaptations listed.

These high viewing levels, of course, reflect the fact that half the Austen list consisted of TV dramas (bearing in mind that the 'film'-viewing habitus of many NTs was in reality overwhelmingly televisual), and the inclusion of the BBC's 1995 serialisation of *Pride and Prejudice* – which had been a ratings phenomenon even on repeat screenings and, predictably, was the favourite period TV drama most widely named by (almost a quarter of) NTs. Indeed, one of the three Austen feature films listed, *Persuasion*, was initially screened on BBC-TV and only later released in (US and then UK) cinemas so that the Austen-mania stoked by *Pride and Prejudice* could be more fully exploited. However, the two Austen films made for the cinema had also been seen, and strongly liked, by virtually all NTs. Of all the ninety-seven period feature films listed in the questionnaire, Ang Lee's 1995 *Sense and Sensibility* was *the* one most seen and most strongly liked by NTs: 95% had seen it, 79% liked it 'a lot' and a further 10% 'liked' it. Even the transatlantic *Emma* (less well received by critics) had been seen by 82% of NTs, 'liked a lot' by 56% and 'liked' by a further 19%, beating *A Room with a View* to fifth place in their hierarchy of favourites.

Although Austen adaptations were also enjoyed by many TO respondents, they did not occupy the same position of excessive centrality as they did for NTs. Hence only 23% of TOs had seen five or six of the listed Austen adaptations (compared to 87% of NTs). *Sense and Sensibility* was, however, as widely seen among TOs as *A Room with a View* (seen by 84%), while *Emma* was as widely seen as *Heat and Dust* and *Maurice* (by 70%). This preference for Austen adaptations made for the cinema rather than TV, is, of course, in line with the strongly film-centred – and cinemagoing – habitus of the TO cohort. The two Austen feature films were, however, received by TOs with more modest enthusiasm than the cohort's most-favoured Ivory films. Thus *Sense and Sensibility* was liked or liked a lot by 75% of the TOs who had seen it – compared to 92% of the TOs who had seen *A Room with a View*.

NOTES

1. The term 'post-classical' of course refers here to the widely accepted – but not uncontested – historical account of the evolution of Hollywood film form which characterised the loosening of the narrative and stylistic conventions of 'classical' Hollywood cinema (from the mid 1950s, but most strongly in the 'New Hollywood' cinema of the late 1960s to 1970s) as 'post-classical'.
2. King, 'Crossing thresholds', p. 217.
3. Jancovich, 'Genre and the audience', p. 35.
4. For a dedicated study of *Gone With the Wind*'s female fans, see Taylor, *Scarlett's Women*.
5. See Chapter 2, Note 8. The two pre-1960 BBC-TV Classic Serials named by respondents were the 1956 *Jane Eyre* (director Campbell Logan), with Daphne Slater as Jane and Stanley Baker as Mr Rochester, and the 1958 *Pride and Prejudice* (director unknown), with Alan Badel as Mr Darcy and Jane Downs as Elizabeth Bennet.
6. Harper, *Picturing the Past*, p. 188.
7. *Sense and Sensibility* was warmly received by many UK critics who did not foreground its heritage status; and by others, like myself, who argued that its merits challenged blanket anti-heritage positions. Andy Medhurst, however, argued forcefully that it catered to 'conservatively nostalgic tastes'. (Monk, '*Sense and Sensibility*' [review]; Medhurst, 'Dressing the part'.)
8. Peachment, '*A Passage to India*' [review], in Milne (ed.), *The Time Out Film Guide*.
9. Roberts, 'They hated the family [etc]'.
10. For example, the Swedish 'quality film' characteristically focuses on childhood (Soila, 'National cinema and notions of quality'), while the class perspectives of 1980s French heritage films – coloured by the socialist values of the Mitterrand era – differed sharply from their British contemporaries (Austin, *Contemporary French Cinema*, pp. 142–70).
11. See, for example, Christie, 'The Scorsese interview', and Cook, '*The Age of Innocence*' [review].
12. *Dangerous Liaisons*, as a Hollywood production with a Hollywood cast, was classed as an ALH film but adapted from an eighteenth-century French source and made by a British director.
13. Merchant–Ivory–Jhabvala's third – higher-budget but less well-received – James adaptation, *The Golden Bowl* (USA/Fr/UK, 2000), was released after the survey's completion.
14. See, for example, Lynch (ed.), *Janeites*.
15. For a fuller analysis of the contemporary critical reception of *Maurice*, see Monk, *Sex, Politics and the Past*, pp. 49–55.
16. See Monk, *Sex, Politics and the Past*, and Monk, 'Sexuality and heritage'.

CHAPTER 6

Audience Pleasures, Attitudes and Perspectives 1: Visual Pleasure and 'Authenticity', Engagement and Escape

INTRODUCTION

What did the survey's respondents enjoy – or dislike – about the period films they watched? What attitudes and perceptions underpinned, and contextually and interpretatively informed, these preferences and responses? Of more specific importance, how far, and in what ways, did respondents' positions and perspectives support or challenge claims about the putative aesthetic and political workings (and even implied 'effects') of heritage films? And in what ways were the wider critical discourses and debates around period films – around the representation and (re-)imagining of past historical periods or events; the reconstruction or simulation of the period mise-en-scène; the process of adaptation from 'classic' literature to screen; and questions of cultural value(s) as well as political orientation – reproduced, revised or resisted by the films' audiences? Last, does the evidence suggest that it is appropriate to conceive of these audiences as *producers* of distinct 'audience' or 'fan' discourses around period films, or was the relationship a less active one of absorption and reproduction of elements of existing (critical, media, promotional) discourses?

The remaining chapters of this book consider and interpret the forms of evidence on the questions of reception posed above that were generated via the survey questionnaire. Chapters 6 and 7 engage directly with the pleasures survey respondents expected from, and reported finding in, period films, drawing out the patterns and divergences in the priorities (or hierarchies of pleasures) favoured by respondents in the TO (*Time Out*) and NT (National Trust) cohorts, and in their attitudes and orientations towards period films. The closing Chapter 8 draws together the study's conclusions, with an emphasis on questions around the coherence or otherwise of the heritage film audience(s); respondents' own self-reflexivity and self-perception as members (or not) of this audience; and the broader implications of the findings for film-audience studies.

Chapter 6 begins with an overview of patterns in the period-film pleasures most highly valued (or not) by respondents in the TO and NT cohorts.[1] My focus then broadens to consider the wider mesh of attitudes within which the two cohorts' film tastes, pleasures and displeasures were located, with particular reference to questions directly or tacitly relevant to the heritage-film debate, in an analysis that continues in Chapter 7. Chapter 6 focuses in detail on the expectations, positionings and attitudes that emerged among TOs and NTs in relation to two areas of potential pleasure offered by period films which the heritage-film debate has conceived of as operating in tension with one another: on the one hand, visual pleasures, including those specific to the period mise-en-scène; on the other, the pleasures of narrative (and wider forms of) engagement that the 'mainstream' viewer normally expects of 'mainstream' cinema. Chapter 7 focuses on respondents' positioning and attitudes in relation to notions of 'quality', what might be termed the 'literary' pleasures of many period films, and discourses around 'faithful' adaptation. As will be clear from this subdivision, the 'discourse of authenticity' closely associated with notions of the 'heritage film' – and respondents' own positions in relation to this – are explored in Chapter 6, but then returned to, with reference to 'classic' literary adaptation, in Chapter 7.

The Heritage Audience Survey questionnaire (presented in Appendix 2.1) generated three forms of evidence which I draw upon in this analysis. It first asked respondents an open question: 'Please describe in your own words what you most enjoy about the period/costume films you watch' (Question 21).[2] A later question (Question 29) then presented respondents with a list of twenty-eight possible 'factors or ingredients' (potential pleasures) and asked them to rate the importance of each of these 'in explaining your personal enjoyment of [period] films'. Last, Question 30, 'Your attitudes to period films', presented respondents with a list of seventy-four statements expressing a range of attitudes, opinions or positions, primarily with reference to recent period films in the British context. The statements sought to ascertain respondents' opinions, attitudes and perceptions on matters such as the relationship between period films and the historical past depicted; issues around the adaptation of classic novels or plays for the screen; the cultural status and critical reception of 1980s–1990s British period films in the UK; respondents' wider attitudes to and tastes in contemporary cinema; and their views on issues salient to the heritage debate. Respondents were asked to indicate how closely each statement matched their own position: did they 'strongly agree', 'agree', hold 'no strong opinion', 'disagree' or 'strongly disagree'?[3]

Analysis of replies to these questions (analysis of recurrent content and discourses in the self-worded replies to Question 21; statistical analysis of

multiple-choice replies to Questions 29 and 30) made it possible to identify structuring patterns, preoccupations and themes in the pleasures and attitudes of the
two sub-samples, and to situate these with reference to respondents' wider identities and patterns of film habitus. It should be noted that the 'pleasures' enjoyed
or prioritised by respondents often meshed symbiotically with their 'attitudes',
whether to period films or on related questions. Respondents' favoured pleasures
tell us much about their attitudes, while many of the attitude statements presented in Question 30 related explicitly or implicitly to pleasures. But the inter-
relationship goes deeper. In many cases – as will emerge from my analysis – the
period-film pleasures respondents named or prioritised were as much expressions of *a priori* positions and beliefs (on matters such as historical authenticity or
cultural value) as they were responses to the qualities of specific films or types of
film. This analysis will show conclusively that while respondents in the TO and
NT cohorts shared some overlapping film tastes – including a shared liking for
many of the core British heritage films – the two groups on the whole perceived
and engaged with these films in radically different ways.

The pre-suggested pleasures in Question 29 and the attitude statements in
Question 30 were, of course, worded to elicit replies that would help clarify
respondents' positions not just as film viewers or consumers in the narrowest
sense, but *vis-à-vis* the heritage-film debate and related questions of cultural
and literary value, cultural politics and taste. Although I strove to eliminate
leading or ambiguous wordings, it would be risky, and methodologically
unsound, to interpret responses to these pre-worded questions in isolation
from respondents' wider replies. Accordingly, Chapters 6 to 8 endeavour to
interpret the patterns of response in the context of respondents' own self-
worded statements in their replies to Question 21, and the wider findings
presented in Chapters 3 to 5.

While ascertaining audience members' tastes and preferences in films is
(practically and methodologically) relatively straightforward, their *reasons*
for enjoying their favoured types of period film, and the particular pleasures
they gain from these, are less readily accessed. As touched upon in Chapter
2, whether the researcher asks open or closed questions, whether or not the
answers are expressed in respondents' own words, and whether insights are
sought via a printed questionnaire, individual interviews, focus groups, or
other methodologies, certain limitations will always remain that recall the
objections to empirical investigation raised (albeit reductively) by 1970s
Screen Theory. As I hope the remaining chapters will demonstrate, respondents' answers, and my analysis of these, give valuable insights into the conscious relationships that particular segments of the (cinematic and televisual)
audience have with period films, and the terms in which they articulate – or
wish to present – these relationships through language. What is less certain
is how far such questions – however carefully formulated – and answers

– however carefully interpreted – can provide access to and understanding of the unconscious pleasures and drives served by period-film viewing. For more prosaic reasons, questionnaires (and, equally, interviews) may also fail to elicit candid replies from some respondents about pleasures which are conscious but inadmissible (for example, due to cultural snobbery or embarrassment). Ultimately, the best the researcher can do is to analyse and interpret respondents' replies with and within a conscious awareness of these limitations.

The full list of twenty-eight potential pleasures viewers might find in period films, and the full list of seventy-four attitude statements, as presented to respondents, can be found in Appendix 2.1 (the questionnaire: Question 29 and Question 30). Appendix 6.1 presents a comparative (and, for reasons of space, selective) summary table showing, in ranked order, which pleasures were rated as ('very' or 'quite') important by the *greatest* and *smallest* numbers of respondents in the NT and TO cohorts respectively. This table, of course, presents composite trends across each of the sub-samples – as do many of the findings reported in Chapters 6 to 8 – and it should be borne in mind that there may be patterns of response across smaller sub-groups, or among individual respondents, within the TO and NT cohorts that are submerged rather than fully revealed in such summaries. The key trends that emerged in the two sub-samples were, however, sufficiently distinct that I have not merged the two to present combined findings for the Heritage Audience Survey sample as a 'whole'.

Each pleasure, and each attitude statement, listed in the questionnaire relates to a wider mesh of pleasures and/or attitudes, and these interrelationships are reflected both in the approach to analysis taken in Chapters 6 to 8 and in the organisation of the chapters themselves. When viewed as clusters – or, more precisely, as a set of overlapping clusters – these grouped pleasures and attitudinal positions serve to indicate particular kinds of disposition towards, relationships with or uses of period films on the part of respondents. Of course, during the process of questionnaire design and piloting, these pleasures were formulated, and wordings chosen, with such analytic groupings already in mind, on the basis of hypotheses about the range of reasons why audience members with different identities might enjoy period films. These hypotheses were, in turn, derived from the heritage-film debate as it has evolved in the UK, and my past thinking about and responses to this. The questionnaire itself, however, was structured *not* to make these hypotheses, or the analytic groupings I will deploy in these chapters, explicit to respondents.

The clusters of pleasures discussed in my analysis will at times intersect, given that the particular significance and meaning we might attribute to a specific 'pleasure' will depend on the contextual mesh of related pleasures valued by the same respondent or cohort. The analytic connections I will draw – and any underlying hypotheses not already elucidated in earlier chapters – will emerge as the discussion progresses.

VISUAL PLEASURES AND THE
PERIOD MISE–EN–SCÈNE

The pre-suggested pleasure given high priority by the greatest number of TO respondents was general 'visual enjoyment' (Question 29 and Appendix 6.1). Around 90% of TOs and NTs alike identified this as important to their enjoyment of period films and, within these, 60% of TOs (and 65% of NTs) rated it 'very important'.

However, the next six pre-suggested pleasures most widely judged important by TOs concerned the quality of the performances (important to 83% of TOs, and 'very important' to 57% of the cohort); various aspects of the narrative, intellectual and/or empathetic engagement offered by the films (important to between 77% and 83%, and 'very important' to between 50% and 63%); and the general 'high quality' of the films (important to 80%, but rated 'very important' by only 40%). Among TOs, these pleasures were followed in popularity by the opportunity to learn from period films about 'life in the past' or 'important historical events'; character identification; the chance to relive novels or plays adapted for the screen; and 'stories which still feel relevant today'. However, although these five ingredients were deemed important by 60% to 67% of TOs, the percentages rating them 'very important' were much lower, ranging from only 17% of the cohort for character identification to one-third for contemporary relevance. The priorities indicated by the pattern of these multiple-choice replies were consistent with TOs' self-worded replies to Question 21, in which the majority articulated their enjoyment of period films in terms of a – varying – blend of narrative, visual, performative, emotional, intellectual, historical and literary pleasures.

TO respondents were less likely, however, to agree that more specific elements of the period mise-en-scène – or efforts to reproduce these with the fastidious accuracy valued and demanded by the 'discourse of authenticity' – were important to their enjoyment of period films. Herein lay the first significant contrast between the priorities and attitudes of most TOs and those of most NTs. Between 57% and 60% of TOs assigned some importance to 'accurate reproduction of details in period settings' and/or 'looking at period costumes'. But the corollary, of course, was that around 40% did *not*, and only 17% of TOs agreed that the 'accurate reproduction' of period detail was *very* important. In contrast, 95% upwards of the NT cohort assigned importance to these two pleasures, and 81% rated 'accurate reproduction' 'very important'.

The remaining three pleasures of period mise-en-scène pre-suggested in Question 29 – 'period furnishings/interiors', 'landscapes/locations' and 'historic buildings' – were agreed to be important by more than 90% of NTs (and rated 'very important' by 60% or more) but only 37% to 40% of TOs (and rated 'very important' by a mere 10% to 17%).

For some purposes in this discussion, the term 'period detail' usefully offers greater elasticity than 'period mise-en-scène'. My use of the former encompasses all the details of the period mise-en-scène – setting or location, costume, styling and the deportment and movement of actors – but also those elements of dialogue and sound (speech and diction, diegetic music, ambient noises) which contribute to the sense of the recreation of a past period. (Of course, the absence of 'anachronistic' sounds – such as modern aircraft noise – can be as crucial to period verisimilitude as the presence of others.) The inclusion of such elements is crucial if we are to take into account the importance of acting to the strategies of period films – and for their audiences. It was notable that many respondents were as preoccupied with the (perceived) historical 'authenticity' (or otherwise) of dialogue, and the speech/diction and deportment of actors, as they were with details of visual styling.

Only one or two TO respondents showed any attachment to the discourse of authenticity in relation to period detail in their self-worded comments.[4] TOs were far more likely to describe the pleasures of period films in the language of hedonism, rapture or abandonment. Some 27% of TOs mentioned the pleasures of 'sumptuous style' (TO1, gay man, 33; corporate account manager, private health insurance), 'visually rich and sumptuous viewing' (TO13, woman, 26, British-Iranian; office manager, property), 'spectacle' and 'visual ravishment' (TO26, man, 38; technical author, strategic management).

A number of points distinguish this TO discourse of 'sumptuous' pleasure from the discourse around 'detail' and 'accuracy' that was more typical among NTs. First, the emphasis is more on the creation of a style, aura or ambience than on period minutiae. Second, the language used by the TOs quoted here – 'rich', 'sumptuous', 'ravish[ing]' – clearly frames period style as a source of sensory or aesthetic pleasure, one that might even rapturously take the viewer by force, not as an object of obsessive or critical scrutiny. Third, period style was almost never mentioned by TOs in isolation from other pleasures such as 'stunning adaptations of classic novels' and 'superb performances' (TO1, as above). TOs' statements tended to focus centrally on narrative or performative pleasures, or other forms of historical or emotional engagement. NTs, by contrast, were far more likely to focus centrally on 'authentic' period detail.

We should recall here that the (period and wider) genre tastes and film preferences of most TOs were not narrowly tied to heritage films. Both their self-worded statements and their self-named favourite period films established that some TOs expressly enjoyed flamboyant period spectacle; or genres, from westerns to sword-and-sandal epics, in which the spectacle derives from expansive scale and landscape rather than exquisite detail; or even films, such as Ken McMullen's *Partition* (UK, 1987) taking a Marxist (and, in this example, non-naturalistic countercinema) approach to the representation of history. (McMullen's films were recommended by TO29, woman, 37; a teacher of prisoners who – uniquely among respondents – was a member of the Socialist Workers' Party and engaged directly and thoughtfully in her reply with questions of film as historiography and related questions of narrative form.)

In this context, 'period detail' was not a ubiquitous focus of interest for TOs, nor were their notions of enjoyable period spectacle always coterminous with or associated with the heritage film. Indeed, a number of TOs echoed anti-heritage-film criticisms on this point, stating their dislike of 'those frock-flicks which look like exhibits from a heritage theme park' (TO10, man, 44; cultural journalist) or where 'strong storyline, plot and sometimes real character conflict are sacrificed in favour of a "look" which is supposed to be able to carry a film' (TO13, woman, 26, British-Iranian; office manager, property).

These comments illustrate a second important distinction between the two cohorts. Most TOs' self-worded Question 21 replies showed an *awareness of the existence* of a critical debate around period films and the representation of the past – and the UK heritage-film debate in particular – which was virtually absent from NTs' replies. This awareness can be viewed as a weakness as well as a strength; most TOs' comments were mediated on some level by an awareness of the debate, and some were heavily constrained by it.

As will become increasingly apparent, there was a tendency among TO respondents to engage in *debate* around cinematic representations of the past, occasionally even dissecting the presumed 'thesis' underpinning my research (one, a solicitor, assumed it was conducted from an anti-heritage-film position, then sought to demolish this) or the questionnaire's terminologies (for example, by proposing their own typologies of period genres). While these critical interventions were often useful, they cumulatively suggested an intense self-consciousness about period films – or, more precisely, the critical debates around them. TOs were, correspondingly, less likely than I had hoped to write directly and personally about their period-film tastes and pleasures. I had not expected to find that any respondents' relationships with period films would be so strongly constrained by knowledge of the debates that few would write in an 'unmediated', un-self-conscious way about why they *enjoyed* the films.[5] In keeping with this, the pattern of TO responses to Question 29's pre-suggested possible period-film pleasures was more fragmentary, and showed less consensus, than among NTs (see Appendix 6.1).

On the other hand, this self-consciousness brought a critical, reflective *self-awareness* to many TO responses that – as we shall see – was considerably less available to NTs. For example:

[My attitude] depends on when the film is set. e.g. Films like *Dangerous Liaisons*, *Orlando*, *Restoration* have a bosom-quivering magnificence about them with their sumptuous sets and costumes and one doesn't *know* if the designers have got everything right but one just marvels

at all that fol-de-rol and extravagance. Later stuff [in terms of historical setting] like *Brideshead, Remains of the Day* or *Jewel in the Crown* I
watch like an old hawk to see if they've got it right and it *matters* to me.
(TO7, woman, 44; arts centre receptionist)

[I enjoy the] strong storylines and characterisation; beautiful costumes,
interiors, furniture and architecture. The possibility of getting a sense of
social history without having to actually *read* social history (I'm intellectually lazy!); escapism; better acting (coherent, grammatical dialogue can
help here); nostalgia for a more 'civilised' age which couldn't have ever
really existed. (TO3, gay man, 38, Irish; civil servant)

In contrast with such irreverence, NT respondents collectively rated the
'accurate reproduction' of period detail even more highly than general 'visual
enjoyment' (Appendix 6.1). The pleasure prioritised most highly by NTs
alongside 'accurate reproduction' was 'quality of the performances or acting' –
both were judged important by almost the entire cohort, and 'very important'
by 81% – followed closely by 'looking at' *specific* elements of the period mise-
en-scène (which, as already noted, were of substantially less interest to most
TOs than general 'visual enjoyment' or the various pleasures of engagement).
Beyond this, the perceived 'quality' of the films, and their 'literacy and wit',
were judged important by 92% to 95% of NTs.

It was only in the next six pleasures (rated important by between 82%
and 89% of NTs) that the pleasures rated most highly by TO respondents
– general 'visual enjoyment' and some of the pleasures of story engagement –
began to make an appearance in NTs' priorities, intermingled with the literary
and historically educative aspects of period films. Even here, however, there
were indications that the films' signifiers of 'quality' and 'authenticity' – and,
in a point I return to below, educationality – were more important to many
NT respondents than more direct pleasures. Here, one of the most distinctive
traits of the NT cohort emerges: many NTs appeared to regard the 'accurate
reproduction' of period details as more important than the *aesthetic* pleasure
these details afforded – and as significantly more important than general 'visual
enjoyment'. Thus where 81% of NTs rated 'accurate reproduction' as 'very
important', this fell to only 65% for 'visual enjoyment' and 'looking at' historic
buildings, and to between 58% and 63% for 'looking at' landscapes/locations,
period furnishings/interiors, or costumes. Countering this, however, some
NTs' *self-worded* replies expressed a primary, even specialist, interest in period
costume and hairstyles and their authenticity.

In line with these priorities, only 39% of NTs (compared to 63% of TOs)
agreed with the statement that 'filmmakers should not be obsessive about
getting every single period detail correct', and only a quarter of NTs (but 60%

of TOs) agreed that 'I enjoy period films for their atmosphere, regardless of whether the historical details are accurate' (Question 30).

In addition, NTs were more inclined than TOs to place high importance on the historically educative function of period films *over* their function as entertainment. Thus around 80% of NTs (and two-thirds of TOs) placed importance on learning about 'life in the past' or 'important events in history' from period films, and – in a more decisive contrast – around 50% of NTs rated these 'very important', compared to around 25% of TOs (Question 29 replies). Although (as I will return to later), respondents' self-worded replies showed that many TOs did, in fact, engage with period films as a form of historiography and social history, they responded to them equally as narratives or entertainment – whereas, by contrast, some NTs conceived of 'history' and entertainment' as mutually exclusive.

A more disconcerting finding was that NTs collectively assigned *less* importance to the historically informative or educative functions of period films (whether in relation to 'big history' or social history) than they did to fidelity of period detail. Indeed, NTs' self-worded and multiple-choice responses alike suggested that most of them were less interested in *social* history than TOs. In stark illustration, only 48% to 56% of NTs thought it 'very important' to be able to learn about historical events or 'life in the past' from period films, compared to the 81% who ticked the 'very important' box for 'accurate reproduction' of period detail.

The remaining two sections of this chapter explore respondents' self-worded statements to probe further into the preoccupation with period detail among NTs, and the different forms of historical engagement with period films both shown and expected by TOs. The polarisation between the two cohorts' dispositions on these questions was such that the first of the two sections, below, engages mainly with the positions and opinions expressed by NT respondents, the section beginning on page 131 most substantially with those expressed by TOs.

PERIOD DETAIL AND THE
DISCOURSE OF AUTHENTICITY

> I enjoy the general 'ambience' – not just costume but room settings – outdoor scenes, etc. I want the impression of being 'transported' to that period. (NT17, woman, 66; retired primary teacher, N England)

> Recreation of a time in history that seems to be well researched and accurate: buildings; clothing; transport; work; living conditions for rich and poor. Brings history alive. (NT6, woman, 51; systems analyst, London)

Accurate details make for enjoyment, the scenery, clothes, furnishings, and also true langue [sic], not pseudo dialects. (NT11, woman, 67; part-time tourist information centre manager, W/SW England)

Enjoyment of history, particularly 18thC – so like seeing the period detail . . . Having seen static historic houses, costumes, artefacts, paintings, I enjoy seeing them 'in use'. (NT2, woman, 48; part-time lecturer, computer-based learning, S/SE England)

I particularly like the *detail* of costumes, hair, interiors, and that is why I like to watch repeats . . . I do like to try to identify the various locations. (NT46, woman, 70; retired teacher, Midlands)

The houses and the horses. The story illustrates a time when society was polite, did not use bad language and the men and women wore hats and acted in an elegant manner. (NT52, man, 78; retired surgeon and chief medical officer in industry, N England)

Two-thirds of NT respondents mentioned pleasure in – or, often, attentive scrutiny of – period detail *unprompted*, in Question 21 replies, as one of the main factors contributing to their enjoyment of period films. However, as shown by the quotations above, the *place* of period detail – in terms of respondents' dispositions towards it and in relation to other pleasures mentioned – varied greatly. Each of the quotations above is indicative of a position expressed by a wider range of NTs. For analytic purposes, these replies can be distinguish in (at least) two ways. First, we can distinguish between those (such as NT2 and NT46) that focused entirely on period detail – often in an obsessive or critical way – and those (NT6) that mentioned it as part of a package of wider pleasures, not always with an emphasis on 'authenticity' of detail. Second, these replies can be subdivided into those (NT8, NT17) that centrally emphasised the respondent's *pleasure* in period styling or ambience; those (like NT11) specifying that '*accurate*' period detail (or, for NT6, historical research) was necessary to enjoyment; and those (like NT2 and NT46) that took a still more specialist, obsessive or critical interest in specific period details. The final quotation (NT52) illustrates a fourth kind of answer in which certain kinds of (very class-specific) period detail were cited by the respondent as a device for expressing distaste for, or alienation from, aspects of present-day society, signalling a use of period films that was candidly escapist and reactionary.[6]

The statements of the NTs who named a 'package' of pleasures, and the remaining third who did not mention period detail at all, focused on pleasures relating to 'quality' and the literary (explored further in Chapter 7). Of these, the most frequently mentioned were 'the recreation on screen of what is usually a well-loved literary classic' (NT29, woman, 61; retired tax accountant, S/SE England), and sets of qualities perceived as flowing naturally from this. These included the classical narrative pleasures of 'a proper story . . . with a beginning, a middle and an end' which has 'stood the test of time' (NT9, woman, 68; retired school secretary, Central England) and 'interesting dialogue' (NT19, man, 74; retired mechanical engineer, Wales).[7] Many NTs also cited the use of 'top quality actors' (NT9, as above), and the 'quality' of the films themselves. Their criteria of 'quality' typically specified that period films were (or should be) 'well-made' (NT83, woman, 67; solicitor, N England) and 'true to the book, if there is one' (NT50, woman, 63; retired teacher, N England).

These comments suggest that, for many NTs, the appeal of period films owed much to classical storytelling and related notions of 'quality' and literary fidelity. In practice, however, few NTs mentioned literary fidelity in isolation from the more widespread obsession with 'accurate' period detail, and their replies characteristically blurred the two authenticities as well as conflating them with further indices of 'quality'.

In some cases – as illustrated in the two replies quoted below – this conflation went considerably further to encompass explicit indicators of *class* distinction – typically articulated by respondents in terms of manners, diction and/ or an absence of 'vulgarity'. Respondent NT9 produces a discourse in which the Reithian 'educative' qualities of period films are held to flow naturally from their 'proper' storytelling, and in which the virtues of classical narrative, 'faithful' reproduction, 'top quality' actors (rather than *acting*), 'the Queen's English' and a return to an idealised pre-feminist patriarchal chivalry are presented as a seamless package. In a similar operation, NT55 yokes the pleasures of period detail expressly to class-specific notions of quality of diction and dialogue, and conflates 'education' with social class:

> Period/costume films invariably have a proper story (*whether fact or fiction*) with a beginning, a middle and an end – *therefore* they can be both entertaining and historically educative. In recent years they have been enhanced by the use of authentic locations and proper research into costumes and props – usually faithfully copied. I enjoy most of all the use, more often than not, of top quality actors who beautifully speak the Queen's English, and the reminder that ladies were once treated as such! (NT9, woman, 68, as above; my emphases)

> The clothes are usually to be admired.
> Hairstyles are a pleasure to look at.
> Speech is fully audible, grammatical and devoid of swear words.
> Good manners are in evidence.

Dialogue indicates education.

Generally, an absence of vulgarity.

(NT55, woman, 77; retired medical secretary, Central England)

While the vision of period films expressed here would not have been accepted by all NT respondents, it was echoed widely enough to place it within the mainstream of NT opinion. These replies are thus very instructive about the bundle of class and cultural values from which NTs' zeal for 'authenticity' and 'quality' sprung, while clarifying some of the underlying thinking (and contradictions).

Among those NTs preoccupied with the specifics of 'authentic' period detail, costume, hairstyles, domestic architecture, props and room settings were all popular choices. However, a significant number also mentioned kinetic and aural details: dancing, the scripting of dialogue or language perceived to be appropriate to the period depicted, and the 'correct' deportment and diction of actors. Their replies demonstrate that this audience segment's fascination with – and critical scrutiny of – period detailing extended beyond inanimate objects, and it seems significant here that respondents wrote of the pleasures of seeing period artefacts 'in use', or of period films bringing history (or sometimes well-loved stories) 'to life'. This notion that films are able to animate that which is inanimate – and perhaps less easy to comprehend – in museums and historic houses or on the printed page recurred in the replies of TOs as well as NTs. Indeed, this was one of the few areas where the stated views of the two sub-samples, and the youngest and oldest survey participants, converged. As we shall see, however, the two cohorts' notions of what 'bringing history to life' *meant*, and their views on how this should be done, diverged considerably.

As the section starting on page 131 discusses further, for most TO respondents, 'history' primarily meant *social* history, and they were drawn to period films that engaged them with this narratively, intellectually, emotionally and personally. A contrasting strand of TOs (two of them quoting L. P. Hartley's famous observation that 'The past is a foreign country')[8] were drawn to films that invoked the *otherness* or *strangeness* of the past. In polar contrast to such positions, a minority of NTs (around 10%) gave the minutiae of period detail such an extreme centrality in their replies as to suggest, perplexingly, that these formed the main, if not sole, *raison d'être* for their period-film viewing. In some cases, this focus was justified in terms of a specialised interest in a particular historical period or aspect of production design, but in others, the motivation remained more enigmatic:

I enjoy period/costume films because I am interested in the clothing and accessories. I particularly like Georgian and Regency room settings, houses, domestic architecture and hairstyles. (NT14, woman, 70; retired laboratory technologist, S/SE England)

Trying to identify locations. Costume detail. Set detail, i.e. furniture, table settings, ornaments, flowers, etc. (NT3, woman 65; retired antique-shop owner, Midlands: full reply)

[I like to see] the costumes – the utensils that were used – the settings especially – the dancing, e.g. quadrilles, etc. (NT62, woman, 76; retired clothing retail buyer, East Anglia: full reply)

I most enjoy an insight into the costumes of the past, wondering how were the garments made, were they practical, comfortable to wear, were [they] worn till they fell to pieces, or were they washed . . . (NT34, woman, 59; retired teacher, Midlands)

Such statements suggest that a certain contingent in the NT cohort did not respond to period films *as films*, narratives or dramas, but more as a pretext for the scrutiny of detail – whether as a form of relaxation or a critical exercise. They also imply a form of spectatorship which from one perspective is very attentive and focused, yet from another appears uncommitted and even naïve.[9] Such responses perhaps becomes less surprising if we recall that the viewing habitus of many NTs was more televisual than cinematic – and that many, accordingly, did not draw a firm distinction between feature films and TV dramas. While I have difficulty imagining anyone travelling to a cinema and paying for a ticket to contemplate 'utensils' or 'ornaments', a (possibly distracted) spectatorship, marked by moments of intense attention to such details, becomes more plausible in the context of domestic viewing.

More typically, NTs expressed their appreciation, or critical scrutiny, of period detail from within a discourse about 'culture' (in the pre-Raymond Williams sense) that sought to display respondents' critical discernment while also serving to express sociopolitical and class positions. NTs' comments about period dialogue, speech, and the diction of actors offer one illustration of this. Some NTs simply wrote that they enjoyed the language used, 'particularly in literary adaptations' (NT4, woman, 69; retired PA, further education college, East Anglia) – a pleasure also cited by some TOs. Other NTs cited the absence of swearing or 'violence of the tongue' (NT10, man, 71; retired removal-company manager, Central England), as a positive pleasure in the period films they watched. Others expressly associated culturally or historically inauthentic language and speech with Hollywood period productions – *Robin Hood: Prince of Thieves* (Kevin Reynolds, USA, 1991) was one prime offender – a linkage also made by some TOs. (The corresponding conflation of 'Britishness' with 'quality' in many replies is explored in Chapter 7.)

As we have seen, however, the notions of 'authentic' speech and diction articulated by some NTs were highly class-specific, suggesting that the past they wished to seeing depicted on film was one peopled solely by the 'elegant', polite, literate classes. Respondents NT9 and NT55 (already quoted) were not alone in requiring both script and actors to deliver 'the Queen's English' or 'fully audible, grammatical' speech rather than 'modern idioms' (NT73, woman, 60; retired company director, West/South-West, and others), collo-quialisms, 'pseudo dialects' (NT7, woman, 72; retired GP's practice manager, Central England) or 'mummerset speech' (NT46, woman, 70; retired teacher, Midlands). NT73 particularly bemoaned 'the way that modern actresses speak so badly in "upper-class" roles, failing to enunciate their terminal consonants'; Tara Fitzgerald and Helena Bonham Carter were the named offenders.

Such comments had a further subtext beyond the class snobbery – and anxieties – of respondents who were in many cases less secure members of the middle or upper-middle classes, and from less 'cultured' class fractions, than their remarks might seek to suggest (see Chapter 3). From NT52's perception that period films depict 'a time when society was polite', to NT9's enjoyment of them as a 'reminder that ladies were once treated as such!', it is clear that a significant minority of NTs were responding from a position of alienation from, and disapproval of, aspects of contemporary society and culture. Period films – obviously of certain kinds but not others – provided this sub-group with a cultural space where they could both openly vent this distaste and indulge in a candidly reactionary escape from the present. NTs' perceptions of the 'elegance' of the past and the 'sloppiness' of the present thus need to be understood as expressions of generational alienation as much as class distinc-tion. 'Former generations would never have spoken so sloppily and ungram-matically,' NT73 complained.

In a further highly significant finding, it was clear from some NTs' com-ments that – far from spoiling their viewing experience – spotting perceived inauthenticities and anachronisms (of period detail more than historical fact) was a source of active enjoyment. Indeed, the criteria of authenticity applied to period films by some respondents were unworkably stringent; and for some NTs, and even one or two TOs, this exercising of cultural or historical knowl-edge was an important – if at times sadistic and fault-finding – pleasure. In support of this, consider the following comments:

> I've chatted to friends about this questionnaire. All but one enjoy period/costume films – two (ex-textile tutors) enjoy as much for the sake of finding mistakes! (NT17, woman, 66; retired primary teacher, N England)

I like the elegance, lack of hurry in everyday life, and comparing film with fact. *I especially like finding a discrepancy* in the history displayed, but I hate any slip in the language which makes it unbelievable. (NT65, woman 68; retired teacher, W/SW England: my emphasis)

It might be argued with some validity that such preoccupations are predictable from a group drawn from committed National Trust members. As one NT respondent herself observed: 'I am a historian, and so of course you will expect me to be prejudiced in favour of historical accuracy over effect' (NT47, woman, 50; historic buildings researcher and participant in Tudor living history enactments). But I would argue, too, that while NT membership may indicate some kind of *a priori* interest in historic buildings, interiors and styling (but, on the evidence of this survey, not *necessarily* in history *per se*), it does not automatically pre-indicate a *particular disposition* towards these. Nor does it explain the relative uninterest in the wider, and more expressly cinematic, aspects of period films that was characteristic among many NT respondents.

Rather, the importance of 'authentic' period detail to so many NTs – and, in contrast with most TOs, their frequent equation of this with 'history' itself – needs to be understood with reference to more complex shaping factors. Central to these were the generational differences between the two cohorts; related differences in educational and cultural capital and class attitudes; and the differing conceptions of cultural value that sprang from these. Although more TO respondents than NTs were degree-educated (see Chapter 3), it may be more pertinent that most NTs had grown up in the era of traditionalist education, when 'the three Rs' and the certainties of the canon still held sway. Most TOs, by contrast, had been degree-educated in the era of postmodernism, cultural studies and the 'trashing' of the high/low culture divide: an era also characterised by a growing awareness of history-writing as a process of interpretation and narrativisation rather than the simple recording of 'fact'. These differences (in educational *culture* as much as educational capital) provide much of the context within which NTs took it as read that period films derive their prestige intertextually from 'higher' cultural forms (centrally, classic literature) – and focused far more on these relationships than on the films' qualities as cinema – while most TOs understood such a position to be deeply problematic. Conversely, the positions expressed by TOs were coloured by an awareness of debates within the modern humanities that were unavailable, and would have seemed alien, to many NTs.

In summary, then, period films and literary adaptations served (in part) as focuses for the exercise of cultural competences and cultural or educational capital for NT and TO respondents alike; but the particular forms of competence and capital being exercised, and the cultural hierarchies thus asserted, differed considerably. While for NTs, cultural competences were characteristically displayed via the close observation of detail and the policing of period or literary fidelity, TOs were more likely to display their educational capital by commenting on *approaches* to the interpretation of history, *strategies* of literary adaptation – or on the heritage debate itself.

PLEASURES OF ENGAGEMENT AND DISENGAGEMENT

As we have already seen, the pleasures of engagement offered by period films were of great importance to most TO respondents but seemed to be less so to many NTs. Beyond the obvious pleasures of engagement with narrative and characters, period films may prompt further, more specialised, forms of engagement between viewer and film: with the social/historical milieu or events being imagined or depicted; with the ideas the film tacitly or overtly proposes about these; and meta-engagement with issues around how the filmmaker chooses to interpret, present or visually reconstruct the events, milieu or period. Cutting across these *objects* of engagement, the viewer's *mode* of engagement may take varied and subtle forms: for example, imaginative engagement; empathetic engagement with characters or situations, or a more Brechtian observant detachment; forms of intellectual engagement; emotional or erotic response; and so on. My exploration of these questions oscillates between considering the relevant multiple-choice findings (Questions 29 to 30) and the – often more interesting – evidence presented in respondents' self-worded replies (Question 21).

Three core points emerged from the replies of TO respondents. First, their Question 29 and 30 responses showed that most TOs routinely expected to be engaged by period films – narratively, intellectually and on other levels – and that, in contrast with many NTs, they prioritised this more highly than period spectacle (Appendix 6.1). Although 'visual enjoyment' was the pre-suggested pleasure judged important by the greatest number of TOs (93%), 'compelling, involving plots and stories' were most widely rated 'very important' (by 63% of TOs, compared to 48% of NTs). Almost as important for TOs were the pleasurable 'literacy and wit' and 'complexity and intelligence' of period films, and their capacity to offer 'human drama' (all judged important by around 80% of the TO cohort, and 'very important' by 50% to 60%).

It must be stressed that NT respondents were not indifferent to the pleasures of engagement: for example, 89% agreed that 'compelling, involving plots' were important. Rather, the salient distinction between the two cohorts was that NTs were less likely than TOs to rate these pleasures '*very* important', and rated factors such as authentic period detail and quality of acting still more highly, a difference in priorities affirmed by NTs' self-worded statements.

Second, TO and NT respondents prioritised the various pleasures of engagement differently. Both cohorts valued the 'literacy and wit' of period films highly (important for 92% of NTs and 80% of TOs), followed closely by 'human drama' (important for 82% of NTs and 77% of TOs). However, the NT cohort responded less positively than TOs to the proposition that period films might be enjoyably challenging intellectually. The perceived 'lack of explicit sex, violence or bad language' in period films was deemed important by more NTs than their 'complexity and intelligence'. And fewer than one-third of NTs (compared to 57% of TOs) rated 'challenging films I have to get involved in to enjoy' as a pleasure, making this one of the three Question 29 pleasures given lowest importance by NTs (although also one on which around 40% of both cohorts held 'no strong opinion'). In a further difference in priorities, NTs collectively rated 'being able to identify with the characters' as even *less* important than 'complexity and intelligence' – and less important than nostalgia, escapism or any of the pleasures of period detail. Despite the importance they attached to 'human drama', only 44% of NTs gave *any* importance to character identification compared to two-thirds of TOs.

It should be added, however, that TOs as well as NTs expressed some ambivalence regarding the importance of character identification in period films. Fewer than 20% of either cohort rated it 'very important'; in addition, 60% of TOs (and 68% of NTs) agreed (although not strongly) that 'I enjoy period films without really identifying with the characters'; and only one TO (and 15% of NTs) agreed that 'the characters in the period films I watch have similar values and concerns to me'. Such responses confirm that the TO cohort – and indeed some individual TO respondents – were divided on the question of whether they expected or required films set in the past to engage them in the same ways as films set in the present, or to invite their social or political engagement. The exact force and meaning of the findings cited above depend, of course, on the kinds of period films respondents had in mind when ticking the boxes in reply to these questions. It is no surprise, for example, that many TO respondents – who were strongly aware of the heritage-film debate and its charges about the films' class bias – denied that the characters in period films shared 'similar values and concerns' to themselves. As we shall see, however, the positions expressed by TOs in their own words reveal more complex reasons for their equivocation around these questions.

The third feature distinguishing the two cohorts' positions was that TOs' self-worded replies by and large engaged *simultaneously* with period films as narrative feature films *and* as representations of history or social history – or, in some cases, more specifically as literary adaptations. NTs, by contrast, tended to stress a package of values (see also pages 125–6) – 'quality', 'authenticity' and educationality – but had less to say about narrative or character engagement. Some TOs' statements departed from this pattern to give primacy to the qualities of period films as entertainment, or to valorise them in terms of psychological complexity (typically defined in contrast with big-spectacle Hollywood blockbusters). The most characteristic TO replies nevertheless synthesised prioritisation of narrative or character engagement with a strong interest in history – centrally, social history – and reflexive commentary on the issues around its representation on film (or on issues of adaptation).

The TO cohort's self-worded statements can be loosely divided into four categories indicating the complexities of their positions on these various issues. The first group – those TO replies coming closest to the dominant NT position, while remaining distinct from it – stressed 'sumptuous' aesthetics, strong performances, literate and coherent scripts, and other indicators of 'quality' that these respondents associated with period films.

The second group responded most powerfully to period films which engaged them narratively – and, for some respondents, politically and/or personally – with characters and the historical situations they faced. TOs in this group expressly responded to the period films they valued via engagement or empathy with characters – but, importantly, this was seen as a conduit for gaining historical insights, or an understanding of the experiences of specific social groups, from which respondents could draw parallels with the present or with their own experiences or identities. Typical replies from this group stressed the universality, or continuing contemporary relevance, of the situations presented in period films and faced by their protagonists:

> They bring history *alive* and allow you to see that people are the same now as they have always been . . . I think only the medium of film/TV can achieve this because we live in a visual culture . . . These are universal stories about people, which people are still playing out today. (TO36, woman, 29; project/drugs worker, street agency)

> Like any other films period films stand or fall on the strength of their narrative and the strength of the ideas behind the film. People have always required narratives set in the past to explain and illuminate the present. It is important not to allow the commercially manipulated heritage-industry aspects of some period films to obscure this. (TO33, woman, 33; solicitor)

Some TOs not only argued for the contemporary value of period films in terms of their 'universal stories' or ability to 'explain and illuminate the present'; in sharp contrast with NTs' demands for 'authentic' (bourgeois or upper-class) period diction and deportment, they explicitly wanted the characters to 'have ways of speaking, thinking, moving that make me remember their kinship with people of the present' (TO5, bisexual woman, 32, Irish; policy worker).

Such notions that narratives and characters of the past should engage us via 'contemporary' or 'universal' resonances or relevance – although conceived as politically progressive by the respondents who proposed them – are not unproblematic; many critical theories of historical representation would view the construction of a (false) 'kinship' between past and present as itself ahistorical. (Indeed, one strand in Craig's objections to the heritage film was that the films elicit structures of identification and sympathy that 'elide' the distance between past and present to 'deny our historical knowledge'.)[10] One response that stood apart from those quoted above came from TO29 (woman, 37; the Socialist Workers' Party member and admirer of Ken McMullen already cited) – who described herself, non-coincidentally, as 'an historian' (by academic training, not occupation), and wrote about period films expressly as representations of history, implying an analytic appreciation of *distance* rather than celebrating 'relevance'.

Most TO respondents, however, preferred period films that engaged with social issues or identity politics in ways they could frame as relevant to the present, or personally relevant to themselves. In a marked contrast with most replies received from (female or male) NTs, a significant number of TOs in this group (of both genders) praised the period films they enjoyed from a feminist perspective. For these respondents, the emphasis on character over action in heritage (and related types of period) films, their nuanced character development and emphasis on character subjectivity – not always confined to a single privileged protagonist – was specifically associated with central and complex female characters:

[I enjoy period films for their] strong female characters. Good character development. Involved and often complex storylines. (TO17, woman, 34, black British; CV counsellor, employment)

Good period films are stimulating to the imagination and historically interesting . . . [Also they] are far more likely than contemporary films to focus on the experiences of strong and central women characters. (TO33, woman, 33; solicitor)[11]

The Portrait of a Lady, *The Silences of the Palace*, and *The Piano* moved me because I could identify strongly with the female characters: the battle against restriction and repression takes different forms for me but hasn't gone away. (TO5, bisexual woman, 32, Irish; policy worker)

Such comments support the arguments presented in my earlier work that active, central and complex female characters were one of the core appeals of many so-called heritage films. Moreover, this appeal was cited by male as well as female TOs. Thus TO26 (straight man, 38; technical author) identified the 'role/position' of women as a theme of recent English (and Chinese) period films – and commended this as 'a change from middle-aged male menopausal detectives on TV!' – while TO1 (gay man, 33; corporate account manager, private health insurance) cited the 'superb performances' of mature British actresses – Vanessa Redgrave, Maggie Smith, Emma Thompson – as a key pleasure, for him, of the Merchant Ivory films.

By contrast, few respondents gave replies that directly illuminated questions of gay, lesbian or queer spectatorship of period films, as I had hoped. However, one bisexual female respondent expressed her enjoyment in terms of 'the visual/aesthetic/erotic pleasure of watching actors I find attractive in interesting clothes/settings/landscapes' (TO5, 32, Irish; policy worker, voluntary sector); while a lesbian respondent proposed the following, more reflective, hypothesis with reference to 1980s–1990s British films (from *Maurice* to *The Wings of the Dove*) set in the Edwardian era:

> In contrast [with the appeal to conservative 'Golden Age' nostalgia] a lot of [these] films show that society in a negative way, as rigidly structured, class-bound, etc. And often focus on characters who are constrained by that, and seek self-expression, etc. (A possible site for audience identification.) There is a strong sense of desire as something transgressive and dangerous, punished by society. Perhaps this is something which appeals to a gay audience – modern society allows free expression of heterosexual love, etc, but gay desire is still much more 'forbidden'. [These films offer] an identification with characters who refuse to conform . . . And constraint focuses eroticism on smaller, coded signs – the touch of a hand or a glance can be more erotic than the explicit scenes featured in a lot of modern films. (And, since less is overtly stated, I suppose there's more room for the viewer to impose their own subtext or reading.) (TO41, 33; poetry librarian)

A third, smaller group of TO respondents favoured period films that invoked for them the *otherness* or *strangeness* of the past. *The Draughtsman's Contract* (Peter Greenaway, UK, 1982) and *Barry Lyndon* (Stanley Kubrick, UK/USA, 1975) were emblematic films cited by the TOs who adopted this position, as in this (self-consciously) sophisticated response from the sole professional cultural commentator to participate in the survey:

> While I enjoy many period films simply because they're well made, my favourites all have one thing in common: they have an exquisite feeling of strangeness. This unsettling or unexpected difference is what makes a frock-flick into a mentally stimulating as well as visual experience. So *Barry Lyndon*'s formality of pose and eerie lighting is what made it seem

like a messenger from the distant past, which, like L. P. Hartley, I see as 'a foreign country, they do things differently there' . . . I want films about the past to give me a sense of a different world. (TO10, man, 44; cultural journalist)

Interestingly, one male NT respondent – a fan of Akira Kurosawa's Samurai masterpieces of the 1950s alongside the 1980s–1990s British TV adaptations of *Brideshead Revisited* and Anthony Powell's *A Dance to the Music of Time* (C4, Alvin Rakoff, 1997) expressed a similar position, observing that 'one major pleasure arises when a period is evoked with a real sense of alienation; when a culture, distant in time and/or location, is compellingly conveyed' (NT48, 68; retired chief educational psychologist, West/South-West).

The fourth type of TO replies engaged with period films centrally as literary adaptations, and are therefore discussed in Chapter 7.

In contrast with the varied and complex TO responses categorised and analysed above, the self-worded comments of most NT respondents on the pleasures of narrative and character provided far less meat for discussion. Many NTs said that they enjoyed the story in period films, the 'interesting and plausible' plots (NT19, man, 74; retired mechanical engineer, Wales) and 'beautifully drawn' characters (NT10, man, 71; retired removals manager, Central England). A few mentioned engagement with generic elements specific to particular favourite films or TV dramas: 'The action, romance and costumes . . . the mystery as well as the setting and good-quality acting' (NT24, woman, 45; part-time clerk to school governors, S/SE England).

However, few NT respondents had more to say than this on the subject. One wrote that he liked 'a good story, the best actors/actresses, excellent settings/costumes . . . These factors enable us to suspend disbelief and enter into the characters and identify [with] them . . . A story dealing with human relationships is the sort I like best' (NT22, man, 60; part-time Crown Court judge, West/South-West) – but he was an isolated exception. As already illustrated, the narrative qualities and characterisation of period films were more usually mentioned by NTs as perceived by-products of the all-important adaptation of 'classic' novels 'which have already survived the test of time' (NT60, man, 63; semi-retired teacher of English as a Foreign Language, S/SE England). Similarly, elements such as dialogue and acting were typically cited as indicators of the quality, perceived cultural status and fidelity/authenticity of period films rather than as sites for empathy or engagement.

Indeed, emotional or personal investment in period films was something that few NTs – in another contrast with TOs – chose to discuss. This can be seen even in the linguistic structure of NTs' replies, which were typically phrased as third-person 'objective', impersonal statements rather than first-person statements of personal opinion or taste. The effect was to present the merits of period films as *self-evident* and in need of no explication; as neither a matter of personal taste nor a site of debate: 'For the most part they are well-produced, well-directed and well-acted. As such they are worth watching' (NT51, man, 70; retired physicist, N England: full reply).

If this impersonal language in part reflects the NT cohort's particular uses of period films as objects for the expression of cultural discernment, the apparent disengagement it expresses had a further dimension. A significant number of NTs expressly *did not want* period films to 'involve' them – emotionally or politically – since they watched them in a spirit of disengaged retreat from social issues and problems – whether personal or societal – which were perceived to be the province of the present. A far higher percentage (and number) of NTs (68%) than TOs (23%) rated 'nostalgia' as an important pleasure in their period-film viewing. While 56% of NTs also rated 'escapism' as important, more decisively, around 20% mentioned elements of escapism or nostalgia unprompted in their self-worded replies: 'Escapism into a world which often seems more elegant and civilised' was a typical phrase (NT73, woman, 60; retired company director, W/SW England). For another such respondent, 'period/costume films are the most pleasant form of escapism, almost as a time traveller with the ability to see and hear *but not be personally involved*' (NT10, man, 71; retired removals manager, Central England: my emphasis).

The practice of some other NTs of defining the pleasures of period films in *double-negative* terms, citing the displeasures they lacked – 'the general absence of explicit violence, sex and bad language – all things which unfortunately appear to be "essentials" in modern offerings' (NT29, woman, 61; retired tax accountant, S/SE England) – seems equally revealing of a desire to escape disliked aspects of the contemporary culture extending beyond cinema. It was clear from such comments that period films were perceived – and used – by such respondents as a safe haven from images of violence or sexual activity, bad language and bad manners. Although NTs objected to all these elements, they were most upset by the prospect of encountering representations of violence on screen (a concern shared by some TOs).

In an undoubted challenge to my own hypotheses when embarking on this audience study, the escapist positions expressed by some NTs showed a desire to retreat from aspects of present-day culture and society in which the underlying impulses were conservative and reactionary. Often these views emerged obliquely or as subtexts – for example, through (double-)negative statements about the elements respondents implicitly did *not* wish to encounter and from which period films provided a respite:

Period dramas . . . tend to be less violent, provide a form of escape from everyday problems. (NT49, woman, 46; part-time special needs classroom assistant, N England)

> [Period films are] a pleasant form of 'escapism' [sic] entertainment and not concerned with moral or social present-day issues. (NT19, man 74; retired mechanical engineer, Wales)[12]

> One friend dislikes period films – only enjoys 'modern reality'. She happens to be not as 'merry' as most I know. (NT17, woman, 66; retired primary teacher, N England)

> There is so little of value on TV these days – when you watch a period piece you know that you will be spared crude jokes, unnecessary violence and explicit sex. (NT61, woman, 67, born New Zealand; retired surgery receptionist, S/SE England)

The escapist impulses expressed by some other NTs were, however, more equivocal and by no means unambiguously reactionary. In many cases, respondents' choices of words signalled that their enjoyment of 'wallowing' in a fantasy 'bygone age' co-existed with a sense of perspective about the hardships of real life in past periods, and so cannot validly be read as a consistent indicator of indifference to the latter:

> [Period films] also [appeal to] some nostalgia for ages when there was more time and space to enjoy life, while recognising that the accident of birth played a larger part in that enjoyment than now. (NT15, man, 60; part-time taxi driver, former software analysis, S/SE England)

> When the drama is authentic . . . it is an entertaining way to learn, rather than read dry accounts by sociologists [sic] . . . Almost as important is one's ability to forget the troubles of day-to-day living and wallow in other people's situations in a bygone age and sometimes another country. (NT50, woman, 63; retired teacher, N England)

In concluding Chapter 6, I want to quote an NT respondent who expressed a position that at first sight seems more extreme than any quoted above:

> When I do watch television, films, etc, I like to feel happy at the end and not depressed, as so many modern programmes do. Although I know the portrayal of life on period dramas is unreal, I enjoy escaping from the unsavoury news media and violence of our present-day society. A 'supposed' calmer and more serene way of life where people had better manners towards each other . . . Even the violence (if any) in the story does not have the same impact psychologically as in modern films. (NT30, woman, 59; retired shopkeeper, Midlands)

If this statement seems depressing, it seems to me that this is precisely why it deserves attention. First, this respondent shows an honesty in expressing fears and anxieties about the world we all inhabit which tend to remain unspoken, and must surely lurk beneath other respondents' reactionary-escapist replies. Second, the contradiction between NT30's desire to escape to a 'calmer and more serene' past and her understanding that the past was not really like that is openly visible – while her words make equally clear that this escapist viewing position certainly does not spring from *indifference* to the problems of the present. Last, the melancholy of this reply forces us to contemplate *why* some viewers should want or need to use period films in this escapist way – the human fears and experiences underlying and perhaps explaining this viewing position – in a way that anti-heritage criticism's objectification of the heritage-film audience cannot. But even this respondent was able to step back from her viewing position and review it critically. In a coda to the questionnaire, she added:

> On a slightly more serious note, if a period film shows a more realistic way of life of the poor, it can be a reminder to us all that we would not really swap our comfortable modern lifestyle for those days.

NOTES

1. For an explanation of the approach taken to identifying individual respondents, see pages 41–2.
2. A further question (Question 22) invited respondents to state in their own words 'anything about (some or all) period/costume films', or to name specific examples, that they *disliked*. As 38% did not reply to this question, and the dislikes expressed typically complemented, illuminated or emphasised the likes or wider views expressed in self-worded answers to Question 21 – and the attitudes revealed in multiple-choice answers to Question 30 – any *stated* dislikes are discussed within the wider analysis of respondents' likes and attitudes.
3. Throughout Chapters 6 to 8, the percentages/numbers stated for respondents who agreed with a given statement in Question 30 *include* those respondents who ticked the 'agree strongly' box in the multiple-choice options *as well as* those who ticked the 'agree' box. Similarly, the percentages/numbers stated for respondents who reported that a pleasure listed in Question 29 was important include those who ticked the 'very important' box as well as those who ticked the 'important' box. The same cumulative approach is taken when patterns in 'disagree' or 'not important' responses are expressed statistically.
4. One of these (TO31, woman, 52; university librarian) expressed a position that was barely distinguishable from the position on 'authenticity' that (as we shall see) predominated among NTs: 'I am very interested in period costume since I wear a copy of an eighteenth-century gown when I am stewarding at Osterley Park House [in west London, as a National Trust volunteer] . . . This is why I feel authentic dress is the only way to accurately present characters from the past. So much is governed by what one wears – then and now!'

5. For example: 'If you are unwilling to see period films you are raising an artificial barrier. I like to see films deal with contemporary issues, but equally . . . film can be good or bad whether it is a period film or not' (TO6, man, 45; policy officer). As a comment this is fair enough, but it reveals almost nothing of the respondent's personal film tastes or the specific pleasures he might find in the films (period or otherwise) he enjoys.

6. NT52 added in a note: 'I found the questions interesting and shedding light on many aspects of society which we older generation find hard to accept. I have no computer, still use cash, and have been called a dinosaur!'

7. Many NT respondents attributed the narrative merits and strong dialogue of period films *directly* to the decision to film a classic novel (or, less often, play: Shakespeare was the only playwright named by NTs). Many also treated classic literary adaptations as synonymous with 'period films' in general. Only one NT drew an explicit distinction 'between plays and dramatisations of fiction . . . and fictionalisation of history' (NT47, woman, 50; part-time historic buildings researcher, West/South-West).

8. Hartley, *The Go-Between*, p. 1.

9. NT34's curiosity to learn about the construction and durability of 'the costumes of the past', for example, suggests – if her comments are to be taken literally – a confusion of cinematic reconstruction with the real thing.

10. Craig, 'Rooms without a view', p. 5.

11. For TO33, the space given to strong female characters in period films had a commercial rationale: 'It is a truism that period films are enjoyed by and marketed towards women.' But she then followed this with a sharp critique of the marginalisation of female characters in mainstream films set in the present:

> It is interesting that . . . the most commercially successful period film [of 1997], *The English Patient*, had two central women characters, whereas say a successful contemporary-set film like *Jerry Maguire* was about the experience of male characters. It is another film cliché that a film which deals with the experience of a contemporary group of people will see a typical group of people as containing at least a three to one ratio of men to women. The women will be in the subordinate roles to the men and under 35.

12. NT19 added: 'It might be helpful to have categories of period film [listed in the questionnaire] to choose preferences, e.g. Seafaring, Tudor, Stuart, Georgian, Victorian, etc. Empire, i.e. India, Africa, etc. Ireland (history). Scotland.' This was not the only NT reply which seemed to conceive of 'India, Africa, etc.' as possible subjects for films (or rather, *genres*) only in the context of the British Empire; while 'Ireland' was consigned to (presumably non-recent, colonial?) history.

Audience Pleasures, Attitudes and Perspectives 2: 'Quality', Literary Pleasures, Adaptation and Cultural Value

NOTIONS OF QUALITY

In a continuation of Chapter 6's analysis, Chapter 7 explores respondents' conceptions of 'quality' in relation to the period films they watched, and their positioning in relation to the 'literary' pleasures offered by many period films (including, but not solely with reference to, literary adaptations), and attitudes and expectations in relation to adaptation itself.

Chapter 6 established that a large majority of Heritage Audience Survey respondents across both cohorts associated period films with 'quality', and that particular importance was placed on the – perceived high – 'quality of the performances or acting' (Question 29 replies: Appendix 6.1). Of course, agreement with such pre-suggestions does not clarify *which* aspects of period films signified 'quality' for respondents, *what* they enjoyed or valued in the acting, which performances or performers they associated with 'quality', and so on. We have already seen, however, that NT and TO respondents' explicit or less explicit conceptions of 'quality' *vis-à-vis* period films differed, as did their mobilisation(s) of the term (or not) in their self-worded statements: NTs were far more likely to mention 'quality' – without ironising or distancing it inside quotation marks – than TOs. Such patterned choices of words and stated priorities, considered against patterns of response to the pre-suggested Question 29 pleasures, suggested that virtually all NTs were unreserved participants in the discourse that positions period films as high-status, 'quality' cultural products as distinct from popular entertainment. TO respondents, by contrast, were less responsive to the promotional or critical discourses that sweepingly frame period films as 'quality films'.

TOs on the whole preferred to conceive of – and tended to articulate – their enjoyment of period films in terms of their 'literacy' or 'complexity and intelligence' rather than 'quality'. Those who voluntarily cited 'quality' did so either to praise specifics – particularly acting, but also 'quality' of literary adaptation or production values – or, as illustrated in the two replies quoted below, deployed the term (or related concepts such as 'craft') with a notable analytical distance. TO41's reply does both in a way that nicely illustrates the conflictual relationships many TO respondents had with period films. TO41 was unusual among TOs in that, while sharing the cohort's typical cine-literacy, she rarely watched mainstream entertainment films, and was clearly more responsive to the complex exploration of emotion and character she found in some period films – traits frequently identified in critical discourse as markers of a 'quality film'. Yet, even so, her deployment of the terms 'quality' and 'cultured' sets up a critical self-distance:

> Another attractive feature of the films is their emotional depth; they are often very moving. They focus on character and emotion rather than 'action' and special effects. The fact that many of the films are literary adaptations lends them an air of 'quality' before they even begin. Which appeals to the viewer's self-image. (Actually, I've read very few of the books on which they're based.) They're very 'cultured' films. (TO41, lesbian woman, 33; poetry librarian)

> Period films are 'crafted' (all that stitching) and some people might think this not 'art'. (TO26, man, 38; technical author, strategic management)

Of those TOs who praised the 'quality' of specific technical or artistic aspects of period films, it must be noted that a few cited exactly the same ingredients favoured by most NTs: namely, quality character acting, and narrative strengths that were assumed to flow from 'classic' adaptation. For TO35, 'the primary reason I watch most period films is that I find it interesting to see how they have adapted the book' – which 'in most cases I have both read and enjoyed' – but *the fact* of adaptation itself was also presented as the guarantor of a successful result: 'I know before I go that it will have a strong storyline and well-scripted dialogue' (woman, 28, born New Zealand; research nurse for drug trials). But other TOs knowingly appropriated notions of quality (if not always the word itself) in terms that departed from – and even consciously challenged – the discourse that equates heritage-type period films with a notion of 'quality' defined by naturalistic realism and restraint:[1]

> The films challenge the actors because they have to act in a certain style that can be unusual for them and the audience. The films don't have to be as tied down to realism as contemporary films and so are sometimes more imaginative and richer emotionally. (TO30, man, 31; unemployed ex-bookseller and part-time student)

In the case of Hammer [films], [I marvel] at the superb production values and cinematography, knowing they were made on low budgets. (TO39, man, 36, Dutch; associate director of market-research company)

The self-worded replies of most NT respondents, by contrast, embraced a simpler, more uncritical – and consistent – discourse about what constituted a 'quality' film. This discourse had two distinguishing traits. First, just as NTs tended to perceive the strong narratives and scripts of period films as flowing naturally from the literary 'classics' from which these films were *assumed* to be adapted, so most NTs' replies assumed that 'quality' flowed naturally from 'authenticity': most often, fidelity to the literary source; sometimes, from the 'authentic reproduction' of period setting, dialogue or language; only rarely from accuracy of historical fact. Second, the specific elements NTs believed to contribute to the 'quality' of the period films they enjoyed were typically *asserted,* as if they required no explication, qualification, analysis or debate.

On the first point, a few NTs did mention criteria of quality that had some specificity to cinema: 'The beautiful photography and colour, which contributes greatly to the setting of the piece and the mood of the time . . . The dialogue: the sheer vitality of *all* the script/screenplay' (NT88, woman, 60; occupation described as 'housewife, mother, harassed slave!', London; with input from her daughter, 21). But even here, beliefs about authenticity of period 'setting' and the origins of 'vital' dialogue in classic literature are embedded in the references to cinematic techniques. (NT88 went on to cite 'the story or original play behind' her favoured period films as a further strength.) NT88 was, however, unusual in referring to film techniques at all. In most NT replies, judgements about the 'quality' of period films were made solely with reference to – indeed, were entangled indistinguishably with – the films' intertextual affiliations with 'higher' cultural forms. Thus in the following responses, the function of period films as a *substitute* for reading classic novels or factual history, or going to the theatre, was given as a – or *the* – primary reason why the respondent enjoyed them:

[I enjoy] classical and historical stories brought to life. An excellent way to enjoy Shakespeare, Austen, Dickens, etc. (NT26, woman, 62; retired teacher, London)

The ability to watch good drama at home without having to visit a theatre. (NT40, man, 69; retired teacher, S/SE England)

The acting is superb, and it does give one the opportunity to see the finest actors at work. (One cannot always get to a theatre.) (NT61, woman, 67, born New Zealand; retired surgery receptionist, S/SE England)

> The period/costume films which I enjoy are those adapted from the classics. This means that both the script [sic] and the plot have stood the test of time . . . I am less interested in costume films made from popular, best-selling, but less literary books such as [the] Poldark [novels] or Catherine Cookson's stories. (NT8, woman, 73; retired social worker, S/SE England)

In an additional note that affirmed the status of films as a substitute for theatre and a less legitimate cultural form, NT61 wrote: 'I wish I had the opportunity to see some of the better films which are not shown in our area – when I do go to London it is usually to go to the theatre.' While this statement presents limited viewing of 'the better' period films as a matter of lack of opportunity, it also implies a clear hierarchy of cultural value. Theatre productions are 'real' culture and merit a special trip to London; films, even 'the better' ones, are not and do not.

In an extension of the quality–authenticity discourse, some NT respondents valued period films in terms of their perceived *educational* value:

> Interesting to learn how people lived and thought in the past, the enormous difference between rich and poor, the rigidity of the class system, the position of women in society and the different moral climate which prevailed. (NT4, woman, 69; retired PA to further education college principal, East Anglia)

However, NT4's statement of *personal* pleasure and engagement in learning about social history from period films made her very unusual in the NT cohort. Indeed, this interest aligned her with a position that was far more widespread among TOs. For NT4, the educationality of period films as sources of 'information about the past' (NT82, woman, age undisclosed, born Germany; artist/writer, London) was evidently a source of personal insight and enjoyment. But the self-worded replies of many other NTs, while nominally positioning period films as educational, did so alongside references to patently incompatible escapist pleasures, suggesting that 'educationality' was being invoked merely as a value to be name-checked.

A further cluster of NT respondents posited period films as 'educational' not for themselves, but for imagined others. For respondents such as NT28, below, those in need of this cinematic/televisual education were not period-film viewers such as herself, but a hypothetical less-educated, unread wider public whose own schooling had left them ignorant of, or indifferent to, 'historical facts' and 'the great classical [sic] books'. Note also the way that 'educational value' is bound up in NT28's comments with notions of the 'well-made' film:

I have always been a dedicated student of history and it is enjoyable to see various periods of history portrayed on screen, *particularly* when they are accurate in fact and detail and have been well-researched . . . I consider that there is great educational value in these films when they are well made, because they illustrate the historical facts and the stories in the great classical books to people of all ages who 'hated history at school' or never read 'those boring old books'. If well done, these films are of inestimable value. (NT28, woman, 75; homemaker/part-time genealogist, London)

This position immediately raises a problem the respondent does not address: why would such viewers choose to watch films based on historical events or 'boring old books'? In a further irony (to which I return on pages 157–8 onwards), the attachment of many NT respondents to period literary adaptations proved to be rooted in a paradoxically narrow familiarity with their 'great classical' sources, while the more widely read TOs were less concerned to invoke ritually the values of educationality, literary authenticity or 'the classics' in relation to period films.

The NT cohort's second distinguishing trait – the tendency to *assert* the 'quality' of films in terms which broached no debate – generated repeated assertions to the effect that period films reliably offer 'a good story' (NT22, man, 66; part-time Crown Court judge, W/SW England) or 'strong storylines with good subplots' (NT21, woman, 50; part-time student and homemaker, Wales), and that 'the characters are beautifully drawn' (NT10, man, 71; retired removals manager, Central England). But, more than this, it was taken for granted that there was a universal understanding of, and consensus about, what this meant; the qualities that constitute a strong storyline or characterisation were, for NTs, self-explanatory – at least to like-minded members of their audience peer group. A few NTs did mention examples of specific adaptation decisions made in particular productions, but did not go so far as to evaluate the relationship between these and the 'strong' or 'proper' story.[2] The only *explanation* offered for these perceived narrative strengths was that 'very often novels etc that form the basis of these films are those that have stood the test of time' (NT21, as above).

The NT respondent quoted below departed from this refusal of analysis insofar as he identified quality of story, actors and settings as *preconditions producing* 'suspen[sion of] disbelief' and 'maximum enjoyment'. But even he saw no need to elaborate on what he meant by a 'good' story, 'the best' actors or 'excellent' settings:

A good story, the best actors/actresses, excellent settings/costumes providing an authentic setting. These factors enable us to suspend disbelief and enter into the characters and identify with them, thus obtaining maximum enjoyment. (NT22, as above)

'QUALITY', BRITISHNESS AND THE
HERITAGE DEBATE

In addition to the question of what it was about period films that respondents – particularly NTs – associated with 'quality', I was interested to test whether any respondents adopted positions on this which were more extreme than those quoted above, or closely aligned with aspects of the conservative pro-heritage-film media discourses prominent in the 1980s. For example, did some respondents associate or conflate the 'quality' of period films or period-film acting specifically with their 'Britishness' or 'Englishness', regard these films as self-evidently the peak of British cinematic (or televisual) achievement, echo the discourse of British/English cultural superiority evident in some 1980s–1990s UK media coverage, or express such patriotic sentiments in anti-Hollywood or anti-American terms? Last, did any respondents agree with the proposition (common in the contemporary media coverage of 1980s British heritage-film successes) that their painstaking pursuit of fidelity made these films superior to the period films of earlier decades? Of course, respondents' stances on such matters also shed light on their understandings of the status of post-1980 heritage films among professional critics, and their consciousness of broader discourses and debates around period cinema.

Most respondents in both cohorts were reluctant to express strong agreement with broad generalisations that 'period films and literary adaptations are definitely films for a discerning audience' or 'rare examples of quality among the films/TV programmes which are made these days' or that 'British cinema is the best in the world' (all Question 30: Appendix 2.1). There was, however, one notable exception to this pattern: almost 60% of NTs agreed – and almost a quarter of the cohort agreed strongly – that period films/dramas were 'rare examples of quality . . .'. In addition, 40% of NTs agreed (although few strongly) that they were films for a 'discerning audience'; and more than a quarter agreed that 'British cinema is the best in the world'. In all, around a third of NTs seemed willing to agree with a cluster of generalisations about the high status of period films and literary adaptations, the 'discerning' taste of their audiences and the unparalleled quality of British cinema.

In addition to the 'British cinema' attitude statement (Question 30), the questionnaire had pre-suggested two pleasures (Question 29) – 'seeing leading British actors/actresses at their best' and 'pride in seeing British cinema at its best' – which conflated notions 'quality' with 'Britishness'. We already know that British films – set in both past and present – formed a significant component of both TO and NT respondents' viewing. However, while for TOs, British films were merely one element in a very varied film diet, NTs' tastes were *dominated* by a very narrow range of British film types: certain popular mainstream films set in the present, plus heritage films set in the past. Indeed, the willingness of almost one-third of NTs to agree that 'British cinema is the best in the world' only makes sense in the context of this narrowly (and, among contemporary audiences, untypically) Anglocentric film diet.

TOs and NTs alike were less likely to assign importance to 'pride in seeing *British* cinema at its best' or 'seeing leading *British* actors/actresses at their best' than to the 'high-quality, well-made' traits and quality of acting in period films in general. But despite this, a large majority of NTs – and more TOs than might be expected – responded to the 'British' statements in ways that could be read as indicating a specifically Anglophilic or patriotic enthusiasm for British period films. Thus almost 80% of NTs and 40% of TOs gave some importance to 'seeing leading British actors/actresses at their best'; and two-thirds of NTs and almost a quarter of TOs assigned some importance to 'pride in seeing British cinema at its best'. However, barely any TOs rated these factors 'very important', compared to 40% to 50% of NTs. Both of these 'British' pleasures were thus rated 'very important' by notably more NTs than the 'complexity and intelligence' of period films or 'being able to identify with the characters'.

Only a few NT respondents explicitly asserted the quality or superiority of *British* period films and TV dramas in their self-worded replies. But this may be because – given NTs' narrowly British film diet, their often largely televisual habitus, and their preference for adaptations from English literary classics – the Britishness of these productions was taken as read. (Certainly, all the favoured source authors named by NTs were English, while even Anglophile Americans such as Henry James went unmentioned.) And, as can be seen in the replies quoted below (particularly the first), NTs often repeated a very well-worn discourse about the quality of British film and television which – in the case of the latter – had crystallised in the 1950s–1970s Reithian 'golden age' of British broadcasting rather than the BBC's populist present:

> They are usually well produced and well acted. I have watched them in USA, Canada and Australia where they are appreciated. BBC seems to do them better in general but ITV has excelled itself occasionally. Period dramas are about the only thing I bother to tape. (NT44, woman, 67; senior social worker, semi-retired, S/SE England)

> The British film industry leads the world in the making of period films and dramas – they are enjoyed worldwide. (NT61, woman, 67; already quoted)

> The fact that they are (almost) all British and they are absolutely brilliant! The British film industry is the best for production of quality films, they are not tackified or sentimentalised, and corny or sugary like all American products. (NT88, woman, 60; already quoted)

More often, however, the association between 'Britishness' and 'quality' emerged more obliquely, through respondents' negative comments or jokes about anachronisms or unsubtleties – both routinely attributed to Hollywood productions, Hollywood commercial imperatives and Hollywood ignorance:

> NB: True story: when *Sense and Sensibility* was doing so well in America an American PR chap made serious enquiries about the possibility of Jane Austen doing a book-signing tour. (TO40, man, 39, Welsh; unemployed, S/SE England)

> Actors and actresses' accents are sometimes wrong for the period or setting, often because 'American' stars are used to sell the film in the USA market (*Much Ado About Nothing* [Kenneth Branagh, UK/USA, 1993], *Robin Hood* with Kevin Costner [Kevin Reynolds, US, 1991]). (NT26, woman, 62; retired teacher, London)

> I particularly dislike (usually American) films which portray women with inappropriate 20thC hair coiffures. I also dislike films where the 'swash buckling' is overdone as for example in many films starring Errol Flynn. I dislike films made to glorify a star rather than telling the story. (NT28, woman, 75; homemaker/part-time genealogist, London)

As these comments illustrate, NTs in particular associated American cinema with an inauthenticity not confined to period detail. NT28's reply implies further criteria of quality which British period films tacitly possess but Hollywood productions do not: restraint in preference to 'swash buckling', storytelling in preference to the 'glorification' of stars. That such comments were made by TO respondents as well as NTs indicates that critical anti-Hollywood sentiment was deemed acceptable among TOs where expressions of pro-British patriotism were not. In fact, the most detailed critique of contemporary Hollywood – and defence of the qualities of certain British heritage films as its antithesis – came from an American TO respondent living in London, although one wonders if she would have written so positively about the 'range and intelligence' of British film and TV output if responding a decade later rather than in the late 1990s:

> I don't really like or dislike films as genres . . . There are good films and bad films . . . [But] it stuns me sometimes at [sic] the sheer virulence that some British critics vent upon period films, spec. Merchant/Ivory . . . They'll do this whilst slavishly sucking up to any American rubbish which crosses their path.

If one must generalise, which I hate doing, period films are generally well written, acted and directed. They can be superficial chocolate boxes lacking any depth of character and concerned with a tiny segment of the upper/middle classes. But look at *Another Country*. Two public school-boys; what could be more elitist? But it was a film of enormous depth, complexity and compassion, which really made you think. My own home-land is so intellectually and morally bankrupt they are remaking remakes and making films 'inspired' by commercials . . . There is more range and intelligence in British film and television than there is in 60 American TV channels and the 400 or so movies they inflict on the public as we speak. (TO25, woman, 47, US–Croatian; dietetic technician in clinical nutrition)

This range of responses shows that, although TOs and NTs alike were appreciative of the qualities of British acting and British period films, few were willing to agree with jingoistic generalisations. Moreover, anti-Hollywood feeling was usually a more significant force in such replies than pro-English or pro-British patriotism *per se*. It is vital to remember, however, that when TO and NT respondents expressed anti-Hollywood views, they did so from within very different film habituses. TOs generally criticised Hollywood from a position of wide knowledge of cinema – extending, in most cases, to an enthusiasm for post-classical and independent US cinema. By contrast, while many NT respondents had once been viewers of Hollywood films, their drift away from a cinemagoing habitus seemed to have coincided with a narrowing and pronounced Anglicisation of film tastes.

As we saw in Chapter 5, a significant number of NTs mentioned Hollywood (or Hollywood-style) period films among their self-named favourites – sometimes of precisely the kind their Question 21 comments appeared to denounce – but these were almost invariably films of distant decades. NTs' criticisms of the inauthenticities of Hollywood period films were similarly as likely to refer to older films or cycles as recent ones: Errol Flynn alongside Kevin Costner. Although NTs were thus more susceptible than TOs to a disposition of (cinematically poorly informed) narrow patriotism that believed that British films, and period films/dramas especially, were 'the best in the world', this disposition was both far from ubiquitous and (as already evidenced) contradicted by the film tastes some NTs recalled from their younger decades. This disposition – where it existed – should therefore be understood as an effect of narrowing film-viewing, coupled with the NT cohort's characteristic attitude to film as at once a substitute for 'higher' art forms and indistinct from television.

To return to my final question posed at the start of this section, NTs' self-worded replies confirmed that at least some of them did indeed believe that recent, particularly post-1980, British period films and TV dramas were superior to those of earlier decades, centrally due to their scrupulous 'authenticity':

> I think costume drama has improved greatly in terms of attention
> to detail, e.g. coaches, costume, lighting, food, furnishings. (NT24,
> woman, 45; part-time clerk to school governing bodies, S/SE England)

> I especially like the films that have been made from the plays of
> Shakespeare. Some made just post-[World War II] seem 'dated', but
> recent ones have been excellent. (NT35, woman, 79; retired teacher, S/
> SE England)

> I do not like the old Hollywood-type period films, i.e. *Dick Turpin*,
> *Scarlet Pimpernel*, Margaret Lockwood, etc. 'Alright' in their day. But
> cannot compare with *our* later adaptations of Jane Austen, etc. (NT30,
> woman, 59; retired shopkeeper, Midlands: respondent's emphasis)

Such replies show clear affinities with 1980s–1990s conservative pro-heritage-film media discourse, which had praised the films both as more authentic and faithful than their precursors (to the 'look' of the past and the words of the adapted author) and in terms of a set of virtues presented as the antithesis of contemporary Hollywood cinema's vices.[3] Significantly, respondents such as NT30 associated the 'inauthentic' older costume and historical films they disliked with 'Hollywood', even when the films they cited were in fact British; *The Scarlet Pimpernel* (Harold Young, 1934) was produced by Korda's London Films, and Margaret Lockwood's star vehicles such as *The Wicked Lady* (Leslie Arliss, 1945) by Gainsborough Studios.[4] While we cannot be sure that such views were influenced by – rather than merely converging with – positions expressed in the conservative British press, almost 50% of NTs (and respondent TO40, source of the Jane Austen book-signing anecdote) were readers of the *Daily Mail*, *Daily Telegraph* and/or their Sunday equivalents, the newspapers that had been most active in promoting this discourse. But not all the respondents quoted above were readers of these papers; and perceptions that recent period films and dramas have 'improved greatly in terms of attention to detail' (NT24) could be read more neutrally, as an acknowledgement of heightened standards of research and production design, assisted by advances in both film technology and scholarship.

ACTORS VERSUS ACTING

Enjoyment of the performances and the appeal of specific performers were undoubtedly among the attractions that had drawn me to (certain) period television dramas and heritage films in my teens to early 20s, and I assumed that this would be true for many members of the wider audience. The *actor*-centred pleasures distinctive to post-1980 British heritage films fall into two categories.

First, films such as *A Room with a View* offered the opportunity to see memorable, entertaining performances by highly regarded established British actors – often classically trained and/or renowned for their work on stage. We have already seen that such performances were one of the primary sources of enjoyment for respondents across both cohorts; and the use of period films by some NT respondents expressly as a substitute for theatregoing signals the important function of the films as a showcase for 'the best' actors. Second, the strategy of casting young, attractive unknowns in central roles alongside the character cameos from distinguished older actors – the 'discovery' of new young talent, which had been a significant ingredient of Merchant Ivory's success from *The Europeans* onwards – extended the films' appeal to younger audiences, added tasteful sexuality to their mix of attractions, and offered a diversified range of publicity and marketing possibilities, from interviews (often in glossy magazines and colour supplements) to fashion shoots featuring both male and female stars.[5]

In their casting rationale and acting styles, then, post-1979 British period films have pursued a dual strategy with a commercial logic; the ensemble casting multiplies the films' points of appeal and promotional possibilities, while (in lower-budget examples such as *A Room with a View*) making it possible to ration the more eminent and expensive actors to smaller roles. However, the kinds of *pleasures* viewers might derive from period-film acting or actors cut across the analytic headings used in Chapters 6 and 7 in ways also facilitated by the dual casting strategy. In some cases (or rather, for some viewers), acting and performance are pleasures of engagement, which in turn shape our engagement with characters and narratives and have implications for the *mode* in which we engage (intellectual, emotional, erotic, and so on). But in other cases, the viewer's relationship with period-film acting (as with other facets of the films) may owe more to 'appreciation' than engagement.

In the latter case, the film and its performances or performers become centrally a focus – even pretext – for the viewer's exercise of cultural judgement, discrimination and taste: in effect, a vehicle for the display of 'cultural competences' (as defined and discussed by Bourdieu), but also for the social/ peer-group and self-validating pleasures associated with this.[6] In this case, acting (or the mere presence of 'classical' actors) functions pre-eminently as a signifier of 'quality', and the pleasures are those that arise from the act of exercising – or displaying – judgement itself.

The NT cohort were primarily *appreciators* of period-film acting, rather than being deeply engaged or moved by performers and performances or, through them, by characters and narrative situations. Fewer than one-third of NTs mentioned actors or acting in their self-worded replies, and the comments of those who did were typically generic – citing 'excellent acting' (NT42, woman, 67; retired clerical officer, credit-card company, S/SE England) or the 'opportunity to see the finest actors at work' (NT61, woman, 67; retired surgery receptionist, S/SE England), and emphasising quality and prestige rather than emotion, identification or erotics. Only rarely did NTs cite specific actors or performances:

> [In *Mrs Brown*] I enjoyed the exploration of the character of John Brown and was pleasantly surprised by the standard of acting of Billy Connolly in the role. Judi Dench was as brilliant as ever. (NT2, woman, 48; part-time lecturer, computer-based learning, S/SE England)

Likewise, fewer than one-third of TOs mentioned acting or actors; but (in contrast with NTs) far more mentioned matters such as character engagement, emotional involvement and general strength of characterisation – strengths not unrelated to performance. TOs' comments about acting were also more varied in their focus and tone than the univocal discourse (re)produced by NTs. While some TOs wrote of the 'quality' of period-film acting, they did so in more enthusiastic language, and with more reference to specifics such as char-acter acting or the performances of named actors – in Ivory's films especially:

> I mostly enjoy the Merchant–Ivory films due to the extensive cast. (TO2, gay man, 32; 'director of secretarial services')

> I greatly enjoy the films of the Merchant/Ivory/Jhabvala 'stable' . . . [not least the] superb performances, i.e. Vanessa Redgrave, Maggie Smith and Emma Thompson. (TO1, gay man, 33; corporate account manager in private health insurance)

> Period films tend to feature top-notch character actors whose perform-ances sometimes outclass the leads. (TO39, straight man, 36; market-research associate director)

This last perception of period films as an *especially* appropriate showcase for character acting was shared by at least one NT respondent, although, in line with the characteristic NT preoccupation with 'quality', she identified period films with a 'standard' (rather than style) of acting:

> There is a standard of acting that seems to go with period films. The players *wrap* themselves round a part in a style that would be inappropri-ate in modern dramas, e.g. adaptations of Dickens. (NT55, woman, 77; retired medical secretary, Central England)

A separate section of the questionnaire asked respondents whether they had favourite actors, including favourites they particularly associated with, or watched in, period films (Question 23). The replies confirmed that TOs' interest in films – period and otherwise – was more actor-centred than that of NTs. Some 80% of TOs stated that they had favourite actors; more than 70% named at least one; 43% said that that the casting of favourite actors was sometimes the factor prompting them to see period films; and 43% followed these actors' careers beyond period films. In keeping with these responses, TOs' actor preferences were eclectic (ranging from Robert De Niro to Bob Peck); mostly not narrowly tied to period films; and showed enthusiasm for strong female performers, past and present (Bette Davis, Katharine Hepburn and Susan Sarandon were cited alongside Helena Bonham Carter).

By contrast, only 55% of NTs said they had favourite actors or named any, but there was a strong consensus about the overwhelming favourites: (Dame) Judi Dench (14 votes) and (Sir) Anthony Hopkins (10 votes), followed by further classically trained names strongly associated (at least by this audience) with the heritage film and/or the Shakespearean (Kenneth Branagh, Derek Jacobi, Nigel Hawthorne, Emma Thompson). The only real convergence in tastes between the two cohorts lay in their shared admiration for Hopkins[7] and, less strongly, around younger British heritage stars such as Thompson.

Fan attachments to actors – or emotional or erotic responses – were, however, acknowledged by few respondents. Fewer than 20% of TOs, and only 10% of NTs, made statements suggesting an attachment that could be classed as fandom. This was a surprising finding given that fan relationships, and attraction to actors, had emerged as strong motivations for some respondents' period-film viewing in my initial pilot study, and that the potential erotic attractions of some heritage films are very evident in online fan/audience discussions.[8] It must be allowed, though, that this is a subject on which some respondents might feel self-conscious, and mute their comments accordingly. In support of this, 42% of NTs and 47% of TOs assigned some importance to 'watching actors/actresses who I find physically attractive'; and around half the TO cohort, and a quarter of NTs, were willing to agree that period films could be 'sexy' (Questions 29 and 30). Some favourite actor choices also signalled or hinted at erotic interests. A number of female TOs who named Harvey Keitel had been moved specifically by his performance – and nudity – in Jane Campion's *The Piano* rather than taking an equivalent interest in his contemporary roles. Among NTs, such interests were limited (predictably) to Colin Firth, Mr Darcy in BBC-TV's 1995 *Pride and Prejudice*.

In concluding this section, it seems clear that the actor tastes of the two cohorts closely reflect the breadth and narrowness of their respective film tastes, the place of period films within these, and NTs' and TOs' generally very different conceptions of cultural value. But what are we to make of the

sizeable proportion of NTs who appeared to have no actor tastes or preferences at all? One possible explanation suggests itself in the comments of TO31,
the National Trust volunteer whose intense attachment to the discourse of
authenticity made her an anomaly within the TO cohort:

> I have no 'favourite performers' – I am more interested in the precise
> historical presentation and look of the performance. Many modern actors
> fail because their walk or overall composure appear 'out of place' for the
> period they are portraying. (TO31, woman, 52; university librarian)

If we hypothesise that this position may have been shared – if tacitly – by some
NTs, this would explain the absence of a fan interest in actors among such
respondents. But TO31's statement goes significantly beyond this, suggesting the possibility of a broader uninterest in the human, emotional and social
dimensions of acting, and the forms of engagement these facilitate for the
viewer. In the position articulated here, the period-film actor is not a *human*
actor, but merely part of the period mise-en-scène.

LITERARY PLEASURES, 'RESPECTFUL' ADAPTATION AND CULTURAL VALUE

This closing section of the analysis presented in Chapters 6 and 7 considers
respondents' responses to what can be termed the 'literary' pleasures of period
films. It must be stressed that the pleasures – and issues – to be considered
here are not confined to those hinging on the films' perceived conformity, or
otherwise, to the discourse of literary authenticity, nor even to those with a
direct relationship to adaptation. Although heritage-film criticism's preoccupation with the discourse of authenticity has proved problematic in that it
marginalises other possible focuses of audience pleasure, it is nevertheless vital
to acknowledge that the discourse of literary authenticity has been powerfully
pre-established for these same audiences – through publicity, media coverage
and criticism – prior to their encounters with the films themselves. On the
other hand, as this section will illustrate, the same films were, and are, enjoyed
by many viewers who escape this discursive trap to engage very differently
with both the issues of adaptation they raise and the broader 'literary' pleasures they offer.

   Just as NT and TO respondents held very different conceptions and expectations in relation to visual 'authenticity' and historical engagement, so the two
cohorts tended to engage differently with the literary qualities and literary prestige of period films. (These differing positions must also, of course, be interpreted with reference to what we already know about the two cohorts' different

and unequal awarenesses of film as a distinct medium or legitimate art form.) This section will seek to crystallise these findings to present some broader conclusions about the notions of cultural value in operation among period-film audiences, and the *kinds* of cultural value they believe these films to embody.

As one indicator of respondents' acceptance or rejection of the discourse of literary authenticity, Question 29 asked them to rate the importance of 'the chance to see *respectful* adaptation of *important* literary works' to their enjoyment of period films (emphasis added). In addition, a range of attitude statements seeking to test attitudes to 'respectful' adaptation and the perceived cultural value of literature, and to clarify how the film–literature relationship figured in respondents' viewing and reading habitus in practice, were presented in Question 30. Attachment to notions such as 'respectful adaptation' or 'important literary works', of course, has a different force from enjoying the 'literacy and wit' of period films or 'reliv[ing] the pleasures' of source novels or plays (both of which were also pre-suggested as possible pleasures in Question 29: see Appendix 6.1). While the latter two pleasures suggest straightforward enjoyment of books, plays or 'literary' language and dialogue, the former suggest a self-conscious awareness of the cultural capital (ostensibly) absorbed by the film – and, implicitly, its viewers – from its high-status literary source.

Although in their Question 29 replies 89% of NTs agreed that 'the chance to see respectful adaptations of important literary works' had some importance, only 58% judged it *very* important (compared to the 81% who found 'accurate reproduction' of the details of period styling 'very important'). Similarly, 92% of NTs gave some importance to the 'literacy and wit' of period films, but only 56% rated it 'very important'. Although such indices, in isolation, implied that 'respectful adaptation' was less vital for NTs than the accurate visual/material reproduction of period detail, the wider evidence – not least, their self-worded statements – made it very clear that most of the cohort subscribed, often rigidly, to the discourse of literary authenticity.

By contrast, fewer than 50% of the TO cohort assigned any importance to 'respectful adaptation' – compared to 80% for the 'literacy and wit' of period films – and only 20% of TOs rated 'respectful adaptation' 'very important', compared to 60% for 'literacy and wit'. A total of 63% of TO respondents also gave some importance to 'reliving the pleasures' of source novels or plays. These patterns suggest, first, a relatively high – but not ubiquitous – interest among TOs in film adaptations *as* adaptations of books they had actually read; but, second, that TOs valued the literary *pleasures* offered by many period films more highly than their perceived 'high' cultural value or respectfulness as adaptations. Although, as we shall see, TO respondents' stances on – and levels of interest in – the film–literature relationship varied considerably, this interpretation was supported by the wider evidence drawn from their self-worded replies.

As with the 'appreciation' of fine acting, period films adapted (or *perceived* to be) from 'the classics' characteristically served, for NTs, as a focus for the exercise of judgements and the display of cultural competences whose points of reference were literary, or sometimes theatrical, but rarely cinematic. These competences included *recognition* of the source author – but not always, it should be noted, detailed familiarity with the source text – and appreciation of the 'beautifully drawn' characterisation, 'proper story' and 'script (i.e. words of author)' (NT41, man, 69; retired bank official, S/SE England).

As we have already seen, for many such respondents, the relationship to a literary 'original' served as a *self-evident* marker of a film's quality and cultural value. NTs' choices of words affirmed that, for them, in the film–literature or film–theatre relationship, the book or play took primacy. The role of the film or TV version was thus to '*follow*' a book (NT67, woman, 65; retired teacher, N England), to 'bring [it] to life' (NT11, woman, 67; part-time tourist information centre manager, W/SW England, and several others), or the '*recreation* on screen of what is usually a well-loved literary classic' (NT29, woman, 61; retired tax accountant, S/SE England) (my emphases). As I established at the start of this chapter, this disposition also framed period films or dramas (which, of course, many NT respondents viewed mostly on television) as opportunities 'to see on TV a *novel* that you have read' (NT16, woman, 61; retired retail manager, N England) or to 'watch good *drama* at home' (NT40, man, 69; retired teacher, S/SE England) (my emphases).

As might be predicted against this background, three-quarters of NT respondents (but only 13% of TOs) agreed that 'it is wrong for adaptations for novels/plays to make too many creative changes to the author's work,' and only 35% of NTs (compared to 83% of TOs) agreed that they enjoyed films which adapt literary works 'in daring and imaginative ways' (Question 30). Despite the stereotype this suggests, some NTs showed perceptive insights into the difficulties of adaptation from a literary medium to a time-constrained visual one. NT48, for example, disliked 'over-condensation to a point where characters and situations become impossible to develop and where the wit and elegance of the original writer is lost' (man, 69; retired chief educational psychologist, county council, W/SW England). However, the more typical NT replies conceived of adaptation very narrowly, as a matter of fidelity (or not) to source or authorial intention rather than a process of interpretation. Moreover, the notion of 'fidelity' displayed was often rigidly literal in ways that suggested limited understanding of the formal constraints of feature films or TV drama serials and the necessary differences between their storytelling techniques and those of the novel. This position led NTs into some unwitting contradictions. For example, NT67, quoted below, was unable to engage with the issue of reader interpretation, the question of how (if at all) the author's intention could conclusively be determined, and who (if anyone) had the authority to pronounce on this. And the logic adopted by NT35 and NT72, if rigorously pursued, would dictate that very few novels should ever be adapted for film or television:

> I do not mind if the story is slightly altered on film if that is the best way of showing a character faithfully to the author's intention [but I dislike it] if a character is unlike that described by the author. (NT67, woman, 65, quoted above)

> I am not too happy when the adaptation from a book takes only one small part of it, but continues to call it by the original name – e.g. *The Remains of the Day* – it was well-acted [and] produced, but bore so little relevance to the book, or relevance in part only. I think it should be re-named. (NT35, woman, 79; retired teacher, S/SE England)

> If a period or costume film demands a certain length to do it justice, it is not worth trying to shorten it to save time and/or money. I think *Tom Jones* [*The History of Tom Jones, A Foundling* (Metin Hüseyin, BBC-TV, 1997)] suffered from this treatment, but it was also not a good choice as the book itself is very verbose and episodic. (NT72, woman, 72; retired modern languages teacher, Wales)

NT35 and NT72 were clearly commenting from a familiarity with the source novels. In some other cases, however, it seemed that approval for 'respectful adaptation' was not necessarily rooted in an avid reading habitus or familiarity with the source works. In support of this, 98% of NT respondents (compared to 83% of TOs) agreed that 'I enjoy film and TV period literary adaptations whether I have read the book or not,' and only one NT (and two TOs) agreed that 'I hardly ever watch literary adaptations unless I have already read the novel or seen the play' (Question 30). It might be inferred from this that at least some NT respondents were less widely read than TOs. Significantly, TO respondents were *more* likely than NTs to agree that adaptations 'often disappoint me because they don't live up to the literary original' (agreed with by 50% of TOs but only 37% of NTs). Yet it was NT respondents, not TOs, who insisted on 'respectful adaptation'.

In such a context, 'respectful adaptation' may serve merely as an abstract value or ideology and a notional, second-hand and middlebrow signifier of cultural prestige: something to be placed (to borrow a phrase from Andrew Higson) 'on display'.[9] The reply from NT79 quoted below is suggestive about the extent to which the attachment to 'the classics' professed by many NT respondents – forcefully instilled, as I hypothesised in Chapter 3 and as is confirmed here, via a certain kind of schooling – might conform to this interpretation. Her comments imply that a classics-loving habitus may be defined by rather narrow, unadventurous reading, while requiring neither persistence nor a particular relish for intellectual challenge from the reader:

> I have always enjoyed reading the classics, both at school where they formed a large part of the curriculum, and since purely for pleasure. Very often the storyline is better than in more modern works! . . . [Films offer] the added bonus of bringing to life those stories which may be more difficult to read because of lengthy descriptive passages. (NT79, woman, 66; retired nursing teacher, W/SW England)

This impression was supported by the relatively narrow and predictable range of favoured 'classic' source authors, or works, named by NT respondents. The self-worded replies of around one-fifth of NTs focused centrally on the pleasures and/or fidelity of period literary adaptations, yet named *no* specific films or source authors in support of this. When NTs did cite specific authors, the name most widely mentioned (by 19%) was Jane Austen – primarily with reference to this cohort's favourite self-named period TV drama serial, BBC-TV's 1995 *Pride and Prejudice*, although there were also two negative criticisms of the BBC's feature-length 1995 adaptation of *Persuasion*. Austen was followed in popularity by Shakespeare, who was also the only playwright named (by 10% of NTs). Beyond this, 8% of NTs mentioned Charles Dickens; 6% mentioned the Brontë sisters (either in the collective abstract, or naming the most obvious novels of Charlotte or Emily, not Anne's *The Tenant of Wildfell Hall*); and 5% mentioned the 1981 Granada TV adaptation of Evelyn Waugh's *Brideshead Revisited*. Beyond this, George Eliot, E. M. Forster, Thomas Hardy and the 1990s adaptations of, on TV, Daniel Defoe's *Moll Flanders* and, on film, Kazuo Ishiguro's *The Remains of the Day* were mentioned by one NT respondent each.

Dickens, however, was a special case; his work, and adaptations from it, emerged as a problematic site for NT respondents. Some associated Dickens with 'good plots and characters' (NT47, woman, 50; part-time historic buildings researcher, W/SW England), and a pleasurably larger-than-life acting style (NT55, woman, 77, as already quoted). But for others, the name 'Dickens' stood as a sign for representations of poverty or violence – and as shorthand for the kind of classic literary adaptation they did not enjoy. It seems significant that Dickens was the only name mentioned by NTs in connection with the representation of working-class experience, whether in literature or film. While few NTs would have been willing to state openly that their enjoyment of period films expressly excluded such representations, the contexts in which the name Dickens was mentioned suggested that this was indeed the case:

I don't relish viewing some films of Dickens novels – e.g. *Little Dorrit* – the general feeling of grimness and poverty – though particular to the plot, of course. (NT17, woman, 66; retired primary teacher, N England)

I do not like extreme violence, e.g. *Oliver Twist* murder of Nancy. (NT52, man, 78; retired surgeon and chief medical officer in industry, N England)

NT17's reaction to Christine Edzard's 1988 film of *Little Dorrit* (at the date of the survey, its sole English-language adaptation since the silent era) notably conflicts with its classification by critics (and by me in Chapter 5) as a core heritage film, a classification prompted for many by Raphael Samuel's renowned critique of the film: 'The malodorous London of *Little Dorrit* has been spring-cleaned . . . The poor have been sanitized . . . The shabby-genteel, too, have been upgraded.'[10] On Samuel's reading, the film's insistent aestheticisation and cleansing of Victorian poverty might have been expected to make the Dickensian subject-matter palatable to viewers such as NT17. But – perhaps *because* this is Dickens? – she recalls only 'grimness and poverty'.

Notwithstanding the narrow, often prescriptive, positions discussed above, a wider and more complex range of responses to the 'literary' pleasures of period films were expressed by a few NT respondents, and more extensively by TOs – whose positions were notably diverse, and consequently not easily pigeonholed. While the self-worded replies of a few TOs echoed elements of the dominant NT discourse about the merits of 'the classics', others made no mention of pleasures relating to literary adaptations (often in cases where these were not central to their genre or film tastes, both period and non-period). But more interestingly from the point of view of the heritage debate (and as already touched upon in Chapter 6), a significant number of TOs either cited pleasures of engagement that had a tacit or explicit relationship to the literary, or engaged with questions of literary adaptation in ways that were more subtle and informed than the reductive 'classics = quality' equation. We have already seen, for example, that (in their self-worded replies) TOs valued period films for their 'complex storylines' (TO17, woman, 34, black British; CV counsellor), 'coherent, grammatical dialogue' (TO3, gay man, 38, Irish; civil servant), strong characterisation and nuanced character development – qualities which are literary or theatrical insofar as they owe more to (screen)writing, acting and the direction of actors than to more film-specific techniques.

A further (overlapping) section of the TO cohort engaged directly and explicitly (in their own words) with period films as literary adaptations – with the distinguishing feature that virtually all TOs understood adaptation as an interpretative *process* requiring the adaptor to make choices, and referenced the specifics of particular film adaptations, in a way most NTs did not. In some cases this was done with a sophistication that clearly drew upon undergraduate or postgraduate study in English Literature or related disciplines. Whether their preference was for adaptations that remained close to source or achieved a 'violent rupture' from it, these TOs (very differently from most NTs) stressed their own active engagement with and subjective responses to texts – as well as the interventions of the film- or programme-makers:

> As I studied English drama at school/college/university, for most of my young adult life I enjoyed engaging with the self-contained world of the individual novels, yet holding the associations and references towards the other works of the period. Watching period films is often about revisiting those works . . . and having my ideas confirmed or changed about how they imagined them . . . [I dislike period films that strive] too hard for formality, thereby neutralising some of the energy of the drama. Having said that, I do get reactionary when directors play too freely with the text as well! (TO4, woman, 33; mental health care services manager)

> I prefer adaptations which are a violent rupture with the original – so I prefer *Clueless* [Amy Heckerling, US, 1995] to [Douglas McGrath's 1996] *Emma*. The reason I like this violent clash is that it forces me to rethink the meaning and value of the original – it doesn't try to lull me into senselessness. (TO10, man, 44; cultural journalist)

> Although I still enjoy most period drama, I have found that *Tom Jones* [BBC-TV, 1997: the production criticised earlier by NT72] has shown how much more engaging a drama can be when it is not treated with so much reverence. Jane Austen had a delicious wit, which often doesn't quite come through because of 'over-respect' in adaptation/direction. (TO28, woman, 36; part-time secretary and psychology student)[11]

> Increasingly I find period/costume films and TV progs [sic] irritating. When I do enjoy them it is because they are authentic and well-researched and are good films in their own right. Quite often they tend to be original screenplays or based on fact rather than literary adaptations. I like it when an adaptation can add something, some fresh insight, to the original text . . . [But] there have been so many [classic adaptations], some badly done. I think I'm just tired of them as a genre . . . The fact that I work in the book trade has something to do with all this, no doubt! (TO24, woman, 35; bookshop manager)

I don't particularly care for Jane Austen adaptations on the whole: 'Mills & Boon with nice frocks' (heresy!) (TO41, lesbian woman, 33; poetry librarian)

For some TOs, and in a trend unique to the TO cohort, the valuing of complex and subtle narratives and characterisation took on a politically progressive – and, more specifically, feminist – dimension. In keeping with the liking among TOs for strong female performers, heritage films were valued by these TOs – male as well as female – for their strong and complex female characters and the narrative centrality given to these. Not only was this not a stated priority for NTs, but also some of the NT perspectives already quoted – most of them from female respondents – have been implicitly anti-feminist (for example, in directing the harshest scrutiny of 'authenticity' at female performers).

In a related vein, when TO respondents named specific source authors, they not only cited a different (although overlapping) range of writers from NTs, but – significantly – they did so with reference to different, and sometimes expressly social or political, preoccupations and concerns. Accordingly, source authors were typically named by TOs with reference either to specific adaptations of their work, or to the specific values their work signified for the respondent. Thus where, for the NT cohort, 'Shakespeare, Austen, Dickens, etc' (NT26, already quoted) primarily signified the cultural prestige of 'classic' literature and literary adaptation, for TO respondents, Austen signified 'wit', while E. M. Forster was associated with liberal social critique and the Leavisite 'Great Tradition' in late nineteenth- to early twentieth-century English literature.[12] Indeed, two TO respondents cited the liberal values and social critique presented in Forster's novels explicitly in order to challenge the anti-heritage-film critical position:

Probably the most successfully adapted authors for period films have been the Merchant–Ivory adaptations of E. M. Forster. Interestingly, although the film adaptations of Forster are seen to be romantic, Forster was seen as a radical writer in his time. He was dealing with social change and the experiences of New Women. Forster's novels concern the difficulties and tensions experienced by people trying to live their lives in a changing society. (TO33, woman, 33; solicitor)

Many British period films, from the much-vaunted 'Great Tradition', revolve around issues of class and sexuality which have remained central to our literary tradition and to the structures of our social, economic and psychological experiences. The complexities of these themes makes [sic] the term 'heritage films' especially redundant/inadequate. (TO38, man, 39; English teacher, S/SE England)

Such interventions demonstrate that TO respondents were far more aware of the heritage-film debate – and cultural–political debates more broadly – than NTs, who, while they had (whether consciously or not) absorbed the late-1980s conservative pro-heritage-film discourse (which flowed through many of their own pronouncements), seemed unaware of the opposing critique. They also demonstrate that some TOs were prepared to enter critically into this debate, bringing in their own sexual-politics or cultural-politics perspectives.

Critics of the heritage film might argue that interventions such as those of TO33 and TO38, quoted above, do not convincingly counter the anti-heritage-film critique due to a tendency to miss, or misrecognise, some of its crucial nuances. (In particular, the critique of the Merchant Ivory adaptations of Forster does not deny Forster's radicalism, but rather claims that the films' aesthetic strategies neutralise it. Moreover, it is unclear from TO33's comments whether or not she intends to argue – against this – that the socially engaged radicalism of Forster the writer does find its way into some of the Forster films.) However, such objections miss the point. The finding that the audiences for heritage films include viewers who engage actively and critically with both the films and the debates around them *in itself* refutes the textual determinism of the anti-heritage-film critique and undermines its core arguments.

The analysis presented in Chapters 6 and 7 has shown that the highly conservative viewing positions and perspectives of a significant contingent of the heritage-film audience – as represented by many members of the NT cohort – do not merely conform with the reading of heritage cinema proposed by critics on the left, but exceed it, at times parodically. But this analysis has also demonstrated that *über*-conservative fans of period films constitute only one segment of the 'heritage film audience'. The TO cohort had seen many of the same films, yet the perspectives they expressed were far more varied and often radically different. Comparisons of these two clusters of contrasting responses – and the contrasts between participants in the two cohorts themselves – demonstrate that the broader 'heritage film audience' encompasses diverse social identities, educational experiences, and political and cultural positioning(s), and that its members bring to their viewing of the films a variety of perspectives and perceptions, formed by and filtered through these diversities and generating polyvalent readings.

A key finding of Chapters 6 and 7, then – and one of the most important findings of this book – is that the perceptions, uses and readings of period (and, more narrowly, heritage) films by their audiences are diverse in ways that cannot validly be viewed as textually determined. On the contrary, the evidence presented here has repeatedly illustrated ways in which these audience engagements are coloured by factors such as educational capital, film and literary habituses, cultural and class attitudes and aspects of peer-group identity – all of which are coloured, in turn by generational experiences and identities as much as differentials such as raw socio-economic class.

To conclude with a final illustration, we have seen that Heritage Audience Survey respondents from both the NT and TO cohorts valued and enjoyed heritage films for their 'literary' qualities. But the meaning and context of this finding differed for the two sub-samples. While many NTs valued the 'literary' qualities of heritage films from a position of limited immersion in film culture – and an attendant hierarchy of cultural value which equated literature and theatre, but not cinema, with cultural prestige – TO respondents enjoyed heritage films because their 'literary' qualities gave them a difference and distinctness from other types of film they also enjoyed. Going beyond habitus and taste, the differing literary-educational capital of the two cohorts provides the explanatory context for the paradox that while TOs were likely to be wider readers than NTs– and more highly trained interpreters of literature and adaptation – it was NTs who invested fanatically in the cultural prestige of literary adaptation.

NOTES

1. This equation of 'quality' with good taste and restraint has its roots, of course, in the discourse valuing British cinema in terms of its supposed 'realism and restraint' which came to dominate British film-critical culture from the 1940s. See Ellis, 'The quality film adventure'; Lovell, 'The British cinema: the known cinema?'; Murphy, *Realism and Tinsel*. TO39's praise for the Hammer horror films echoes the revisionist reversal of this discourse in the 'new' British film history, which has re-valorised British film cycles, genres and directors associated with fantasy and excess. See also Chapter 1, Note 67.

2. Thanks are due to Francis Mulhern for pointing out that notions of the 'proper' or 'well-told' story have specific origins in the culture of the nineteenth-century novel, and therefore already refer implicitly to the novelistic. This may account for the assumption – so widely internalised by NTs – that the connection needed no elaboration.

3. See, indicatively, Usher, 'The gentle English conquering America', and Montgomery-Massingberd, '*A Handful of Dust*'.

4. For a definitive textual, contextual and reception study of the Pimpernel films and Gainsborough period melodramas, among others, see Harper, *Picturing the Past*.

5. See, for example, Clinch, 'James and Hugh and Maurice too' [interview feature], and Hoare, 'Actors' tweeds' [fashion shoot], both featuring the three 'new' male stars of *Maurice*, James Wilby, Hugh Grant and Rupert Graves.

6. Bourdieu, *Distinction*; see Chapter 3, pages 52–3.

7. As noted in Chapter 5, Hopkins's popularity among NTs was such that 39% had seen him as Hannibal Lecter in *The Silence of the Lambs* (despite NTs' almost unanimous aversion to screen violence).

8. For one example, see David K., 'Re-seeing *Maurice*'. See also YouTube user comments

(and fan-video uploads) in response to *Maurice,* such as those at: http://www/youtube.com/watch?v=ufS4-nkdSSM&feature=related

9. Higson, 'Re-presenting the national past', p. 115.

10. Samuel, 'Dockland Dickens', pp. 402–5.

11. TO28 identified herself as a fan of westerns and sword-and-sandal epics, but (as her comments here establish) her wider tastes extended to novelistic classic literary adaptations.

12. Forster, Henry James and (via *The Remains of the Day*) Kazuo Ishiguro were all named by TO respondents as favourite adapted authors. Austen adaptations, by contrast, were widely mentioned but almost never favourably (indicatively, see TO28's and TO41's comments already quoted on pages 160–1).

CHAPTER 8

Conclusions: Period Film Audiences, the Heritage Film Debate and Audience Studies

INTRODUCTION

This concluding chapter draws together the key findings and insights that have emerged from this book's detailed investigation and analysis of the late-1990s 'heritage film audience' – or rather, 'audiences' – as represented by the two groups who participated in the Heritage Audience Survey, and considers their implications: for our understanding of period-film audiences, for the critical debate around heritage cinema which first motivated this project, and for the wider field of empirical film-audience studies.

If we define this field as comprising work that engages directly with 'real audiences' to generate the material for its analysis – usually with a qualitative emphasis on audience testimony – and/or draws on other sources of empirical data on real audiences, the 'wider' field of empirical film-audience studies is, in fact, a relatively new, small and emerging one. (*Participations*, the main specialist journal of 'cultural and media' audience and reception studies, was launched only in 2003, and continues to describes its mission as one of 'developing' a field 'not at present well supported' within academia.[1]) The new work defining this field has emerged across a timeframe that parallels the genesis of the *Heritage Film Audiences* project. However, its most prominent trends to date have been driven by markedly different preoccupations and agendas to which the findings of my own study present some unpredicted challenges, centrally around the 'active audience' thesis and questions of audience autonomy.

In seeking to distil the defining characteristics, tastes, positions and attitudes of the two sub-groups of the period-film audience represented in my study – in relation to both period films and the heritage-film debate – Chapter 8 focuses particularly on the following areas.

First, how far did the two cohorts of respondents who participated in the survey exhibit distinct sets of characteristics, or responses, that make it valid to conceive of the viewers of period films – or some sub-groups of these viewers – as a coherent, distinct audience or audiences? What were the distinguishing features of the two audience segments exemplified by the National Trust (NT) and *Time Out* (TO) respondents, and what features, if any, set them apart from the putative 'mainstream' film/cinema audience – or does such a distinction prove unhelpful or problematic? To go further, did some sections of these audiences display characteristics that make it pertinent to understand their viewing of 'heritage films' or other period films – within a surrounding discursive, social and cultural-consumption context – as an appropriative or subcultural activity?

Second, Chapter 8 engages with the question of respondents' self-consciousness and self-perception in relation to the questions just posed. How far did respondents *self*-identify as members – or not – of 'the' period-film or heritage-film audience, and did NT and TO respondents show different tendencies in this respect?

A third question, following from the second, is that of respondents' self-consciousness and self-reflexivity in relation to the heritage debate itself. How did respondents' self-positioning (particularly in their self-worded comments) relate to their levels of awareness, and their perceptions, of the critical debates around heritage cinema and the critical status of heritage films? Did some show a self-conscious or distanced relationship to period films, likely to be coloured by awareness of the existence of a negative critical debate and 'cultural cringe' around heritage cinema, or did their self-positioning suggest unawareness of, or imperviousness to, these negative discourses?

Via the consideration of this third issue, Chapter 8 will move towards a concluding crystallisation of the implications of *Heritage Film Audiences*' findings for both the heritage-film debate and film-audience studies. The conclusions to be drawn hinge not merely on the cohesiveness and distinctness – or not – of the audience(s) studied, and the accumulated evidence about their complex, polyvalent relationships with period films, but also on their relationships with existing cultural, critical and media discourses and debates. Given the textual-determinist view of the audience embedded in the original heritage-film critique, this discussion will also revisit the complex factors and influences conditioning – and, I will argue, at least in part explaining – the viewing positions of the two audience sections represented in this study.

A fourth and last question – of some importance in the light of the top-down, critic-led origins of both the heritage-film debate and the very idea of 'heritage cinema' as a genre – is that of audience autonomy. How far did respondents seem able to produce their own (relatively autonomous) audience, or even fan, discourses in relation to the period films they watched? Conversely, how far did they replicate, or seem constrained by, the terms of established journalistic, promotional, critical or academic discourses around the 'heritage film'? The answers to such questions also have implications for the assumptions about the activity, interpretative freedom and even creativity of film audiences that have coloured much of the emergent work in film-audience, fan and reception studies since the mid to late 1990s.

IS THERE A DISTINCT AND COHERENT 'HERITAGE–FILM AUDIENCE' – OR AUDIENCES?

Chapters 3 to 7 have cumulatively established that there is not a single, cohesive audience for period films – nor even for the narrower and more contested category 'heritage films' – defined by neat, static boundaries or stable shared characteristics which distinguish it from the wider – and nominally more 'mainstream' – film audience. Rather, my portrait of the demographics and educational capital of survey respondents, as well as their film-consumption habitus, breadth/narrowness and specifics of film tastes, cultural positioning and wider attitudes, suggests that the audiences who enjoy period films consist of overlapping, dynamic groups, positioned in varied relationships to both commercial and art cinema, who make sense of the films from a variety of cultural–political perspectives. As Andrew Higson rightly notes, for the contemporary film industry (ever since the rise of mass TV ownership, but now ever more so in the digital, multi-channel, multi-platform era), 'the "mass audience" is necessarily an agglomeration of niches.'[2] The findings presented in this book suggest that this is equally true of the contemporary UK (and, we can infer, wider) audience for heritage films.

This study has demonstrated that at least two distinct sub-groups exist within this audience. And, in analysing the marked contrasts in identity, taste and attitude – but also some similarities – between them, it has shown not just that a diversity of identities, tastes and attitudes can be found among the audiences for period films, but that order and pattern can be found in this diversity. It does not follow, of course, that the trends found within the two specific groups who took part in the Heritage Audience Survey necessarily represent the totality of all possible trends within contemporary audiences for period films, whether in the UK or beyond. Although the many contrasts between the TO and NT cohorts certainly provide valid insights into the spectrum of orientations among period-film audiences, this does not rule out the existence of further sub-groups, tendencies or 'niches' – or shifts in the trends noted here – to be uncovered by future researchers.

One of this book's most important findings, however, is precisely that the 'period-film audience' is not a homogeneous entity. We have seen that even the narrower range of British period films regarded – by consensus – as 'heritage films' do not appeal solely to a homogeneous audience with unified tastes and views. Nor is heritage-film spectatorship characterised by a monolithic viewing position, and certainly not one which can be 'read off' as a textual 'product' of the films themselves, as early-1990s critics tended to do. From the forms of evidence presented in Chapters 6 and 7, we can see that agreement about the enjoyability of the most popular (culturally) British heritage films did not, alone, symptomatise or dictate a particular orientation towards these films (as seen, for example, in the ways in which these orientations were inflected by the opposing sexual politics expressed by NTs and TOs). It would be more correct to say that respondents in the two cohorts – and sometimes smaller sub-groups within these – enjoyed (some of) the same heritage films from within very different wider contextual meshes of tastes and attitudes, which were in turn coloured by equally complex meshes of social identity, educational and cultural capital, and life experiences.

A further crucial finding, then, is that audiences' viewing and ideological positions in relation to period films – and the surrounding debates – need to be understood in relation to a complex social, educational and cultural intertext extending beyond the films themselves. My analysis has illustrated in detail the ways in which some of the strands of this mesh interweave to define the contexts within which different viewers – or sections of the audience – can like the same films, yet respond to them from different and complex reception positions.

Although a variety of taste and opinion was evident within both the TO and NT cohorts (albeit in a more limited way among NTs), it emerged clearly that both sections of the period-film audience can be defined and understood in terms of relatively coherent sets of broadly shared characteristics, both demographically and in terms of similarities of educational capital, film tastes or cultural–political orientation. Thus while there is no homogeneous period-film (or even heritage-film) audience, there *are* relatively coherent period-film *audiences* or audience sectors, albeit with dynamic and overlapping relationships both to each other and to the wider (and putatively 'mainstream') film audience.

With this dynamism and overlap in mind, how should we sketch the key features of the NT and TO cohorts as relatively coherent 'audiences'? We can see that in their film tastes, opinions and cultural–political positioning, the NT cohort emerged as a considerably more cohesive 'audience' than their TO counterparts. The NT audience was defined, at its core, by narrow (predominantly British and Anglophone) film tastes and viewing that were dominated by period films, and by equally narrow core tastes within the latter. TOs, by contrast, were an audience that enjoyed period films – indeed, TOs had typically seen a wider range of them than NTs – but period films did not define their identity, and (for most) were watched in the context of very varied, often cinephilic, film tastes. For three-quarters of TOs, most of the films they had seen, of those listed in the questionnaire, were *not* period films; for two-thirds of NTs, most of the films they had seen *were*. For the NT audience, the most commercially successful of the post-1980 British heritage films (plus analogous TV dramas/serials) formed the core, or 'mainstream', of their tastes around which other, limited, niche film tastes clustered: Anglophone, mainly British, popular genre films, centrally upper-middle-class 'contemporary heritage' comedy hybrids and dramas of female redefinition classified by Justine King as contemporary British woman's films.[3] By contrast, the equivalent core position in the TO audience's tastes was occupied (for most) by post-1970, post-classical and auteurist Hollywood cinema.

Although the ideological–aesthetic positioning and attitudes of NTs conformed significantly with the conservative pro-heritage-film discourses of the Thatcher era, neither Merchant Ivory's films – nor E. M. Forster adaptations from other directors – figured as prominently in their core tastes as the 1980s media or early-1990s critique would have predicted. It may be significant that around three-quarters of NTs had (or named) no favourite directors. They were less likely to have seen Ivory's films beyond the core crossover hits (*Howards End*, *A Room with a View*, *The Remains of the Day*) than the ubiquitous Jane Austen adaptations or other 1990s period films less strongly marketed on the director/producer's name.

Instead, it was the younger, more liberal or left-wing, and more sexually diverse TO audience who showed a strong brand awareness of Ivory's films and were likely to have seen a broader range of them. These unanticipated findings on the 'place' of Merchant Ivory – in relation to both cohorts – have interesting implications for our understanding of the field of heritage cinema, and also throw into question the academic critique's conjectural bracketing of Ivory's films to a conservative, uncritical spectatorship. On the contrary, among TOs (and in the pilot study for the survey), a liking for Ivory's films coincided with a critical spectatorship, which frequently engaged with period films in terms of their exploration of social issues and dilemmas through the prism of the past – in contrast with the NT audience's narrowly heritage-centred disposition and attitudinal alignment with established assumptions about heritage cinema and its audiences.

Despite such contrasts, the overlapping core of agreed British 'heritage films' that were widely liked by both TOs and NTs provides sound justification for identifying and discussing both groups as components of the 'heritage film audience'. However, when the two cohorts' differing hierarchies of favourite period (and even Merchant Ivory) films are cross-referenced with the differing hierarchies of period-film pleasures they prioritised, and the significantly different attitudes and orientations that emerged from their self-worded comments, a credible interpretation is that the tastes of many TOs emphasised those heritage films most readable in terms of a social and/or sexual-politics critique (such as *A Room with a View*, *Another Country*, *Maurice* and *Orlando*).

NTs, by contrast, favoured those most easily assimilated into a (culturally, politically and/or aesthetically) conservative viewing position.

DEFINING POSITIONS AND AUDIENCE (SUB)CULTURES

The evidence presented and interpreted in this book has shown that overlapping tastes in heritage films can co-exist with substantially different social identities, cultural–political orientations and viewing positions. It has also illustrated the ways in which these audiences are defined, and distinguished from one another – and, to differing degrees, from the broader film audience – by the identities and orientations they *bring to* their choices, and viewing, of period films. This cumulative evidence demonstrates decisively that the various audiences for period films are not defined solely by their film tastes, nor are their viewing positions 'produced' or dictated textually by the films they enjoy. But the particular case of the heritage film audience has also demonstrated abundantly that these prior identities and orientations (and, ultimately, the mesh of social, educational, cultural and critical–discursive intertexts that form them) *mediate and constrain* respondents' relationships with the films – at the levels of both interpretation and pleasure – in ways that unexpectedly throw into question the universal validity of the active audience thesis and the celebratory insistence of the 'new' film audience studies on the autonomy and interpretative freedom of audiences.

The NT audience showed a stronger, narrower and more emphatic consensus than their TO counterparts both in their shared film tastes and about the qualities that were important in period films. But, more than this, their replies were almost uncannily unified in articulating very familiar – if problematic and unfashionable – discourses which harnessed period 'authenticity' to the 'quality' of period films and 'respect' for the 'classic' literary source. Inconveniently for my own hypotheses – which had expected (or hoped) to find an 'active', 'autonomous' heritage-film audience culture – the discourses channelled by NTs aligned them in many ways with the ideological–aesthetic positioning of the hypothetical heritage-film spectator projected by the early-1990s critique of heritage cinema. Chapters 6 and 7's exploration of respondents' self-expressed attitudes takes on a particular importance in this context, putting flesh on our understanding of such (easily caricatured) views to reveal their complexities, ambivalences and contradictions, while Chapter 3 has shed light on the facets of respondents' identities and life experiences which underpin and condition them.

The attitudes and tastes expressed by the TO audience showed considerably less consensus and cohesion, and were more resistant to neat categorisation, but were unified by their shared – and usually pronounced – disjuncture from the attitudes and positioning of the hypothetical 'heritage-film spectator'. Although there was strong consensus among TO respondents that 'quality', strong performances, visual pleasure, literate, witty dialogue, and complexity of characterisation all contributed to the pleasures offered by period films – preferences most NTs would, superficially, agree with – almost no TOs shared the NT cohort's (usually) mechanistic conception of 'quality' or shared their zeal for 'authentic' period reproduction and 'respectful' adaptation. The most significant distinguishing trait of the TO audience, however, was critical self-reflection; TOs were far more likely than NTs to think critically about terms such as 'quality' and to define them in their own – at times expressly revisionist – terms. The 'culture' of the TO audience was further distinguished from that of NTs by a strong prioritisation of narrative engagement and a valuing of complexity – and (in some cases) political or social engagement, and contemporary or personal relevance – in the period films TOs enjoyed.

These defining traits of the two 'audiences' – self-consciousness, critical reflexivity and the desire for engagement and 'relevance' among the TO cohort, versus the (near-)ventriloquism of existing conservative critical positions and a very specific appropriation of period films as *vehicles* for the assertion of 'discriminating' taste and 'proper' class and generational values among NTs – have implications for how we understand and locate these two audiences in relation to the heritage-film debate. As signalled by the term 'appropriation', the NT audience's particular relationship with heritage films, coupled with their narrow, particular film tastes, is validly understood as a distinct audience culture – perhaps even a subculture. Certainly NTs' characteristic mode of spectatorship, the specific gratifications they prioritised, and their relative uninterest in period films *as films* (or seemingly, in some cases, even as narratives) distinguished – and distanced – them from the majority audience for 'mainstream' films.

To conceive of the NT audience as a subculture, however, raises a paradox from which spring two problems. On the one hand, as we have seen, the behaviour of the NT audience was 'subcultural' in that NTs in many respects appropriated heritage films for their own shared purposes rather than engaging with them centrally as films. On the other, past critical writing on heritage cinema has, by implication, presented the 'discriminating', authenticity-obsessed mode of engagement epitomised by the NT audience as the *normal* mode of spectatorship textually encouraged by heritage films, not a marginal form of fan appropriation. If the NT audience, in its behaviour, closely resembles the *core* audience for heritage films envisioned by heritage-film criticism, can its relationship with the films simultaneously be subcultural? In a further problem, how should we locate and understand an audience (sub)culture characterised for most of its participants by a 'discerning' self-distanciation from popular cinema and popular culture?

The NTs' particular uses of period films, and the apparent gratifications they gained from them, were 'subcultural' in the sense that their distinguishing features set them apart from 'normal' film-viewing behaviour. The responses explored in Chapters 6 and 7 showed that a significant number of NTs watched heritage and other period films less for pleasures such as narrative or character engagement than in order to scrutinise and police small details (of the period mise-en-scène or actors' speech and deportment) and to gain pleasure from this – including self-admitted pleasure in identifying errors and lapses, and the social pleasure of discussing such details with friends.

This behaviour was subcultural in that it was both clearly appropriative, and inflected by a different, and specialised, set of priorities compared to mainstream film-viewing behaviour. But – in contradiction of the assumptions of much work on audience (and other) subcultures, which has taken its cue from the notion of subculture mobilised by Dick Hebdige (which Hebdige had, in turn, adopted from Phil Cohen) – the 'subcultural' behaviour of the NT audience was emphatically *not* subversive of dominant values or oppositional to elite class positions. Cohen, Hebdige and the body of subcultural studies work that followed in their wake were pre-eminently (even exclusively) invested in working-class and youth subcultures and their perceived resistance to hegemonic values (including, in Ken Gelder's account, resistance to class-conscious identities).[4] The NT audience's use of period films can certainly be construed as 'resistant' – and some NTs would even perceive themselves in those terms. But they were clearly resistant from a (middle-) class and cultural–political position neither envisaged nor favoured by Cohen, Hebdige and most of their successors. Theirs was a resistance *to* the popular and the 'vulgar' – not a resistance to a dominant 'legitimate' culture expressed through popular culture.

Despite this, the NT audience's particular, specialised orientation towards period films fits well with Cohen's observation that the function of subcultures is 'to express or resolve, albeit magically, the contradictions which remain hidden or unresolved in the parent culture', and equally with Hebdige's conception of subcultural practices as an arena where class (and, implicitly, class tensions) is 'work[ed] out in practice as a material force'.[5] However, the NT audience is perhaps most appropriately understood – in terms not envisaged by Hebdige or most of his successors – as a *subaltern* subculture rather than a *subversive* one.[6] By this, I mean that the characteristic viewing practices and attitudes of the NT cohort (with occasional exceptions) were broadly those of a group, subordinate to (or uncertainly located in relation to) the true social or cultural elites, whose self-elected role was to police and defend conservative, established values – and notions of cultural value – perceived to be under threat, whether from the forces of the popular and the trashing of old cultural hierarchies, or from 'sloppy' standards and crumbling moral certainties.

In marked contrast with this specialised, subaltern–subcultural disposition, the TO audience's breadth of film tastes, and expectation that period films should engage them in similar ways to any other film, showed that most of its members were integrated into both the wider film culture and the wider film audience in a way that most members of the NT cohort were not. The behaviour and taste patterns of the TO audience thus located them as (a distinctively cinematically well-informed) *part* of the 'mainstream' film audience rather than separate from it, in ways that strongly challenged many of the assumptions about the heritage-film audience established in the text-centred academic critique.

SELF-IDENTIFICATION AND SELF-CONSCIOUSNESS

In keeping with the above findings, NT respondents were considerably more likely than TOs to identify consciously as members of a distinct 'period-film audience', and to do so fairly indiscriminately and without embarrassment. Although two-thirds of TOs (and 92% of NTs) agreed (in response to the Question 30 attitude statements) that they had 'enjoyed literary adaptations/costume dramas on film/TV for as long as I can remember' – and this book's findings on the range of period films TOs were familiar with confirm this longevity of habitus – they were also more likely than NTs to agree that 'I don't think of myself as typical of the kind of person who watches' them (agreed with by 53% of TOs compared to 27% of NTs). TO respondents were also substantially less likely than NTs to 'usually make an effort to see' new period-film releases (27% of TOs, 76% of NTs) or to 'generally know that' they 'will be my kind of film' (20% of TOs, 77% of NTs). More than this, 20% of TO respondents agreed that 'I sometimes feel embarrassed [to admit] that I enjoy period films' – a sentiment not endorsed by *any* NTs. Although this was not a high percentage, it affirmed a sensitisation among the TO cohort to negative critical discourses around heritage cinema which was seemingly not shared by NTs – a self-consciousness which, as we saw in Chapters 6 and 7, was also manifested in many TOs' self-worded comments.

Most TO respondents positioned themselves as members of a discriminating – rather than alienated – audience in relation to contemporary mainstream cinema. More than 90% agreed that they liked 'many other kinds of contemporary films' as well as period films – but around a quarter of TOs also 'usually prefer[red] period and costume films' to those of 'modern Hollywood'. Two-thirds of the NT cohort, too, agreed that they liked 'many other kinds of contemporary films as well as costume or period films', and just over two-thirds agreed that 'I usually prefer period and costume films to modern Hollywood films' (with one-third of NTs agreeing with both statements). But, as we saw in Chapters 5 to 7, only the second of these claims was substantiated by NTs' wider expressed attitudes or recent film viewing.

One possible reading is that one-third of NT respondents considered that they had varied film tastes beyond period films, but – like around a quarter of TOs – were lukewarm about present-day Hollywood mainstream product. However, the wider evidence showed this to be true only up to a very limited point. Some NTs' favourite self-named period films –notably *Gone With the Wind* – dated from the classical Hollywood period, and a few NTs had been in the 1950s–1960s audience for European art cinema. But few had a signifi-cant current art-cinema habitus; only 45% (compared to almost 90% of TOs) agreed that they 'like[d] to see foreign-language films'; and their non-period film viewing beyond the UK clustered strongly around the same popular genres as their British tastes (comedies and comedy hybrids: indicatively, the major Australian export comedy hit *Crocodile Dundee* was especially popular). In this context, NTs' attitude-statement replies signalled a dissonance between the desire to *project* varied, yet 'discerning', film tastes, and the narrower – and more populist – reality of their present-day viewing.

The identity of the NT audience was further defined by a thread of consciously reactive – even reactionary – alienation from aspects of contem-porary cinema that emerged in NTs' responses to the Question 30 attitude statements as well as their self-worded comments. Although respondents in both cohorts expressed a critical, and to varying extents oppositional, rela-tionship to contemporary Hollywood, fewer than one-fifth of TO respond-ents agreed it to be 'usually true that there are very few new films I want to see' – yet this statement attracted agreement from almost 70% of NTs. One reason for this can be found in the NT audience's strong aversion to 'bad lan-guage', 'vulgarity', explicit sexual representations and – most of all – screen violence, which many NTs perceived to be commonplace in contemporary cinema, and 90% did not wish to see (Question 30 replies). Almost one-third of TOs too were 'put off' by screen violence, but (in contrast with around 70% of NTs) only one TO respondent objected to sexual representations or 'bad language'.

As the discussion in Chapter 6 made clear, however, many of the NT cohort's attitudes to contemporary cinema need to be understood in the context of – and, in many ways, as an expression of – an alienated reaction against aspects of contemporary *society* that they found regrettable or disturb-ing. NTs' particular uses and perceptions of heritage films similarly need to be understood in this wider light – alongside the particular, generational forms of class consciousness and educational and cultural capital that had shaped this cohort – rather than caricatured.

While equivalent determinants were at work within the TO audience, in practice TOs' more eclectic positions in relation to period films seemed less sharply conditioned by their social identities. Rather, the determining factor most strongly shaping the TO cohort's distinctively self-conscious relationship with period films was their heightened awareness of the critical climate and debates, particularly around heritage cinema. With this in mind, the next section now returns to this debate to evaluate the findings of the Heritage Audience Survey in relation to the main contentions of the anti-heritage-film critique, and my own opposing arguments and hypotheses about 'the heritage-film audience'.

PERIOD FILM AUDIENCES AND THE HERITAGE DEBATE

A core aim of this book has been to address the methodological hiatus in text-centred critiques of 'the heritage film' by conducting a concrete and detailed study engaging with real members of the period-film audience. More precisely, this study has established the existence of at least two, very different, 'audiences' for heritage cinema, and explored how their distinct and complex respective identities can be mapped, and need to be understood, in relation to a complex mesh of factors, social and contextual as much as textual. The implications of these findings for the heritage-film debate, however, hinge not only on the complex evidence accumulated and presented about these audiences and their relationships with period films, but also on the positioning of the NT and TO audiences in relation to the existing discourses and debates around 'heritage cinema'.

The evident self-consciousness, and even dissociative embarrassment, of many TO respondents about enjoying period films confirmed their consciousness of a negative critical debate and 'cultural cringe' around heritage cinema. Although few members of the TO audience were deeply immersed in the heritage debate or displayed a full grasp of its detail, most showed some sense of the kinds of criticisms that had been directed at 'heritage films'. Some TOs responded to this critical climate directly, others more indirectly, for example by ironising their enjoyment of period films or framing it from a critical or self-reflective distance. By contrast, the responses of the NT audience suggested a widespread unawareness of, or imperviousness to, these criticisms. On the contrary, the responses of many NTs were clearly aligned with aesthetically, culturally – and often politically – conservative celebratory discourses in which the period films which formed the bulk of their own viewing – British ones and those adapted from English literary 'classics' – were equated with 'quality' itself.

NT and TO respondents' replies to attitude statements that criticised the class politics of heritage films, their bourgeois or upper-class representational bias and their approach to the representation of the past revealed a similar split – not merely along political lines, but between the two cohorts' differing degrees of political consciousness in relation to the heritage-film debate. Although few respondents committed themselves to *strong* agreement or disagreement with these statements, more than three-quarters of TOs agreed that period films/TV dramas 'nearly always show events from the point of view of the middle/upper classes' compared to fewer than half of NTs; and 40% of TOs – but only 10% of NTs – agreed that this bias was a cause for concern. Almost 60% of TOs but few NTs agreed that period films 'can be damaging because they present an idealised, unrealistic vision of the past', while a quarter of TOs but barely any NTs were willing to agree that they 'do nothing to help us really understand history' (all Question 30: Appendix 2.1).

But equally, respondents across both cohorts held more nuanced positions than these replies might suggest in isolation. Thus only 10% of TOs or NTs credited period films with the power of 'encourag[ing] us to retreat into the past rather than face important issues of the present' – as had been strongly implied in both Tana Wollen's critique of the ideological workings of 'nostalgic screen fictions' and Andrew Higson's initial 1993 critique of the 'heritage film'.[7] And a quarter of NTs – as well as two-thirds of TOs – agreed that 'the period films I enjoy are often critical of the hypocrisies and class attitudes of the past.' Such patterns suggest that TOs, while aware of anti-heritage-film criticisms, were resistant to their most reductive, condemnatory claims, or willing to disregard these in the interests of enjoyment; and that NTs did not invariably respond to heritage films from unequivocally conservative or wholly uncritical viewing positions.

A core implication of the founding early-1990s critiques had been that heritage films operated textually/aesthetically – via their spectacular display of the class-specific (bourgeois or upper-class) mise-en-scène – to 'produce' a certain kind of spectatorship or spectator positioning that was strongly ideological, and ideologically conservative. In contrast with this textual-determinist model, I had anticipated that an empirical study of period-film audiences would reveal a diversity of responses to the films, equating with a diversity of ideological–aesthetic viewing positions – including positions less conservative, more progressive and more iconoclastic. The findings presented in this book confirm this to be true. In particular, the findings on the TO audience demonstrate clearly that enjoyment of (at least some of) the core heritage films is fully compatible with critical and progressive viewing positions. But the responses of NTs as well as TOs show that neither cohort was a cultural–political monolith. Just as some TO respondents were resistant to responding to period films in the (guilty, politicised) terms encouraged by the heritage-film critique, so some NT respondents preferred socially critical period films.

CONCLUSION: *HERITAGE FILM AUDIENCES*, FILM–AUDIENCE STUDIES AND THE MYTH OF AUDIENCE FREEDOM

The theorisation of spectator positioning as textually determined has, of course, fallen decisively from favour in Film Studies, a fall accelerated since the mid 1990s under the influence of two main disciplinary shifts. The first of these is the rise of 'post-theory' (and its affiliate, neo-formalist film analysis): a strategic move to depoliticise and pluralise film theory which (accordingly) rejected psychoanalytic–Althusserian models of film spectatorship in favour of an approach influenced by cognitive psychology which instead conceives of the film viewer as a 'rational individual'.[8] Critics of this move point out, however, that cognitivist film theory's 'rational individual' bears uncanny similarities to the 'rational consumer' of free-market economics, and exhibits similar shortcomings.[9] Moreover, these shortcomings include the exclusion from discussion of all the socially rooted elements of the viewer's identity (such as class or gender) that have proved so central to the audience analysis presented in this book.[10] The second is the methodological shift towards an increasing use of empirical audience and reception studies methodologies within Film Studies (methodologies which were hitherto applied predominantly – and continue to be applied more widely – with the disciplines of Media and Cultural Studies), as evidenced by the growing (if still small) body of 'new' film audience studies research which has been conducted and published since the mid- to late 1990s.

My own study of the heritage film's plural audiences adds to the emerging pool of empirical work vindicating this shift in methodological emphasis, and elaborating on the specifics and complexities of audience identities and viewing positions. This book has been able to offer insights in five particular which textual methodologies alone cannot.

First, and obviously, it has offered insights into period-film audience members' own accounts of their viewing pleasures and positions rather than textually derived speculative constructions of these, while acknowledging that these empirical insights cannot be treated as unmediated or unproblematic. Second, it has elucidated the *detail and nuances* of respondents' viewing positions – including areas of contradiction or equivocation – and, third, the complex mesh of social and cultural determinants inflecting and partly explaining these positions. Insights in these areas have proved particularly important in developing a deepened understanding of the conservative viewing positions and specialised, appropriative uses of heritage films found among the NT audience, and the social and cultural influences and vulnerabilities that under-pin and begin to explain this.

Fourth, within this, my study has offered insights into the relationship between educational capital – many aspects of which are generational, and coloured by generational class experiences and class cultures – and the respec-tive attitudes of the TO and NT audiences towards period films. Last, it has offered insights into respondents' awarenesses or unawarenesses of the critical debate around heritage cinema, and their (presumably unconscious) ven-triloquism of, or conscious dialogue with, existing discourses around period films. Here, insights into the younger TO audience's frequently self-conscious awareness of this debate have been of particular importance in understanding this audience's equally self-conscious and equivocal relationship with period films.

If (some) heritage films have been guilty of peddling a bourgeois or aris-tocratic hegemonic vision of 'the national past', as their critics have argued, the findings presented in this book make clear that they do not appeal to, nor work ideologically upon, all of their audiences in these terms. They also show that the audiences to whom idealised representations of a bourgeois/aristo-cratic past appealed most strongly, or who were most disposed to respond to heritage films in such terms – represented most prominently in this study by the NT cohort – were more likely to be insecurely or marginally middle-class than drawn from a securely privileged elite. Thus almost half the NT cohort, and more than 60% of TOs, were concentrated in household social grade B rather than A, with a significant class C1 presence in both cohorts; and 43% of all class B respondents, and one-third of all NTs, were drawn from a single, highly revealing, occupational culture: teachers.

When period-film audiences' attitudes and viewing positions are inter-preted in the light of such specifics – and when we learn that, for significant parts of this audience, membership of the middle classes has been contingent on social mobility and/or concentrated in non-elite pedagogic occupations – such insights shed a different light on the NT audience's embrace of (and, indeed, over-investment in) the discourses of class, quality and authenticity around heritage cinema than if such respondents were securely upper-middle-class. Indeed, the combined prevalence of upward social mobility (frequently *via* education), class B occupations and a pedagogic occupational culture sug-gests why TOs and NTs alike might be motivated to assert a middle-class, or at least 'educated', identity through forms and practices of cultural consump-tion which lend themselves to the forms of exercise of cultural competences and assertion of cultural distinction explored in this book.

We have seen, however, that this assertion took radically different forms in the TO and NT audiences. These differences were coloured by most TOs' experience of the post-World War II British state education system versus

NTs' experience of a traditionalist, academically selective education: hegemonic in the sense of teaching strong certainties about cultural value and social consensus, delivered in a more rigid and explicit class society than that experienced by TOs, and in an imperial rather than post-colonial era. The contrasts between the NT audience's traditionalist schooling in an era of certainties about cultural value, the literary canon, social class and British superiority, and the TO audience's more varied (but predominantly state) school experiences and degree study in the post-1960s, post-structuralist era – characterised by a more critical, questioning attitude to these certainties – are of key significance to our understanding of the two audiences' distinct forms of engagement with period films, and their contrasting cultural–political positions in relation to the heritage debate and beyond. Yet NT respondents' huge investment in these certainties can only be fully understood if we take into account their many vulnerabilities: their generational alienation, tacit class insecurities, and in certain cases a limited education.

And while TOs engaged with period films in ways that demonstrably exercised their particular forms of cultural and graduate educational capital – for example, drawing on debates in literary criticism (around adaptation, the canon, or 'the Great Tradition') or Cultural Studies – this same capital spawned their defining self-consciousness as an audience. For virtually all TOs, their relationships with period films – and, crucially, the terms in which they felt able to articulate and justify their enjoyment of them – were mediated and burdened by prior knowledge.

In conclusion, a major unanticipated finding of this study has been the extent to which both the National Trust and *Time Out* audiences' very different relationships with period films – and their own articulations of these relationships in their survey replies – were permeated and constrained, if in different ways, by existing media, critical or scholarly discourses around heritage cinema. I had hoped that at least some respondents would write in a personal way about their enjoyment of period films, in terms that broke away from the established binarisms of the heritage-film debate, perhaps even to establish a distinct, *audience*-led reception discourse or discourses. But in practice this occurred relatively little in the replies from either cohort. Where NT respondents absorbed existing conservative and traditionalist discourses – to write in an impersonal tone that presented the merits of both heritage films and the literary 'classics' as self-evident fact, rather than a matter of personal taste – TOs' overriding (self-)consciousness around the heritage-film debate too often left the question of their personal enjoyment of (or displeasure in) period films frustratingly evaded. Some TOs did, however, react creatively to the debate to engage with issues around adaptation or genre definition in ways that sought to stretch – or occasionally trash – its boundaries; while others referenced or recommended iconoclastic films (from Kubrick's 1975 *Barry Lyndon* to Ken

McMullen's 1987 *Partition*) that might form the basis of alternative period-film canons.

The most visible strand in the body of 'new' academic work in audience and reception studies that has emerged since the mid 1990s has insisted above all on the interpretative – and wider – *activity* and *freedom* of audiences. Key influences on the field, such as Henry Jenkins's 1992 study of fan subcultures and fan fiction in *Textual Poachers*, and foundational *film* audience studies such as *Knowing Audiences* – Martin Barker and Kate Brooks's 1998 account of the engagements of 'friends, fans and foes' with the big-screen comic-strip adaptation (of) *Judge Dredd* (Danny Canon, USA, 1995) – have all tended to envision audiences as autonomous, highly participatory, *knowing* and even creative makers of meaning.[11] It is no coincidence that so much of this foundational work has focused on fandom, cult genres or texts, and the participatory (and interventive) cultures that come with this, rather than audiences who might not identify themselves in these terms, or genres – such as documentary – less likely to attract such forms of engagement.[12] As the cover blurb for Mat Hills's 2002 book *Fan Cultures* states outright, fans 'are the ultimate active audience'; and the motivations powering much of the 'new' audience scholarship (in Media as much as Film Studies) – whether anti-censorship/social-libertarian, celebratory/consumerist, or (in the case of the fan-academic) personal – give it a notably heavy investment in the active, knowing audience.[13]

The findings presented in *Heritage Film Audiences* demonstrate strongly, however, that there are film audiences, cultures or subcultures and niches, for which such an emphasis (or certainly overinvestment) may be inappropriate or even misguided. This book has demonstrated beyond doubt the diversity and complexity of identities, responses and viewing positions among the (plural) audiences who watch and enjoy period films – including their activity and, at times, creativity. But, far from showing the NT and TO audiences to be free to respond to these films and use them creatively as they wish, unconstrained by dominant or 'legitimate' readings, it has illustrated in detail how their responses and positions are unavoidably mediated and shaped by the existing discourses around period films – not least those around 'heritage cinema'. If the guilelessness of the NT audience in relation to these discourses was far from 'knowing', the TO cohort proved to be not so much a 'knowing' audience as an audience who knew too much.

One possibility is that the particularities of the audiences who are attracted to 'quality' period films and 'heritage films', the films themselves, and the dictatorial nature of the critical and media discourses around them – not least, the top-down, critic-led origins of the very idea of the 'heritage film' – may conspire to produce an overdetermined, far from autonomous audience culture or cultures. A parallel possibility, however, is that there may be a current tendency in empirical film-audience studies – born, understandably, of its eagerness to jettison the last vestiges of textual determinism and to celebrate the power of the audience/fan/consumer as a maker of meaning – to overinvest in, or overstate, the autonomy and freedom of film audiences.

NOTES

1. www.participations.org (homepage) and www.participations.org/introduction.htm [2 August 2010].
2. Higson, *English Heritage, English Cinema*, p. 105.
3. King, 'Crossing thresholds'.
4. Gelder, *Subcultures*.
5. Cohen, quoted by Hebdige in *Subculture*, p. 77; Hebdige, *Subculture*, p. 78; both cited in Turner, *British Cultural Studies*, p. 105.
6. Thanks are due to Francis Mulhern for his suggestion, and discussion, of the notion of 'the subaltern' as an appropriate terminology for the specific form of subculture represented by the NT audience.
7. Wollen, 'Over our shoulders'; Higson, 'Re-presenting the national past'.
8. Bordwell and Carroll (eds), *Post-Theory*.
9. Branston, *Cinema and Cultural Modernity*, p. 143.
10. This point is argued by Bill Nichols in 'Form wars', p. 64.
11. Jenkins, *Textual Poachers*; Barker with Brooks, *Knowing Audiences*. Jenkins's work (for example, 'Reception theory and audience research') at times pushes the 'interpretative freedom' ethos much further to focus on fans as proactive rewriters of accepted textual meaning (for example, via the writing of 'fanfic' – fan fiction – and, within this, sub-genres such as slash fiction), raising radical questions about whether the line between legitimate and illegitimate interpretation has any validity at all.
12. Two studies of the audiences for big-screen documentaries have, in fact, now been published: see Austin, *Watching the World* and Hardie, 'Rollercoasters and reality'.
13. This 'heavy investment' extends to the body of (libertarian) work – initially prompted by opposition to the 'media effects' tradition – concerned with audience responses to 'extreme' violent and/or sexual material. See, for instance, Barker and Petley (eds), *Ill Effects*; Barker's 2006 study (commissioned by the British Board of Film Classification) of audience responses to five films featuring problematic depictions of sexual violence, as reported in Selfe, 'Inflected accounts and irreversible journeys'; and Barker's small study, 'Loving and hating *Straw Dogs*' (conducted with his own students as respondents).

Appendices

The Heritage Audience Survey Questionnaire

PART 1: YOUR FILM-VIEWING HABITS AND GENERAL FILM TASTES

Q1: How often do you watch a film **of any kind**, at the cinema or at home on TV or video? Please tick the **one** box for each question which best reflects your film-viewing habits.
(Multiple-choice options: 2 times a week or more / Once a week / About 2-3 times a month / About once a month / Once every 2 months / 2-5 times a year / Once a year or less / Never.)

Q1a: How often do you see a film **at the cinema**?
Q1b: How often do you watch a feature film (i.e. full-length film) **on TV**?
Q1c: How often do you **rent/hire** a feature film to watch on video?
Q1d: How often do you watch a film which you (or someone else) have **bought or home-taped on video**?

Q2: Out of **all** the films you watch – in the cinema, on TV or on video – what proportion would you say are **period films**? Please tick the **one** box which applies best to you. (By '**period films**', I mean any films made recently but **set in past times** – or older films which were set in the past at the time when they were made.)
(Multiple-choice options: Only a few / Less than half / About half / Most / Virtually all.)

Q3: If you go out to see films at the cinema, **what kinds of cinema** do you tend to visit (**Q3a**) to see **films in general** and (**Q3b**) if you go to see **period films**? Please tick the boxes which best describe your usual film-going habits.
For both Q3a and Q3b, the tick-box options were:
Commercial cinemas *(Never / Sometimes / Mostly.)*
Independent or 'art' cinemas *(Never / Sometimes / Mostly.)*

Q4: Please list the names of the main cinemas (or other film venues) which you visit **regularly** or **most often**, giving the name of the town/city (and, for London cinemas, area) where they are located.

Q5: Are you a member – or mailing-list member – of any cinemas, cinema clubs or other venues which show films (e.g. arts centres)? *(Options: Yes / No.)*
If you answered **yes**, please give the names of these cinemas/film clubs/venues, naming the town/city (and, for London, area) where they are located.

Q6: Do you ever see films at film festivals? *(Options: Yes / No.)*

Q7: Do you ever **buy** feature films or TV programmes/series **on video**, or buy other kinds of pre-recorded video (or have them bought for you)? *(Options: Yes / No.)*
If you answered **no**, please go straight to **Q12**.

> **Q8**: Approximately how many **bought** videos of **feature films** (of all kinds) do you currently own (or share with your household)?
>
> **Q9**: Approximately how many of your bought videos are of **period films**?
>
> **Q10**: Please say roughly how many **bought** videos of **television period/costume dramas or drama serials** you currently own (or share with your household).
>
> **Q11**: Do you own or have use of any **other** kinds of bought videos – including other kinds of TV programmes – not covered by Q8–10 above? *(Options: Yes / No.)*
>
> If **yes**, please say roughly **how many** and give examples of programme/video titles or types.

Q12: Do you ever **home-tape/record** feature films or TV programmes on video **to keep** (rather than just recording them to watch when convenient and then erasing the tape for re-use)? *(Options: Yes / No.)* If you answered **no**, please go straight to **Q16**.

> **Q13**: How many **home-taped** videos of **feature films** (of any kind) do you currently own (or share with your household) and expect to keep?
>
> **Q14**: How many **home-taped** videos of **period films** do you currently own (or share with your household) and expect to keep?
>
> **Q15**: How many **home-taped** videos of **television** period/costume dramas or drama serials do you currently own (or share) and expect to keep?

Q16: A selection of (mostly recent) films from the USA, Britain, Ireland and other countries **set in the present or recent past** are listed below. Please **tick** the relevant boxes A–C to indicate which films you have **seen** (in the cinema, on video or on TV), and **circle** one number for each film (2, 1, 0 or –1) to indicate your **opinion** of it.
(Optional: if you wish, you can also circle numbers 1, 0 and –1 to express your impressions of films you have **not** seen.)
(Multiple-choice options: A: Have seen / B: Have not seen / C: Not sure or haven't heard of it / 2: Liked a lot / 1: Liked / 0: No strong opinion / –1: Disliked.)

> **Q16** listed 145 non-period films, subdivided under the following five headings and then listed A–Z by title. **For these lists of films, see the Selective Filmography** (pages 217–20).
>
> **Q16a: US and Canadian films** (58 films)
>
> **Q16b: British and Irish films** (44 films)
>
> **Q16c: Australian/New Zealand films** (9 films)
>
> **Q16d: European films** (27 films)
>
> **Q16e: Other non-English-language films** (7 films)

PART 2: YOUR TASTE IN PERIOD FILMS: WHICH DO YOU LIKE OR DISLIKE, AND WHY?

Q17: A selection of period films, mostly from the 1980s and 1990s, are listed below. Please **tick** the relevant boxes A–C to indicate which films you have **seen** (in the cinema, on video or on TV), and **circle** one number for each film (2, 1, 0 or –1) to indicate your opinion of it.
(Optional: if you wish, you can also circle numbers 1, 0 and –1 to express your impressions of films you have **not** seen.)

(Multiple-choice options: A: Have seen / B: Have not seen / C: Not sure or haven't heard of it / 2: Liked a lot / 1: Liked / 0: No strong opinion / −1: Disliked.)

Q17 listed 97 period films, subdivided under the following three headings and then listed A–Z by title. **For these lists of films, see the Selective Filmography** (pages 220–2).

Q17a: British and Irish films (52 films)

Q17b: European and non-English-language films (22 films)

Q17c: US, Australian and New Zealand films (23 films)

Q18: Do you have any special **favourite** period films? They can be of any kind, made in any decade and from any country – **including** films **not** listed in Q17. *(Options: Yes / No.)*

If you answered **yes**, please list these favourite films here. Please give approximate years in which they were released and say roughly how many times you have seen them.

Q19: Please **tick** the relevant box(es) A–F to indicate which of these British period TV drama serials you have watched, bought on video, home-taped to keep, etc.

(Multiple-choice options: A: Bought on video / B: Home-taped on video to keep / C: Watched all or part of and enjoyed / D: Watched all or part of but lost interest / E: Haven't seen / F: Not sure or haven't heard of it.)

Q19 listed the following decade options and selected drama serials. **For production credits for the latter, see the Selective Filmography** (page 223).

Any pre-1960 period TV drama

The Forsyte Saga (1960s)

Any other 1960s period TV drama

The Duchess of Duke Street (1970s)

Elizabeth R (1970s)

The Mayor of Casterbridge (1970s)

The Pallisers (1970s)

Poldark (1970s)

Upstairs Downstairs (1970s)

Any other 1970s period TV drama

Brideshead Revisited (1980s)

The Far Pavilions (1980s)

Fortunes of War (1980s)

The Jewel in the Crown (1980s)

Pride and Prejudice (1980s)

[Elizabeth Garvie/David Rintoul]

The Singing Detective (1980s)

Any other 1980s period TV drama

Clarissa (1990s)

Middlemarch (1990s)

Pride and Prejudice (1990s)

[Jennifer Ehle/Colin Firth]

The Tenant of Wildfell Hall (1996)

Emma (1996 – ITV)

Moll Flanders (1996)

Rhodes (1996)

Ivanhoe (1997)

Nostromo (1997)

Any other 1990s period TV drama

Q20: Do you have any special favourite **TV period/costume dramas or serials**? These can be of any kind, from any decade, and need not be listed in Q19. *(Options: Yes / No.)*

If you answered **yes**, please list these favourites here. Please give the approximate years in which they were shown and say roughly how many times you have seen them.

Q21: Please describe in your own words **what you most enjoy** about the period/costume films you watch. (Your answer to this question is especially important for my research, so please try to answer it as fully as possible. Please continue on a separate sheet if you need to. If you usually **dislike** period films, please indicate this in your answer and treat **Q22** as the more important question instead.)

Q22: Is there anything about (some or all) period/costume films that you particularly **dislike**, or specific period/costume films you really dislike? *(Options: Yes / No.)*

If **yes**, explain here what you dislike, naming specific films if you feel this is useful.

Q23a: Do you have any favourite actors and/or actresses? *(Options: Yes / No.)*

Q23b: Do you have favourite actors and/or actresses who appear in period films or TV period drama? *(Options: Yes / No.)*
    If you answered **yes** to Q23a or Q23b, please write in these performers' names here. (If the names for Q23b are the same as those for Q23a, just write 'same' in the box for Q23b.)

Q24: Do you **mainly** associate the actors and/or actresses you named in Q23b with period films and period TV drama? *(Options: Yes / No.)*

Q25: Have you ever watched period films or TV dramas **mainly because** any of the actors or actresses you named in Q23b were in them? *(Options: Yes / No.)*
    If **yes**, say which performer(s).

Q26: Do you also follow the careers of any of the actors or actresses you named in Q23b **outside** period films and TV dramas (e.g. in films set in the present or stage plays)? *(Options: Yes / No.)*
    If **yes**, say which performer(s).

Q27: *(Optional)* If you would like to say more about **one** favourite performer out of those you have mentioned above, please do so below, continuing on a separate sheet if you wish.

Q28a: Do you have any favourite film directors? *(Options: Yes / No.)*

Q28b: Do you have any favourite film directors who you especially associate with period/ costume films? *(Options: Yes / No.)*
    If you answered **yes** to Q28a or Q28b, please write in these directors' names here. (If the names for Q28b are the same as for Q28a, just write 'same' in the box for Q28b.)

Q29: Thinking about the particular kind(s) of period films you enjoy, which of the factors or ingredients listed below are **important** in explaining **your personal enjoyment** of these films? Which are less important, or irrelevant? Please circle **one** number for each factor listed to indicate how important or unimportant that factor is **for you**.
(If you **dislike** most period films, you may want to ignore this question and go straight to Q30.)

1. Compelling, involving plots (or stories).
2. Human drama and a focus on human dilemmas and problems.
3. Visual enjoyment.
4. Being able to identify with the characters in the films.
5. Stories which still feel relevant today.
6. Romance.
7. Looking at the landscapes and locations.
8. Looking at historic buildings.
9. Looking at period furnishings and interior decoration.
10. Looking at period costumes.
11. The films entertain me without making me work too hard.
12. They are challenging films which I have to get actively involved in to enjoy.
13. Complexity and intelligence of the films.
14. Literacy and wit of the films.
15. The pleasures of nostalgia.
16. The pleasures of escapism.
17. *(Films set since the late nineteenth century)* Personal memory or family history: they remind me of my life when younger or how my family used to live.
18. The fact that they are high-quality, well-made films.
19. The quality of the performances/acting.
20. Seeing leading British actors/actresses at their best.
21. Watching actors/actresses whom I find physically attractive.
22. Accurate reproduction of details of the period settings (e.g. buildings, transport methods, costumes).
23. The chance to learn more about life in the past (e.g. how society worked and how people lived).

24. The chance to learn more about important events in history.
25. *(Literary adaptations only)* The chance to relive the pleasures of the original novels or plays.
26. *(Literary adaptations only)* The chance to see respectful adaptations of important literary works.
27. Pride in seeing British cinema at its best.
28. Lack of explicit sex, violence or bad language.

(Multiple-choice options: 2: Very important to my enjoyment / 1: Quite important / 0: No strong feelings / −1: Not important / −2: Totally irrelevant to why I like period films.)

PART 3: YOUR ATTITUDES TO PERIOD FILMS

Q30: Listed below are some statements which people might make about their attitudes to recent British period films, their wider tastes, and their views on some related issues. Please tick the **one** box next to each statement which most closely reflects your own attitude, taste or opinion. (You may feel that some statements are more true of some kinds of period films than others. Please tick the answers which apply to **the kinds of period films you enjoy and see**. If you would like to add comments, please do so.)
(Multiple-choice options: A: Strongly agree / B: Agree / C: No strong opinion / D: Disagree / E: Strongly disagree / F: Not sure or don't know.)

1. I have enjoyed watching literary adaptations and costume dramas on TV and film for as long as I can remember.
2. When I hear that a new period or costume film has come out, I generally know that it will be my kind of film.
3. I'm only interested in certain kinds of period film; some don't appeal to me at all.
4. Watching period films/TV dramas enables me to escape from the routine of everyday life.
5. The look of period films is *the main* thing I enjoy about them.
6. I often find period films emotionally moving.
7. Period films and TV dramas can be very sexy.
8. Period films and TV dramas can be comic/funny.
9. I enjoy some period films because I find them visually or emotionally excessive, over-the-top or camp.
10. The characters in the period films I watch have similar values and concerns to me.
11. When people enjoy period films, it's because they identify with the lifestyles they show.
12. I get most involved in period films when they show situations and behaviour which I can identify with today.
13. Some of the period films I watch show exactly how people from my background would have lived in the past.
14. I enjoy period films without really identifying with the characters.
15. I don't think of myself as typical of the kind of person who watches period films or TV period drama.
16. I sometimes feel embarrassed about admitting that I enjoy period films.
17. I love the look of period films and TV dramas, and try to recreate elements of that style in my home.
18. I enjoy the visual style of period films and TV dramas, but my decorative and furnishing tastes in real life are quite different.

19. Some period decorative and furnishing styles don't appeal to me at all. (If you wish, give examples of likes/dislikes.)
20. I prefer modern design to the decorative styles of the past.
21. I would love to have lived in the times depicted in some of the period films I've seen.
22. The period films I enjoy show Britain as it was in better times.

Statements 23–31 refer to film and television literary adaptations only:

23. I enjoy film and TV period literary adaptations whether I have read the book or not.
24. I hardly ever watch adaptations unless I have already read the novel or seen the play.
25. I sometimes read novels *because* I have enjoyed adaptations of them on film or TV.
26. TV and film literary adaptations often disappoint me because they don't live up to the pleasures of the original novel or play.
27. Period films and dramas based on classic novels or plays are nearly always inferior to the literary originals.
28. I enjoy films (such as *Orlando* or *Richard III*) which adapt classic books and plays in daring and imaginative ways.
29. It's wrong for film adaptations from novels and plays to make too many creative changes to the author's work.
30. Literary adaptations on film and TV are valuable because they encourage people to read more classic literature.
31. Films which are adapted from great novels or plays are usually artistically superior to those which are not.

32. I like to see period films which are critical of how things were in the past and give me an insight into the harsh realities of life then.
33. I enjoy period films for their atmosphere, regardless of whether the historical details are accurate or not.
34. It is very important for filmmakers to ensure that all the historical information in period films is accurate.
35. It is very important for filmmakers to ensure that all the details of costumes and settings in period films are accurate.
36. Filmmakers should not be obsessive about getting every single period detail correct.
37. I enjoy period films (such as *Orlando*) which make daring and creative use of period styles in their design.
38. Costume films and TV dramas are just harmless entertainment.
39. The period films I enjoy are often critical of the hypocrisies and class attitudes of the past.
40. I generally prefer films which are about ordinary people.
41. Most critics regard period films as British cinema at its best.
42. I'm always pleased when British period films do well abroad.
43. It's exciting when contemporary British films like *Trainspotting* are successful.
44. Period films and literary adaptations are definitely films for a discerning audience.
45. Period/costume films and TV dramas are rare examples of quality among the films and TV programmes which are made these days.
46. Period films and TV dramas and literary adaptations are valuable because they promote British culture and traditions.
47. The classics of English literature should be at the heart of our education and culture.

48. Period films and TV dramas represent the right kind of image of Britain to the rest of the world.

49. British cinema is the best in the world.

50. Period films and TV dramas are valuable because they make people realise the importance of preserving our great historic buildings.

51. It's very important that new architecture should be encouraged and funded in Britain.

52. We should not be preserving the buildings and heritage of our past at the expense of investing in our future.

53. Period films and TV dramas encourage us to retreat into the past rather than facing up to the important issues of the present.

54. Period films and TV dramas nearly always show events from the point of view of the middle and upper classes.

55. It worries me that period films and TV dramas are more interested in the lives of the privileged than in the concerns of ordinary people.

56. Period films and TV dramas do nothing to help us really understand history.

57. Period films and TV dramas can be damaging because they present an idealised, unrealistic vision of the past.

58. Most period films made in Britain today are just commercials for the National Trust and heritage industry.

59. A lot of critics seem to have a really low opinion of period films and TV dramas.

The last 15 statements concern your wider taste in films:

60. It's usually true that very few new films come out which I want to see.

61. When a new costume or period film comes out, I usually make an effort to see it.

62. I like many other kinds of contemporary films as well as costume or period films.

63. I usually prefer period and costume films to modern Hollywood (American) films.

64. I prefer older films (e.g. films made in the 1940s, 1950s, etc.) to most of the films being made today.

65. I like to see new British films which are set in the present day.

66. I like to see foreign-language films from other countries.

67. I enjoy seeing blockbuster films with spectacular special effects (such as *Independence Day* or *Mission Impossible*).

68. I enjoyed the British comedy film *Four Weddings and a Funeral*. (If you have not seen this film, state 'not seen'.)

69. I feel that most of the films made today are aimed at people like me.

70. Too many new films today are aimed more at men than at women.

71. Films these days seem to be aimed at younger and younger audiences.

72. Over-explicit screen sex puts me off seeing a lot of the films shown today.

73. Screen violence puts me off seeing a lot of the films shown today.

74. Bad language puts me off seeing a lot of the films shown today.

PART 4: YOUR OTHER CULTURAL AND LEISURE INTERESTS

Questions 31 to 33 asked respondents about indices of their cultural consumption and committed interests beyond film – such as arts, club or charity memberships – but this information was not systematically analysed in the study.

Q34: Which of the following (British) daily or weekly newspapers do you read regularly or look at during the week and on Saturday or Sunday?

Daily Mail	*Star*
Mirror	*Daily Sport*
Daily Telegraph	*The European* (Published in 1990–8)
Guardian	*The Voice* (Black-interest weekly newspaper)
Financial Times	*Evening Standard* (London)
Independent	Any free local weekly paper
The Times	Any paid-for local weekly paper
Sun	Any paid-for local daily paper
I don't read a daily/weekly paper	*Sunday Mirror*
Mail on Sunday	*Sunday People*
Sunday Express	*News of the World*
The Observer	*Sunday Sport*
Sunday Telegraph	I don't read a Sunday paper
Sunday Times	

Questions 35 to 36 asked respondents which magazines/periodicals they read (open question) and about their leisure activities and interests (multiple-choice), but this information was not systematically analysed in the study.

Q37: Are you a member – or a supporter – of any political party?
(Options: Yes – member / Yes – supporter / No.)
   If you ticked either of the **yes** boxes, please say which party you support or are a member of.

PART 5: MORE ABOUT YOU

Q38: Are you: *Male / Female?*

Q39: Please give your current age and year of birth.

Q40: Please give your place/country of birth.

Q41: Where do you live now? *(City or town / Area (if in a city) / County.)*

Q42: How would you describe your **(Q42a)** nationality and **(Q42b)** race/ethnicity?

Q43: Are you currently: *Employed full-time / Employed part-time / Self-employed full-time / Self-employed part-time / Studying full-time / Studying part-time / Unemployed / Retired / Homemaker / Other (please specify)?*

Q44: Please describe your current occupation or employment.

Q45: If retired, what was your most recent previous occupation before retirement?

Q46: Do you currently live in: *Your own house or flat owned or mortgaged / A rented house or flat / Other (please specify)?*

Q47: Are you currently: *Single / Married / In a relationship but not married / Divorced or separated / Widowed / Other (please specify)?*

Q48: Do you currently live: *Alone / With husband/wife/partner / With husband/wife/partner plus child/ren / With child/ren only / With other family member(s) / Sharing with friend(s) / Other (please specify)?*

Q49: If you are married or in a relationship, please give your partner's current occupation.

Q50a: If currently in a relationship, is your partner: *The opposite sex to you / The same sex as you?*

Q50b: When you are in a relationship, is your partner likely to be: *The opposite sex to you / The same sex as you / Could be either sex?*

Q51: Which of the following school qualifications do you have?
(Old) School Certificate / (Old) CSE(s) / (Old) 'O' Level(s) / GCSE(s) / Scottish (SCE) Ordinaries / 'A' Level(s) / (Old) Higher Certificate / (Old) Matriculation / Scottish (SCE) Higher(s) / Other (please specify).

Q52: Which of the above qualifications (if any) do you have in: **Q52a** English Language? **Q52b** English Literature?

Q53: Have you undertaken any further or higher education at college, polytechnic or university? *(Options: Yes / No.)*
    If you answered **yes**, please give details: *Name of college or university / Subject(s) studied or researched / Type(s) of qualification.*

Q54: If you have any qualifications **not** covered by Q51–Q53 – e.g. professional or work-related qualifications, or gained abroad – please list them here.

Q55: What kind(s) of secondary school did you attend?
Comprehensive / Grammar (non-fee-paying) / Secondary modern / Technical school / Grant-maintained/voluntary aided (non-fee-paying) / Direct-grant (pre-1976) or fee-paying grammar / Other private day school / Public school / Other private boarding school / Other (please specify).

Q56: What have been the main **occupation(s)** of your parent(s), including their current (or, if they have retired or died, most recent) occupation(s)?
(Mother / Father / Other parent figures where relevant.)

PART 6: AND FINALLY . . .

Most of the information you supply in this questionnaire will be referred to in my research only in ways which will not reveal your identity. However, I may want to quote from some of your more detailed answers (mostly in Part 2) by name.

Q57: Are you happy for me to quote you in my research findings? *(Options: Yes / No.)*
    If **yes**, would you rather be quoted: *By Name / Anonymously?*

Q58: Would you be prepared to be quoted if this research is published in a book or article? *(Options: Yes / No.)*
    If **yes**, would you rather be quoted: *By Name / Anonymously?*

Thank you for taking the time to help with this research project. If there is any further information you wish to add, please continue below and/or attach additional sheets (stating which questions they relate to).

Your comments on this questionnaire itself are also very welcome; they will help me to take account of any problems with the wording of my questions when I analyse your answers.

Demographic profiles of source populations for the survey: the National Trust (NT) membership

Sex	NT members	National profile*
Male	51%	48%
Female	49%	52%

Age	NT members	National profile**
Under 25	1%	17%
25–34	9%	20%
35–44	17%	17%
45–54	2%	15%
55–64	22%	12%
65+	31%	20%

Marital status	NT members	National profile**
Married	74%	64%
Single	13%	22%
Separated/divorced	4%	6%
Widowed	9%	8%
Have children	71%	–
Living at home	29%	–
Not living at home	47%	–

Socio-economic class (on previous employment)	NT members	National profile*
AB	50%	20%
C1	36%	27%
C2DE	14%	53%
Occupational status		
Retired	45%	17%

Source: National Trust postal survey, sent out to members in 16 NT regions with the *National Trust Magazine*, Autumn 1993.

The National Trust's comparative data sources: * = National Readership Survey, January–December 1993. ** = Target Group Index October 1992–September 1993.

Demographic profiles of source populations for the survey: *Time Out* (TO) magazine readership

All	Universe profile*		*Time Out* readers profile	
	1,000s	%	1,000s	%
Total	16,259	100%	602	100%
Male	7,909	49%	376	63%
Female	8,351	51%	226	38%
Age				
15–24	2,492	15%	208	35%
18–24	1,714	11%	182	30%
25–34	3,512	22%	224	37%
35–44	2,942	18%	79	13%
45+	7,314	45%	91	15%
Class				
AB	4,300	26%	233	39%
C1	4,994	31%	214	36%
C2DE	6,966	43%	156	26%

Women	Universe profile*		*Time Out* readers profile	
	1,000s	%	1,000s	%
Total	8,351	100%	226	100%
Age				
15–24	1,215	15%	80	35%
18–24	853	10%	68	30%
25–34	1,742	21%	81	36%
35–44	1,519	18%	23	10%
45+	3,875	46%	42	19%
Class				
AB	1,973	24%	80	35%
C1	2,723	33%	91	40%
C2DE	3,654	44%	55	24%
Men	Universe profile*		*Time Out* readers profile	
	1,000s	%	1,000s	%
Total	8,351	100%	226	100%
Age				
15–24	1,277	16%	80	34%
18–24	857	11%	68	30%
25–34	1,769	22%	81	38%
35–44	1,423	18%	23	15%
45+	3,439	44%	42	13%
Class				
AB	2,326	29%	153	41%
C1	2,270	29%	123	33%
C2DE	3,439	42%	101	27%

Source: *Time Out* Magazine Readership Survey 1997.

*Universe profile = all adults, London and South-East England.

The Heritage Audience Survey sample: age/gender distribution of the two (National Trust and *Time Out*) cohorts, compared to age/gender distribution of the overall UK cinemagoing population (1994)

THE UK CINEMAGOING POPULATION (1994)			Age group					Summary	
		Total	7–24	25–34	35–44	45+		25–44	45+
% **Distribution**: *Caviar 12* respondents claiming to 'ever go' to the cinema	Male	50%	19%	11%	8%	12%		19%	12%
	Female	50%	16%	10%	8%	16%		18%	16%
	Both sexes	100%	35%	22%	16%	28%		38%	28%

HERITAGE AUDIENCE SURVEY RESPONDENTS

WHOLE SAMPLE

				Age group						Summary		As a % of the whole sample	
		Total	7–24	25–34	35–44	45–54	55–64	65–74	75+	25–44	45+	25–44	45+
% Distribution	Male	26%	0	3%	8%	2%	3%	8%	2%	11%	15%		
Numbers by age/sex		24		3	7	2	3	7	2	10	14		
% Distribution	Female	74%		10%	5%	10%	17%	26%	5%	15%	59%		
Numbers by age/sex		68		9	5	9	16	24	5	14	54		
% Distribution	Both sexes	100%		13%	13%	12%	21%	34%	8%	26%	74%		
Numbers by age/sex		92		12	12	11	19	31	7	24	68		

TO SUB-SAMPLE

		Total	7–24	25–34	35–44	45–54	55–64	65–74	75+	25–44	45+	25–44	45+
% Distribution	Male	43%	0	10%	23%	7%	3%	0		33%	10%	11%	3%
Numbers by age/sex		13		3	7	2	1			10	3		
% Distribution	Female	57%		30%	17%	7%	3%			47%	10%	15%	3%
Numbers by age/sex		17		9	5	2	1			14	3		
% Distribution	Both sexes	100%		40%	40%	13%	7%			80%	20%	26%	7%
Numbers by age/sex		30		12	12	4	2			24	6		

NT SUB-SAMPLE

		Total	7–24	25–34	35–44	45–54	55–64	65–74	75+	25–44	45+	25–44	45+
% Distribution	Male	18%	0			0%	3%	11%	3%	0	18%	0	12%
Numbers by age/sex		11				0	2	7	2		11		
% Distribution	Female	82%				11%	24%	39%	8%		82%		55%
Numbers by age/sex		51				7	15	24	5		51		
% Distribution	Both sexes	100%				11%	27%	50%	11%		100%		67%
Numbers by age/sex		62				7	17	31	7		62		

Sources: Claire Monk, analysis of own Heritage Audience Survey data (1998); and 1994 survey data from *Caviar 12* (1995), Volume 1: Table 1/3 and Appendix A.

The Heritage Audience Survey sample: age/ gender distribution of the two (National Trust and *Time Out*) cohorts, compared to UK cinema audiences for selected 'period drama' feature-film releases (1994 and 1992)

Caviar 12 (1994) and *Caviar 10* (1992) respondents who had seen selected period films at the cinema*	Male	Female	Age group		
			7–24	25–44	45+
The Piano (3% of *Caviar 12* respondents = 100%)	35%	65%	22%	41%	37%
Shadowlands (4% of *Caviar 12* respondents = 100%)	38%	62%	18%	33%	49%
The Remains of the Day (3% of *Caviar 12* respondents = 100%)	39%	61%	18%	39%	44%
The Age of Innocence (2% of *Caviar 12* respondents = 100%)	48%	52%	24%	38%	37%
Howards End (2% of *Caviar 10* respondents = 100%)	49%	51%	24%	44%	31%
Schindler's List (9% of *Caviar 12* respondents = 100%)	51%	49%	22%	41%	37%
Distribution averaged across the 6 films	43.3%	56.7%	21.3%	39.3%	39.2%

Heritage Audience Survey respondents		Total	Age group			
			7–24	25–44	45+	65+
WHOLE SAMPLE	**Male**	26%		11%	15%	10%
% Distribution		24		10	14	9
Numbers by age/sex	**Female**	74%		15%	59%	32%
		68		14	54	29
	Both sexes	100%		26%	74%	41%
		92		24	68	38
TO SUB-SAMPLE	**Male**	43%		33%	10%	0
% Distribution		13		10	3	
Numbers by age/sex	**Female**	57%		47%	10%	
		17		14	3	
	Both sexes	100%		80%	20%	
		30		24	6	
NT SUB-SAMPLE	**Male**	18%			18%	15%
% Distribution		11			11	9
Numbers by age/sex	**Female**	82%			82%	47%
		51			51	29
	Both sexes	100%			100%	61%
		62			62	38

Sources: Claire Monk, analysis of Heritage Audience Survey data (1998).
Survey data from 1992 on *Howards End* from *Caviar* 10 (1993). Survey data from 1994 on all other films from *Caviar* 12 (1995), Volume 1: Table 1/3 and Appendix A.

*Caviar sample sizes: 2,799 respondents in 1992, 2,737 respondents in 1994. The *Caviar* reports express data in 1000s and/or as percentages, as if they had surveyed the entire UK population in the years concerned. For a fuller presentation, and discussion, of the *Caviar* data, see Monk, 'Heritage films and the British cinema audience in the 1990s'.

ABC1 socio-economic class of Heritage Audience Survey respondents (last occupation of Household Review Person) compared to ABC1 class distribution of the overall UK cinemagoing population (1994)

				ABC1 social grade						ABC1 summary
THE UK CINEMAGOING POPULATION (1994)	(100%)	A	B	AB	C1	C2	DE			summary
Cavar 12: % distribution by class of total UK cinema visits per year				26%	30%	23%	21%			56%
HERITAGE AUDIENCE SURVEY: ALL RESPONDENTS		A	B	AB	C1	C2	Unemployed	Not known		ABC1 summary
WHOLE SAMPLE	Total									
% Distribution	(100%)	16%	53%	70%	26%	1%	1%	2%		96%
Numbers	92	15	49	64	24	1	1	2		88
TO SUB-SAMPLE	Total									
% Distribution	(100%)	7%	63%	70%	27%	0%	3%	0		97%
Numbers	30	2	19	21	8	0	1	0		29
NT SUB-SAMPLE	Total									
% Distribution	(100%)	21%	48%	69%	26%	2%	0	3%		95%
Numbers	62	13	30	43	16	1	0	2		59

% DISTRIBUTION FOR AUDIENCES CLAIMING TO VISIT THE CINEMA TWICE A YEAR OR MORE

	A	B	AB	C1	C2	DE		ABC1 summary
Caviar 12 respondents (1994) claiming to visit the cinema twice a year or more (= 44% of all *Caviar 12* respondents)								
% Distribution by ABC1 class (100%)			29%	30%	22%	19%		59%

HERITAGE AUDIENCE SURVEY RESPONDENTS	A	B	AB	C1	C2	Unemployed	Not known	ABC1 summary
WHOLE SAMPLE Total								
% Distribution (100%)	13%	56%	69%	25%	1%	1%	3%	94%
Numbers (= 74% of all) 68	9	38	47	17	1	1	2	64
TO SUB-SAMPLE Total								
% Distribution (100%)	7%	62%	69%	28%	0%	3%	0	97%
Numbers (= 97% of all TOs) 29	2	18	20	8	0	1	0	28
NT SUB-SAMPLE Total								
% Distribution (100%)	18%	51%	69%	23%	3%	0	5%	92%
Numbers (= 63% of all NTs) 39	7	20	27	9	1	0	2	36

Sources: Claire Monk, analysis of Heritage Audience Survey data (1998). Data for 1994 from *Caviar 12* (1995), Volume 1: Table 1/2 and Appendix A.

ABC1 socio-economic class of Heritage Audience Survey respondents (by household) compared to ABC1 class distribution of UK cinema audiences for selected 'period drama' feature–film releases (1994 and 1992)

Caviar 12 (1994) and Caviar 10 (1992) respondents who had seen selected period films at the cinema*	AB	C1	C2	DE	ABC1 summary
The Piano (NZ) (3% of Caviar 12 respondents = 100%)	51%	32%	9%	7%	83%
The Remains of the Day (UK) (3% of Caviar 12 respondents = 100%)	50%	27%	14%	9%	77%
Howards End (UK) (2% of Caviar 10 respondents = 100%)	37%	37%	18%	8%	74%
Shadowlands (UK) (4% of Caviar 12 respondents = 100%)	44%	29%	15%	12%	73%
Schindler's List (USA) (9% of Caviar 12 respondents = 100%)	38%	35%	15%	13%	73%
The Age of Innocence (US) (2% of Caviar 12 respondents = 100%)	41%	28%	17%	14%	69%
Distribution averaged across the 6 films	43.5%	31.3%	14.7%	10.5%	74.8%

HERITAGE AUDIENCE SURVEY RESPONDENTS	Total	AB	C1	C2	Other	ABC1 summary
WHOLE SAMPLE **% Distribution** / Numbers	(100%)	**70%**	**26%**	1%	3%	**96%**
	92	64	24	1	3	88
TO SUB-SAMPLE **% Distribution** / Numbers	(100%)	**70%**	**27%**	**0**	3%	**97%**
	30	21	8		1	29
NT SUB-SAMPLE **% Distribution** / Numbers	(100%)	**69%**	**26%**	2%	3%	**95%**
	62	43	16	1	2	59

Sources: Claire Monk, analysis of Heritage Audience Survey data (1998).
Data for 1992 on *Howards End* from *Caviar 10* (1993), Volume 1: Table 12/11. Data for 1994 on all other films from *Caviar 12* (1995), Volume 1: Table 1/2 and Appendix A.

*See note to Appendix 3.2.

Nationality and race/ethnicity of Heritage Audience Survey respondents

Nationality (as self-reported by respondents)	All respondents		TO		NT	
	%	No.	%	No.	%	No.
British	72%	66	50%	15	82%	51
English	15%	14	10%	3	18%	11
Welsh	1%	1	3%	1	None	
Scottish	1%	1	3%	1		
Irish	2%	2	7%	2		
British–American	2%	2	7%	2		
American and American–hyphenated nationalities	2%	2	7%	2		
British–Iranian	1%	1	3%	1		
British–Danish	1%	1	3%	1		
Dutch	1%	1	3%	1		
New Zealand	1%	1	3%	1		
Race/ethnicity (self-reported)	**All respondents**		**TO**		**NT**	
	%	No.	%	No.	%	No.
White British or Irish (and similar descriptions)	63%	58	63%	19	63%	39
Unspecified (In all cases, stated nationality was British, English or part-British)	20%	18	10%	3	24%	15
White European or European	9%	8	3%	1	11%	7
White Other (USA, New Zealand)	4%	4	13%	4	None	
Black (Caribbean or African)	2%	2	7%	2		
Jewish	1%	1	0	0	2%	1
Iranian	1%	1	3%	1	None	

Source: Claire Monk, analysis of Heritage Audience Survey data (1998).

UK regions where Heritage Audience Survey respondents lived at the date of completing the questionnaire

	All respondents		TO		NT	
	%	No.	%	No.	%	No.
Greater London	37%	34	90%	27	11%	7
South-East or Southern England	20%	18	7%	2	26%	16
Northern England	16%	15	None		24%	15
Central England and the Midlands	11%	10			16%	10
West or South-West England	9%	8	3%	1	11%	7
Wales	5%	5	None		8%	5
East Anglia	2%	2			3%	2
Scotland and Northern Ireland	None					

Source: Claire Monk, analysis of Heritage Audience Survey data (1998).

Neighbourhood types where Heritage Audience Survey respondents lived

NEIGHBOURHOOD TYPE Derived from the 54 Acorn postcode-based residential neighbourhood classifications in the *Acorn User Guide 2001*	All respond-ents		TO		NT	
	%	No.	%	No.	%	No.
Urban affluent (UA) (2001 Acorn neighbourhood types 16, 19–21, 23)	18%	17	43%	13	6%	4
Urban, socio-economically 'average' or varied (U) (Acorn type 24)	8%	7	20%	6	2%	1
Urban, some poverty (UP) (Acorn types 38, 47, 53)	7%	6	20%	6	None	
Small/regional town centres (T) (Acorn types 8, 22, 35, 37)	9%	8	None		13%	8
Suburban affluent (SA) (Acorn types 1, 3–5, 10–11, 13–14, 26, 28–29, 36)	36%	33	10%	3	48%	30
Suburban, socio-economically 'average' or varied (S) (Acorn type 17)	2%	2	7%	2	None	
Suburban intermediate/blue-collar (SB) (Acorn types 30–32, 34)	7%	6	None		10%	6
Affluent 'commuter villages' (RA) (Acorn type 2)	8%	7			11%	7
Rural (R) (Acorn types 6–7, 27)	7%	6			10%	6
Summary: **Urban** (UA, U, UP)	33%	30	83%	25	8%	5
Summary: **Suburban** (SA, S, SB)	45%	41	17%	5	58%	36
Summary: **Rural** (RA, R)	14%	13	None		21%	13
Summary: **'Affluent'** (UA, SA, RA)	62%	57	53%	16	66%	41
Summary: **Less affluent** (U, UP, S, SB, R, T)	38%	35	47%	14	34%	21

Source: Claire Monk, analysis of Heritage Audience Survey data (1998), using the CACI Acorn (A Classification Of Residential Neighbourhoods) schema.

The neighbourhood types were derived from respondents' home postcodes using the CACI Acorn classifications in the *Acorn User Guide 2001* (www.caci.co.uk/pd-caci-brochures.htm, 12 November 2002), which fit each UK postcode into one of 54 'typical' Acorn neighbourhood types (nested within 17 broader groups).

The Acorn neighbourhood descriptions applicable to individual postcodes were accessed via www.upmystreet.com (12–16 November 2002). Heritage Audience Survey respondents were drawn from 35 of Acorn's 54 neighbourhood types. To simplify interpretation, these are clustered into nine larger groups in the table presented in this Appendix.

Since this analysis was completed, CACI has revised the Acorn schema more than once. As these revisions have involved reclassification of some postcodes, revised definitions, and an increase from 54 to 56 neighbourhood types, the 2001-2 ACORN types utilised in my analysis do not map precisely on to the more recent ACORN schemas. For a map of the 2009 Acorn classifications, see www.caci.co.uk/acorn2009/acornmap_ext.asp. For further information, see http://www.caci.co.uk/ACORN.aspx (14 September 2010).

Classificatory groupings used in analysis of respondents' period film tastes

For the lists of films in the form they were presented to respondents in Question 17 of the Questionnaire (**Appendix 2.1**), and production details, see the **Selective Filmography** (page 216).

BRITISH AND IRISH PERIOD FILMS

BH1 Core British Heritage Films (11 films)

Films generally agreed to be exemplars of heritage cinema.

Another Country   *A Passage to India*
Chariots of Fire   *The Remains of the Day*
A Handful of Dust   *A Room with a View*
Howards End   *The Shooting Party*
Little Dorrit   *Where Angels Fear to Tread*
Maurice

BH2 British Borderline Heritage Films (12 films)

Films dating from the late 1980s to 1990s with heritage characteristics, but whose status as heritage cinema is more variably and less clearly established in reception discourses.

Enchanted April   *Persuasion** (See note on page 211)
The English Patient   *Restoration*
Hamlet   *Sense and Sensibility*
Heat and Dust   *Tom & Viv*
The Madness of King George *White Mischief*
A Month in the Country   *Wilde*

BPH British Post-Heritage Films (5 films)

Films with clear 'post-heritage' characteristics (see page 23 and Note 65 to Chapter 1), seeking to distance themselves in some sense from 'heritage' filmmaking.

Angels and Insects   *Orlando*
Carrington   *Richard III*
Jude

BHY British and Irish Historical Films (8 films)

The genre characteristics of these films, their (often political) concerns and their modes of historical engagement clearly distinguish them from 'heritage cinema'.

Anne Devlin *Hedd Wyn*
Century *Land and Freedom*
Comrades *Michael Collins*
December Bride *Rob Roy*

BR1 British Retro Films Type 1 (5 films)

British films set in the decades during or after World War II (1939 onwards), regarded by at least some critics as offering a comfortable perspective which permits nostalgic viewing.

Dance with a Stranger *The Krays*
Distant Voices, Still Lives *Shadowlands*
Hope and Glory

BR2 British Retro Films Type 2 (5 films)

British films set in the decades during or after World War II, but depicting these recent past periods from a more provocative, subversive or critical perspective.

Another Time, Another Place *Scandal*
Intimate Relations *Wish You Were Here*
Prick Up Your Ears

EUROPEAN AND NON-ANGLOPHONE PERIOD FILMS

EPA Period Art Cinema (6 films)

British or international art-cinema films set in the past.

Caravaggio *Prospero's Books*
The Conformist *Quartet*
Edward II *The Sheltering Sky*

EH1 Core European and Non-Anglophone Heritage Films (11 films)

Broadly equivalent to the core British heritage film category BH1.

Babette's Feast *Il Postino*
Belle Epoque *Jane Eyre*
Cinema Paradiso *Jean de Florette*
Cyrano de Bergerac *Like Water for Chocolate*
Farinelli: Il Castrato *Manon des sources*
The Fencing Master

EH2 European and Non-Anglophone Borderline Heritage Films (8 films)

Films with some claims to heritage status, but with other characteristics (e.g. a critical perspective on the past) that problematise this.

L'Accompagnatrice	*Madame Bovary*
Antonia's Line	*La Reine Margot*
Camille Claudel	*Ridicule*
Les Enfants du paradis	*The Silences of the Palace*

US, AUSTRALIAN AND NEW ZEALAND PERIOD FILMS

ALH American Literary Heritage Films (5 films)

The US core heritage category; typically classic literary adaptations.

The Bostonians	*The Europeans*
Dangerous Liaisons	*Little Women*
Emma	

ANP US and New Zealand Postmodern/Self-Aware Heritage Films (3 films)

The Age of Innocence	*The Portrait of a Lady*
The Piano	

AGL US-made Gothic Literary Adaptations (3 films)

Bram Stoker's Dracula	*Mary Shelley's Frankenstein*
Interview with the Vampire	

AHY American History Films (8 films)

The US equivalent to the British and Irish Historical Film category.

The Crucible	*JFK*
Dances with Wolves	*The Last of the Mohicans*
Evita	*Malcolm X*
Jefferson in Paris	*Schindler's List*

ANR1 US and New Zealand Retro Films (6 films)

Overlap category (drawing in films from across other analytic categories): a catch-all classification for US and New Zealand films set in the period during or after World War II.

Evita	*JFK*
Heavenly Creatures	*Malcolm X*
I Shot Andy Warhol	*Schindler's List*

ANR2 US and New Zealand Critical Period Films (4 films)

Overlap category: films offering a critical, minority or unorthodox perspective on recent or distant historical events.

Daughters of the Dust	*I Shot Andy Warhol*
Heavenly Creatures	*Malcolm X*

CROSS-NATIONAL PERIOD FILM CLASSIFICATIONS

The following cross-national – and overlap – categories were also used in analysis, bringing together films already classified under other primary categories in this Appendix. (For example, many of the James Ivory films listed below are also BHI – British 'Core' Heritage – films, while others are ALH – American Literary Heritage – films.)

JIV All listed films directed by James Ivory (11 films)

The Bostonians
The Europeans
Heat and Dust
Howards End
Jefferson in Paris
Maurice

Quartet
The Remains of the Day
A Room with a View
Slaves of New York
Surviving Picasso

JAU All listed post-1980 period adaptations from Jane Austen (6 films)

Including significant adaptations for British television as well as feature films.

Films:
    Emma (1996)
    Persuasion (1995)*
    Sense and Sensibility (1995)
TV dramas:
    Emma (also 1996)
    Pride and Prejudice (BBC-TV, 1980)
    Pride and Prejudice (BBC-TV, 1995)

*Made for BBC-TV, but subsequently released in cinemas as a feature film.

Hierarchies of period film taste among the two survey cohorts

Period films (as listed in Question 17 of the Questionnaire) **most widely liked** by NT and TO respondents, ranked by the percentages who had **liked** them (**L**) and **seen** them (**S**). Films widely liked/seen by respondents in only **one** of the two survey cohorts are presented in *italics*.

National Trust respondents (62 = 100%)			*Time Out* respondents (30 = 100%)		
	Film	%L (S)		Film	%L (S)
1	**Sense and Sensibility** (1995) *(Austen)*	89 (95)	1	**Schindler's List**	87 (93)
2	**A Passage to India** (1984)	87 (94)	2	*Prick Up Your Ears* (1986)	83 (83)
			3	**A Room with a View** *(Ivory)*	77 (83)
=3	**Chariots of Fire** (1981)	79 (85)			
=3	**The Madness of King George** (1995)	79 (89)	=4	*The Remains of the Day* (1993) *(Ivory)*	73 (80)
			=4	*Dance with a Stranger* (1984)	73 (87)
4	*Howards End* (1992) *(Ivory)*	76 (89)			
5	*Emma* (1996) *(Austen)*	75 (82)	=5	**Babette's Feast**	70 (80)
6	**A Room with a View** (1986) *(Ivory)*	68 (71)	=5	*Another Country* (1984)	70 (77)

=7	Schindler's List (1993)	60 (66)
=7	Shadowlands (1993)	60 (68)
=8	The Remains of the Day (1993) (*Ivory*)	55 (56)
=8	The Piano (1993)	55 (61)
9	*Jane Eyre* (1995)	52 (61)
10	*The English Patient* (1996)	47 (56)
11	*Little Dorrit* (1987)	42 (47)
12	Les Enfants du paradis (1945)	39 (39)
13	Jean de Florette (1986)	35 (42)
=14	Cyrano de Bergerac (1990)	34 (37)
=14	Manon des sources (1986)	34 (35)
=15	*Richard III* (1995)	31 (34)
=15	*Evita* (1996)	31 (34)
16	Hope and Glory (1987)	27 (34)
17	Babette's Feast (1987)	24 (29)
=18	Heat and Dust (1982) (*Ivory*)	23 (24)
=18	A Handful of Dust (1988)	23 (29)

=6	Howards End (*Ivory*)	67 (77)
=6	Cyrano de Bergerac	67 (80)
=6	The Piano	67 (83)
=6	Sense and Sensibility (*Austen*)	67 (83)
=7	Manon des sources	63 (77)
=7	The Madness of King George	63 (83)
=7	A Passage to India	63 (90)
=8	*Scandal* (1989)	60 (70)
=8	Jean de Florette	60 (73)
=8	Chariots of Fire	60 (93)
=9	Shadowlands	57 (60)
=9	Les Enfants du paradis	57 (60)
=9	Heat and Dust (*Ivory*)	57 (70)
=9	*Maurice* (1987) (*Ivory*)	57 (70)
=9	*Orlando* (1992)	57 (73)
=10	A Handful of Dust	53 (60)
=10	Hope and Glory	53 (67)
=10	*Emma* (*Austen*)	53 (70)
=10	*Bram Stoker's Dracula* (1992)	53 (73)

Source: Claire Monk, analysis of Heritage Audience Survey data (1998).
For director credits and national origins of films, see the **Selective Filmography**.

Hierarchies of period film pleasures among the two survey cohorts

Comparison of the pleasures rated by NT and TO respondents as 'very' or 'quite' important to their enjoyment of period films (in response to Question 29), ranked to show which pleasures were important for the *greatest* and *smallest* proportions of NTs and TOs respectively. Pleasures which were important for respondents in one cohort but of low importance for the other are highlighted in **bold**.

	National Trust respondents (62 = 100%)		Time Out respondents (30 = 100%)		
	Most important pleasures	%	%	Most important pleasures	
1	Quality of performances/acting.	98	93	Visual enjoyment.	1
2	Accurate reproduction of period details.	97	83	Compelling, involving plots or stories.	=2
3	Looking at period costumes.	95		Quality of performances/acting.	=2
=4	**Looking at historic buildings.**	94	80	Literacy and wit of the films.	=3
=4	**Looking at landscapes/locations.**			Complexity and intelligence of the films.	=3
=5	They are high-quality, well-made films.	92		They are high-quality, well-made films.	=3
=5	Looking at period furnishings/interiors.		77	Human drama/a focus on human dilemmas.	4
=5	Literacy and wit of the films.		67	The chance to learn more about life in the past.	=5
=6	Visual enjoyment.	89		Being able to identify with the characters.	=5
=6	The chance to see respectful adaptations of important literary works.		63	The chance to learn more about important events in history.	=6
=6	Compelling, involving plots or stories.			The chance to relive the pleasures of the original novels/plays.	=6
7	The chance to relive the pleasures of the original novels/plays.	87	60	**Stories which still feel relevant today.**	7
=8	The chance to learn more about important events in history.	82		Accurate reproduction of period details.	=7
=8	Human drama/a focus on human dilemmas.		57	**They are challenging films which I have to get actively involved in to enjoy.**	=8
9	Seeing leading British actors at their best.	79		Looking at period costumes.	=8
10	The chance to learn more about life in the past.	76	50	**The pleasures of escapism.**	9
11	**Lack of explicit sex/violence/bad language.**	73	47	The chance to see respectful adaptations of important literary works.	=10
12	Complexity and intelligence of the films.	69		Watching actors/actresses I find physically attractive.	=10
	Least important pleasures			Least important pleasures	
18	**Watching actors/actresses I find physically attractive.**	42	23	Romance.	=13
19	Romance.	34		**Pride in seeing British cinema at its best.**	=13
20	**Challenging films I have to get actively involved in to enjoy.**	31		The pleasures of nostalgia.	=13
21	The films entertain me without having to work too hard.	29	17	Personal memory or family history.	14
22	**Stories which still feel relevant today.**	26	10	The films entertain me without having to work too hard.	15
			3	**Lack of explicit sex/violence/bad language.**	16

Source: Claire Monk, analysis of Heritage Audience Survey data (1998).

Selective Filmography

This selective filmography lists the films and television dramas/serials that were presented to respondents in Questions 16, 17 and 19 of the Heritage Audience Survey Questionnaire (see Appendix 2.1), following the headings and subdivisions used in the Questionnaire itself. Production details of other films and television productions that are cited in this book but were not listed in the Questionnaire are given in the text of the book itself.

The Filmography presents the lists of films and television dramas/serials for Questions 16, 17 and 19 in the order in which they were seen by respondents, as follows:

Non-period films listed in Question 16:
    US and Canadian
    British and Irish
    Australian and New Zealand
    Continental European
    Other non-Anglophone
Period films listed in Question 17:
    British and Irish
    European and non-Anglophone
    US, Australian and New Zealand
British period television dramas/serials listed in Question 19

Data for each entry are presented in the following order: UK release title; director(s); registered country/ies of origin; year (usually the date of the first public screening). As the registered nationalities of films are determined by production companies and funding sources, these may differ from the nationality/region under which films were classified in the Questionnaire (with reference to cultural, as much as economic, criteria).

Here and throughout the book, the following abbreviations are used:

BBC: British Broadcasting Corporation
BFI: British Film Institute
C4: Channel Four television, UK
ITV: Independent Television network, UK
LWT: London Weekend Television
TV: Television
Aus: Australia

Bel: Belgium
Can: Canada
Den: Denmark
Fin: Finland
Fr: France
Ger: Germany
HK: Hong Kong
Ire: Ireland
It: Italy
Jap: Japan
Mex: Mexico
Neth: Netherlands
Nor: Norway
NZ: New Zealand
Pol: Poland
Por: Portugal
Sp: Spain
Swe: Sweden
Swi: Switzerland
Tai: Taiwan
UK: United Kingdom
USA: United States of America
USSR: Union of Soviet Socialist Republics

NON-PERIOD FILMS

Non-period films listed in Q16a: US and Canadian (58)

Amateur (Hal Hartley, USA, 1994)
Basic Instinct (Paul Verhoeven, USA, 1992)
Big Night (Stanley Tucci, USA, 1994)
Blade Runner (Ridley Scott, USA, 1982)
Blood Simple (Joel and Ethan Coen, USA, 1984)
Clueless (Amy Heckerling, USA, 1995)
The Confessional (Robert Lepage, Can/UK/Fr, 1995)
Crash (David Cronenberg, Can/USA, 1996)
Desert Hearts (Donna Deitch, USA, 1985)
Do the Right Thing (Spike Lee, USA, 1989)
Edward Scissorhands (Tim Burton, USA, 1990)
Everyone Says I Love You (Woody Allen, USA, 1996)
Exotica (Atom Egoyan, Can/UK/Fr, 1994)
Fargo (Joel and Ethan Coen, USA, 1995)
Fatal Attraction (Adrian Lyne, USA, 1987)
The Fifth Element (Luc Besson, Fr, 1997)[a]
First Wives' Club (Hugh Wilson, USA, 1996)
Forrest Gump (Robert Zemeckis, USA, 1994)
Goodfellas (Martin Scorsese, USA, 1990)
Groundhog Day (Harold Ramis, USA, 1993)

Independence Day (Roland Emmerich, USA, 1996)
Jesus of Montreal (Denys Arcand, Can, 1989)
Jurassic Park (Steven Spielberg, USA, 1993)
Kids (Larry Clark, USA, 1994)
The Last Action Hero (John McTiernan, USA, 1993)
Lethal Weapon (Richard Donner, USA, 1987)
Mars Attacks! (Tim Burton, USA, 1996)
The Mask (Chuck Russell, USA, 1994)
Mean Streets (Martin Scorsese, USA, 1973)
Men in Black (Barry Sonnenfeld, USA, 1997)
Mighty Aphrodite (Woody Allen, USA, 1995)
Mrs Doubtfire (Chris Columbus, USA, 1993)
My Own Private Idaho (Gus van Sant, USA, 1991)
The Naked Lunch (David Cronenberg, Can/UK/Jap, 1991)
Natural Born Killers (Oliver Stone, USA, 1994)
Nine Months (Chris Columbus, USA, 1995)
The People vs Larry Flynt (Milos Forman, USA, 1996)
Philadelphia (Jonathan Demme, USA, 1993)
The Player (Robert Altman, USA, 1992)
Pulp Fiction (Quentin Tarantino, USA, 1994)
Reservoir Dogs (Quentin Tarantino, USA, 1991)
Se7en (David Fincher, USA, 1996)
Short Cuts (Robert Altman, USA, 1993)
The Silence of the Lambs (Jonathan Demme, USA, 1991)
Slaves of New York (James Ivory, USA, 1989)
Sleepless in Seattle (Nora Ephron, USA, 1993)
Speed (Jan de Bont, USA, 1994)
Star Wars (George Lucas, USA, 1977) (reissued in the late 1990s)
SubUrbia (Richard Linklater, USA, 1997)
The Sweet Hereafter (Atom Egoyan, Can, 1997)
Taxi Driver (Martin Scorsese, USA, 1977) (reissued in the late 1990s)
Thelma and Louise (Ridley Scott, USA, 1991)
To Die For (Gus Van Sant, USA, 1995)
True Lies (James Cameron, USA, 1994)
The Usual Suspects (Bryan Singer, USA, 1995)
Vertigo (Alfred Hitchcock, USA, 1958) (reissued in the late 1990s)
Waiting to Exhale (Forest Whitaker, USA, 1995)
William Shakespeare's Romeo + Juliet (Baz Luhrmann, USA, 1996)

Non-period films listed in Q16b: British and Irish (44)

Bhaji on the Beach (Gurinder Chadha, UK, 1993)
Blue (Derek Jarman, UK, 1993)
Brassed Off (Mark Herman, USA/UK, 1996)
The Browning Version (Mike Figgis, UK, 1994)
Butterfly Kiss (Michael Winterbottom, UK, 1994)
Carla's Song (Ken Loach, UK/Sp/Ger, 1996)
Close My Eyes (Stephen Poliakoff, UK, 1991)
The Cook, the Thief, his Wife and her Lover (Peter Greenaway, Fra/Neth/UK, 1989)

The Crying Game (Neil Jordan, UK/Jap, 1992)
Damage (Louis Malle, Ger/UK/Fr, 1992)
Darklands (Julian Richards, UK, 1996)
Educating Rita (Lewis Gilbert, UK, 1983)
Face (Antonia Bird, UK, 1997)
Fever Pitch (David Evans, UK, 1997)
A Fish Called Wanda (Charles Crichton, UK, 1988)
Four Weddings and a Funeral (Mike Newell, UK, 1994)
The Full Monty (Peter Cattaneo, USA/UK, 1997)
Funny Bones (Peter Chelsom, UK/USA, 1995)
Hear My Song (Peter Chelsom, Ire/UK, 1992)
Hidden Agenda (Ken Loach, UK, 1990)
High Hopes (Mike Leigh, UK, 1988)
I.D. (Philip Davis, UK, 1994)
In the Bleak Midwinter (Kenneth Branagh, UK, 1995)
In the Name of the Father (Jim Sheridan, Ire/UK, 1993)
Life Is Sweet (Mike Leigh, UK, 1990)
Leon the Pig Farmer (Vadim Jean and Gary Sinyor, UK, 1992)
London (Patrick Keiller, UK, 1994)
The Long Good Friday (John Mackenzie, UK, 1979)
My Beautiful Laundrette (Stephen Frears, UK, 1985)
My Left Foot (Jim Sheridan, Ire/UK, 1989)
Naked (Mike Leigh, UK, 1993)
Nil By Mouth (Gary Oldman, UK/Fr, 1997)
Personal Services (Terry Jones, UK, 1987)
Peter's Friends (Kenneth Branagh, UK, 1992)
The Pillow Book (Peter Greenaway, Neth/Fr/UK, 1996)
Priest (Antonia Bird, UK, 1994)
Secrets and Lies (Mike Leigh, Fr/UK, 1996)
Shallow Grave (Danny Boyle, UK, 1994)
Shirley Valentine (Lewis Gilbert, UK, 1989)
Shooting Fish (Stefan Schwartz, UK, 1997)
Shopping (Paul Anderson, UK, 1993)
Trainspotting (Danny Boyle, UK, 1996)
True Blue (Ferdinand Fairfax, UK, 1996)
Twin Town (Kevin Allen, UK, 1997)

Non-period films listed in Q16c: Australian and New Zealand (9)

The Adventures of Priscilla, Queen of the Desert (Stephan Elliott, Aus, 1994)
An Angel at My Table (Jane Campion, NZ, 1990)
Babe (Chris Noonan, Aus/USA, 1995)
Crocodile Dundee (Peter Faiman, Aus, 1986)
Muriel's Wedding (P. J. Hogan, Aus/Fr, 1994)
Once Were Warriors (Lee Tamahori, NZ, 1994)
Shine (Scott Hicks, Aus, 1996)
Strictly Ballroom (Baz Luhrmann, Aus, 1992)
Sweetie (Jane Campion, NZ, 1989)

Non-period films listed in Question 16d: Continental European (26)

Antonia's Line (Marleen Gorris, Neth/Bel/UK, 1996)[b]
L'Appartement (Gilles Mimouni, Fr, 1997)
Beyond the Clouds (Michelangelo Antonioni and Wim Wenders, It/Fr/Ger, 1995)
Breaking the Waves (Lars Von Trier, Den/Swe/Fr/Neth/Nor, 1996)
Un Cœur en hiver (Claude Sautet, Fr, 1991)
Dear Diary (Nanni Moretti, It, 1994)
Delicatessen (Marc Caro and Jean-Pierre Jeunet, Fr, 1991)
Drifting Clouds (Aki Kaurismäki, Fin, 1996)
French Twist (Gazon maudit) (Josiane Balasko, Fr, 1995)
La Haine (Mathieu Kassovitz, Fr, 1995)
High Heels (Pedro Almodóvar, Sp, 1991)
Jamón, Jamón (Bigas Luna, Sp, 1992)
Man Bites Dog (Rémy Belvaux, Andre Bonzel and Benoît Poelvoorde, Bel, 1992)
Mina Tannenbaum (Martine Dugowson, Fr, 1993)
Monsieur Hire (Patrice Leconte, Fr, 1989)
Nelly and Monsieur Arnaud (Claude Sautet, Fr, 1996)
The Proprietor (Ismail Merchant, Fr/UK/USA, 1996)[c]
Savage Nights (Les Nuits fauves) (Cyril Collard, Fr, 1992)
Stealing Beauty (Bernardo Bertolucci, It/UK/Fr, 1995)[d]
Three Colours: Blue (Krzysztof Kieslowski, Fr/Pol/Swi/UK, 1992)
Three Colours: Red (Krzysztof Kieslowski, Pol/Fr/Swi, 1993)
Three Colours: White (Krzysztof Kieslowski, Fr/Pol/Swi, 1994)
The Vanishing (George Sluizer, Neth, 1988) (original Dutch version)
Les Visiteurs (Jean-Marie Poiré, Fr, 1993)
Wild Target (Cible émouvante) (Pierre Salvatori, Fr, 1993)
Women on the Verge of a Nervous Breakdown (Pedro Almodóvar, Sp, 1988)

Non-period films listed in Q16e: Other non-Anglophone (7)

Bandit Queen (Shekhar Kapur, India/UK, 1994)
Chungking Express (Wong Kar Wei, HK, 1994)
Eat, Drink, Man, Woman (Ang Lee, Tai/USA, 1994)
El Mariachi (Robert Rodriguez, Mex, 1992)
Sonatine (Takeshi Kitano, Jap, 1993)
The Wedding Banquet (Ang Lee, Tai/USA, 1993)
Yaaba (Idrissa Ouedraogo, Burkina Faso/Swi/Fr, 1989)

PERIOD FILMS AND PERIOD TELEVISION DRAMAS/SERIALS

Period films listed in Q17a: British and Irish (52)

Angels and Insects (Philip Haas, UK/USA, 1995)
Anne Devlin (Pat Murphy, Ire, 1984)
Another Country (Marek Kanievska, UK, 1984)
Another Time, Another Place (Michael Radford, UK, 1983)
Caravaggio (Derek Jarman, UK, 1986)

Carrington (Christopher Hampton, UK/Fr, 1995)
Century (Stephen Poliakoff, UK, 1993)
Chariots of Fire (Hugh Hudson, UK, 1981)
Comrades (Bill Douglas, UK, 1987)
Dance with a Stranger (Mike Newell, UK, 1984)
December Bride (Thaddeus O'Sullivan, UK/Ire, 1990)
Distant Voices, Still Lives (Terence Davies, UK, 1988)
Edward II (Derek Jarman, UK, 1992)
Enchanted April (Mike Newell, UK, 1992)
The English Patient (Anthony Minghella, USA, 1996)
Hamlet (Kenneth Branagh, UK/USA, 1996)
A Handful of Dust (Charles Sturridge, UK, 1988)
Heat and Dust (James Ivory, UK, 1983)
Hedd Wyn (Paul Turner, UK, 1992)
Hope and Glory (John Boorman, UK, 1987)
The Hour of the Pig (Leslie Megahey, Fr/UK, 1993)
Howards End (James Ivory, UK/Jap, 1992)
Intimate Relations (Philip Goodhew, UK/Can, 1996)
Jude (Michael Winterbottom, UK, 1996)
The Krays (Peter Medak, UK, 1990)
Land and Freedom (Ken Loach, UK/Sp/Ger/It, 1995)
Little Dorrit (Christine Edzard, UK, 1988)
The Madness of King George (Nicholas Hytner, UK, 1994)
Maurice (James Ivory, UK, 1987)
Michael Collins (Neil Jordan, UK/Ire/USA, 1996)
A Month in the Country (Pat O'Connor, UK, 1987)
Orlando (Sally Potter, UK/Russia/Fra/It/Neth, 1992)
A Passage to India (David Lean, UK, 1985)
Persuasion (Roger Michell, BBC-TV, UK/Fr/USA, 1995)[c]
Prick Up Your Ears (Stephen Frears, UK, 1987)
Prospero's Books (Peter Greenaway, Fr/It/Neth/UK/Jap, 1991)
Quartet (James Ivory, UK/Fr, 1981)
The Remains of the Day (James Ivory, USA/UK, 1993)
Restoration (Michael Hoffman, USA, 1995)
Richard III (Richard Loncraine, UK/USA, 1995)
Rob Roy (Michael Caton-Jones, USA, 1995)
A Room with a View (James Ivory, UK, 1985)
Scandal (Michael Caton-Jones, UK, 1989)
Sense and Sensibility (Ang Lee, USA/UK, 1995)
Shadowlands (Richard Attenborough, UK, 1993)
The Shooting Party (Alan Bridges, UK, 1985)
Surviving Picasso (James Ivory, USA, 1996)[f]
Tom & Viv (Brian Gilbert, UK, 1994)
Where Angels Fear to Tread (Charles Sturridge, UK, 1991)
White Mischief (Michael Radford, UK/Kenya, 1987)
Wilde (Brian Gilbert, UK/Ger/Jap, 1997)
Wish You Were Here (David Leland, UK, 1987)

Period films listed in Q17b: European and non-Anglophone (23)

L'Accompagnatrice (Claude Miller, Fr, 1992)
Antonia's Line (Marleen Gorris, Neth/Bel/UK, 1996)
Babette's Feast (Gabriel Axel, Den, 1987)
Belle Epoque (Fernando Trueba, Sp/Por/Fr, 1992)
Camille Claudel (Bruno Nuytten, Fr, 1988)
Cinema Paradiso (Giuseppe Tornatore, It/Fr, 1989)
The Conformist (Bernardo Bertolucci, It/Fr/West Ger, 1970)
Cyrano de Bergerac (Jean-Paul Rappeneau, Fr, 1990)
Les Enfants du paradis (Marcel Carné, Fr, 1945)
Farinelli: Il Castrato (Gérard Corbiau, It/Bel/Fr, 1994)
The Fencing Master (Pedro Olea, Sp, 1992)
Jane Eyre (Franco Zeffirelli, UK/It/Fr/USA, 1996)
Jean de Florette (Claude Berri, Fr/Swi/It, 1986)
Like Water for Chocolate (Alfonso Arau, Mex, 1992)
Madame Bovary (Claude Chabrol, Fr, 1991)
Manon des sources (Claude Berri, It/Fr/Swi, 1986)
Mediterraneo (Gabriele Salvatores, It, 1991)
Il Postino (Michael Radford, Fr/It/Bel, 1994)
La Reine Margot (Patrice Chéreau, Fr, 1995)
Ridicule (Patrice Leconte, Fr, 1996)
A Self-Made Hero (Jacques Audiard, Fr, 1996)
The Sheltering Sky (Bernardo Bertolucci, UK/It, 1990)[g]
The Silences of the Palace (Moufida Tlatli, Fr/Tunisia, 1994)

Period films listed in Q17c: USA, Australian and New Zealand (22)

The Age of Innocence (Martin Scorsese, USA, 1994)
The Bostonians (James Ivory, USA/UK, 1984)
Bram Stoker's Dracula (Francis Ford Coppola, USA, 1992)
The Crucible (Nicholas Hytner, USA, 1996)
Dances with Wolves (Kevin Costner, USA, 1990)
Dangerous Liaisons (Stephen Frears, USA, 1988)
Daughters of the Dust (Julie Dash, USA, 1991)
Emma (Douglas McGrath, USA/UK, 1996)
The Europeans (James Ivory, UK, 1979)
Evita (Alan Parker, USA, 1996)
Heavenly Creatures (Peter Jackson, NZ, 1994)
Interview with the Vampire (Neil Jordan, USA, 1994)
I Shot Andy Warhol (Mary Harron, USA/UK, 1996)
Jefferson in Paris (James Ivory, Fr/USA, 1995)
JFK (Oliver Stone, USA, 1992)
The Last of the Mohicans (Michael Mann, USA, 1992)
Little Women (Gillian Armstrong, USA, 1994)
Malcolm X (Spike Lee, USA, 1992)
Mary Shelley's Frankenstein (Kenneth Branagh, USA, 1994)
The Piano (Jane Campion, Aus/NZ/Fr, 1993)
The Portrait of a Lady (Jane Campion, UK/USA, 1996)
Schindler's List (Steven Spielberg, USA, 1993)

BRITISH PERIOD TELEVISION DRAMAS/SERIALS LISTED IN Q19 (22)

Brideshead Revisited (Michael Lindsay-Hogg and Charles Sturridge, ITV: Granada, 1981)
Clarissa (Robert Bierman, BBC-TV, 1991)
The Duchess of Duke Street (Bill Bain, Cyril Coke et al, BBC-TV, 1976–7)
Elizabeth R (Roderick Graham et al, BBC-TV, 1971)
Emma (Diarmuid Lawrence, ITV: Meridian, 1996)
The Far Pavilions (Peter Duffell, C4, 1984)
The Forsyte Saga (James Cellan Jones and David Giles, BBC-TV, 1967)
Fortunes of War (James Cellan Jones, BBC-TV, 1987)
Ivanhoe (Stuart Orme, BBC-TV, 1997)
The Jewel in the Crown (Christopher Morahan and Jim O'Brien, ITV: Granada, 1983)
The Mayor of Casterbridge (David Giles, BBC-TV, 1978)
Middlemarch (Anthony Page, BBC-TV, 1994)
Moll Flanders (David Attwood, ITV: Granada, 1996)
Nostromo (Alastair Reid, BBC-TV, 1996)
The Pallisers (Hugh David and Ronald Wilson, BBC-TV, 1974)
Poldark (Paul Annett, Kenneth Ives et al, BBC-TV, 1975–7)
Pride and Prejudice (Cyril Coke, BBC-TV, 1980)
Pride and Prejudice (Simon Langton, BBC-TV, 1995)
Rhodes (David Drury, BBC-TV, 1996)
The Singing Detective (Jon Amiel, BBC-TV, 1986)
The Tenant of Wildfell Hall (Mike Barker, BBC-TV, 1996)
Upstairs Downstairs (Bill Bain, Christopher Hodson et al, ITV: LWT, 1971–5)

NOTES

a. Although *The Fifth Element* was a French film in terms of funding and its director's nationality (with costumes designed by Jean-Paul Gaultier), it combined a futuristic New York setting, Hollywood stars and a blockbuster aesthetic with no evident French cultural characteristics.
b. *Antonia's Line* was classified as both a period and a non-period film in the questionnaire and subsequent analysis.
c. Although most continental European films listed in the questionnaire were non-Anglophone, *The Proprietor* and *Stealing Beauty* (included because both had ingredients which might, hypothetically, appeal to heritage-film viewers) were exceptions, combining English-language dialogue with European settings, themes and (in part) casting.
d. See Note c.
e. BBC-TV production, later released in cinemas.
f. *Surviving Picasso* – US-funded, with British stars but a European narrative setting – was classified as 'British' in the questionnaire but, on reflection, could sensibly have been placed in the European period films list.
g. European co-production with American protagonists and stars, a North African setting and multilingual dialogue.

Bibliography

Ackroyd, Peter, 'Pictures from Italy' [review: *A Room with a View*], *Spectator*, 19 April 1986, p. 38.

Althusser, Louis, 'Ideology and Ideological State Apparatuses' in *Lenin and Philosophy and other Essays*, by Althusser, translated by Ben Brewster (New York: Monthly Review Press, 1971), pp. 121–76.

Anon., 'From argument to abuse' [editorial], *Sunday Times*, 24 January 1988, p. B2.

Anon., 'The class war is over' [editorial], *Guardian*, 22 August 2002, p. 19.

Ashby, Justine and Andrew Higson (eds), *British Cinema, Past and Present* (London: Routledge, 2000).

Austin, Guy, *Contemporary French Cinema: An Introduction* (Manchester: Manchester University Press, 1996).

Austin, Thomas, 'Gendered (dis)pleasures: *Basic Instinct* and female viewers', *Journal of Popular British Cinema*, 2, 1999, pp. 4–21.

Austin, Thomas, *Hollywood, Hype and Audiences: Selling and Watching Popular Film in the 1990s* (Manchester: Manchester University Press, 2002).

Austin, Thomas, *Watching the World: Screen Documentary and Audiences* (Manchester: Manchester University Press, 2007).

Barker, Martin, 'Loving and hating *Straw Dogs*: the meanings of audience responses to a controversial film', Parts 1 and 2, *Participations*, 2.2, 2005, and 3.1, 2006 [www.participations.org].

Barker, Martin with Kate Brooks, *Knowing Audiences: Judge Dredd, its Friends, Fans and Foes* (Luton: University of Luton Press, 1998).

Barker, Martin and Julian Petley (eds), *Ill Effects: The Media and Violence Debate*, 2nd edn (London: Routledge, 2001).

Barr, Charles, 'Introduction: amnesia and schizophrenia' in *All Our Yesterdays: 90 Years of British Cinema*, ed. Barr (London: British Film Institute, 1984), pp. 1–30.

Bastin, Giselle, 'Filming the ineffable: biopics of the British royal family', *a/b: Auto/Biography Studies*, 24.1, 2009, pp. 34–52.

Baudry, Jean-Louis, 'Ideological effects of the basic cinematic apparatus', *Film Quarterly*, 28.2, 1974–5. Reprinted in *Film Theory and Criticism: Introductory Readings*, 5th edn, ed. Leo Braudy and Marshall Cohen (Oxford: Oxford University Press, 1999), pp. 345–55.

Bazin, André, 'In defence of mixed cinema' in *What Is Cinema? Volume 1*, by Bazin, ed. and translated Hugh Gray (Berkeley: University of California Press, 1967), pp. 53–75.

Bennett, Tony, 'The Bond phenomenon: theorizing a popular hero', *Southern Review*, 16.2, 1983, pp. 195–225.

Bordwell, David and Noel Carroll (eds), *Post-Theory: Reconstructing Film Studies* (Madison, WI: University Press of Wisconsin, 2007).

Borgmeier, Raimund, 'Heritage film and the picturesque garden' in *Janespotting and Beyond*, ed. Eckart Voigts-Virchow (Tübingen: Gunter Narr, 2004), pp. 65–74.

Bourdieu, Pierre, *Distinction: A Social Critique of the Judgement of Taste*, translated Richard Nice (London: Routledge & Kegan Paul, 1984).

Bourne, Stephen, 'Secrets and lies: black histories and British historical films' in *British Historical Cinema*, ed. Claire Monk and Amy Sargeant (London: Routledge, 2002), pp. 47–65.

Branston, Gill, *Cinema and Cultural Modernity* (Buckingham: Open University Press, 2000).

Brindle, David, 'Teachers get more class in social shake-up', *Guardian*, 1 December 1998, p. 3.

British Film Institute National Library, *Directories and Reference Works for UK Film, Television, Video and Media*, October 1999: www.bfi.org.uk/filmtvinfo/library/publications/bibliographies/directories.pdf [5 October 2005].

Bruzzi, Stella, *Undressing Cinema: Clothing and Identity in the Movies* (London: Routledge, 1997).

CACI Limited, *Acorn User Guide 2001* (London: CACI, 2001): www.caci.co.uk/pd-caci-brochures.htm [12 November 2002].

CACI website: www.caci.co.uk [12 November 2002, 10 August 2006 and later dates].

Cardwell, Sarah, *Adaptation Revisited: Television and the Classic Novel* (Manchester: Manchester University Press, 2002).

Caviar (Cinema and Video Industry Audience Research), *Caviar 10*, Volumes I–III (London: Caviar/BMRB International [British Market Research Bureau], 1993).

Caviar, *Caviar 12*, Volumes I–III (London: Caviar/BMRB International, 1995).

Christiansen, Rupert, 'Biting the dust', *Harpers & Queen*, June 1988, pp. 119–21.

Christie, Ian, 'The Scorsese interview', *Sight & Sound*, 4.2, February 1994. Republished as 'Passion and restraint' in *Film/Literature/Heritage*, ed. Ginette Vincendeau (London: British Film Institute, 2001), pp. 66–72.

Church Gibson, Pamela, 'Fewer weddings and more funerals: changes in the heritage film' in *British Cinema of the 90s*, ed. Robert Murphy (London: British Film Institute, 2000), pp. 115–24.

Church Gibson, Pamela, 'From dancing queen to plaster virgin: *Elizabeth* and the end of English heritage?', *Journal of Popular British Cinema*, 5, 2002, pp. 133–41.

Church Gibson, Pamela, 'Otherness, transgression and the postcolonial perspective: Patricia Rozema's *Mansfield Park*' in *Janespotting and Beyond*, ed. Eckart Voigts-Virchow (Tübingen: Gunter Narr, 2004), pp. 51–63.

Clinch, Minty, review of *A Room with a View*, *Midweek* [London], 10 April 1986, p. 8.

Clinch, Minty, 'James and Hugh and Maurice too' [feature on *Maurice*], *Observer* magazine, 25 October 1987, pp. 42–4.

Cohen, Nick, 'How our schools are failing the poor', *Evening Standard* [London], 17 January 2005, p. 15.

Comolli, Jean-Luc and Jean Narboni, 'Cinema/ideology/criticism', *Screen*, 12:3, 1971, pp. 27–36. Reprinted in *Film Theory and Criticism: Introductory Readings*, 5th edn, ed. Leo Braudy and Marshall Cohen (New York: Oxford University Press, 1999), pp. 752–9.

Cook, Pam, *Fashioning the Nation: Costume and Identity in British Cinema* (London: British Film Institute, 1996).

Cook, Pam, 'Neither here nor there: national identity in Gainsborough costume drama' in *Dissolving Views*, ed. Andrew Higson (London: Cassell, 1996), pp. 51–65.

Cook, Pam, '*The Age of Innocence*' [review], *Sight & Sound*, 4:2, February 1994. Republished in *Film/Literature/Heritage*, ed. Ginette Vincendeau (London: British Film Institute, 2001), pp. 161–4.

Corner, John and Sylvia Harvey (eds), *Enterprise and Heritage: Crosscurrents of National Culture* (London: Routledge, 1991).

Craig, Cairns, 'Rooms without a view', *Sight & Sound*, 1:2, June 1991. Republished in *Film/Literature/Heritage*, ed. Ginette Vincendeau (London: British Film Institute, 2001), pp. 3–6.

Dave, Paul, 'The bourgeois paradigm and heritage cinema', *New Left Review*, 224, 1997, pp. 111–26.

Dave, Paul, *Visions of England: Class and Culture in Contemporary Cinema* (Oxford: Berg, 2006).

Dinsmore-Tuli, Uma, *The Domestication of Film: Video, Cinephilia and the Collecting and Viewing of Videotapes in the Home*, PhD thesis, Goldsmiths College, University of London, 1998.

Dodd, Philip, 'An English inheritance' [editorial], *Sight & Sound*, 1:2, June 1991, p. 3.

Dyer, Richard, 'Feeling English', *Sight & Sound*, 4:3, March 1994, pp. 16–19.

Dyer, Richard, 'Heritage cinema in Europe' in *Encyclopedia of European Cinema*, ed. Ginette Vincendeau (London: British Film Institute/Cassell, 1995), pp. 204–5.

Dyer, Richard and Ginette Vincendeau, leaflet publicising *The European 'Heritage' Film: A Workshop Conference*, University of Warwick, 24 June 1995.

Dyja, Eddie (ed.), *BFI Film and Television Handbook 2001* (London: British Film Institute, 2001).

Ellis, John, 'The quality film adventure: British critics and the cinema, 1942–1948' in *Dissolving Views*, ed. Andrew Higson (London: Cassell, 1996), pp. 66–93. Expanded and revised from Ellis, 'Art, culture, and quality', *Screen*, 19:3, 1978, pp. 9–49.

Ezard, John, 'Underclass now knows its place in revised social classification', *Guardian*, 15 December 1997, p. 5.

Finch, Mark and Richard Kwietniowski, 'Melodrama and *Maurice*: homo is where the het is', *Screen*, 29:3, 1988, pp. 72–80.

Forbes, Jill, '*Maurice*' [review], *Monthly Film Bulletin*, November 1987, pp. 338–9.

French, Philip, 'The Forster connection' [review: *A Room with a View*], *Observer*, 13 April 1986, p. 23.

Friedman, Lester (ed.) *British Cinema and Thatcherism,* 1st edn (London: University College London Press, 1993).

Fuller, Graham, 'Battle for Britain', *Film Comment*, 24:4, July/August 1988, pp. 62–8.

Gelder, Ken, *Subcultures: Cultural Histories and Social Practice* (Abingdon: Routledge, 2007).

Giddings, Robert and Keith Selby (eds), *The Classic Serial on Television and Radio* (Basingstoke: Palgrave, 2001).

Gottschalk, Peter and Timothy S. Smeeding, *Empirical Evidence on Income Inequality in Industrialized Countries*, Luxembourg Income Study Working Paper No. 154 (New York: Maxwell School of Citizenship and Public Affairs, Syracuse University, 1999).

Hardie, Amy, 'Rollercoasters and reality: a study of big screen documentary audiences 2002–2007', *Participations*, 5:1, 2008 [www.participations.org].

Harper, Sue, 'Historical pleasures: Gainsborough costume melodrama' in *Home Is Where the Heart Is: Studies in Melodrama and the Woman's Film*, ed. Christine Gledhill (London: British Film Institute, 1987).

Harper, Sue, *Picturing the Past: The Rise and Fall of the British Costume Film* (London: British Film Institute, 1994).

Hartley, L. P., *The Go-Between* (London: Hamish Hamilton, 1953).

Hebdige, Dick, *Subculture: The Meaning of Style* (London: Methuen, 1979).

Hensher, Philip, 'Only gay in the village? Not quite', *Independent*, 27 September 2010 [www.independent.co.uk/opinion/commentators/philip-hensher/philip-hensher-only-gay-in-the-village-not-quite-2090321.html].

Hewison, Robert, *The Heritage Industry: Britain in a Climate of Decline* (London: Methuen, 1987).

Higson, Andrew, 'Re-presenting the national past: nostalgia and pastiche in the heritage film' in *British Cinema and Thatcherism*, ed. Lester Friedman (London: University College London Press, 1993), pp. 109–29.

Higson, Andrew, *Waving the Flag: Constructing a National Cinema in Britain* (Oxford: Oxford University Press, 1995).

Higson, Andrew (ed.), *Dissolving Views: Key Writings on British Cinema* (London: Cassell, 1996).

Higson, Andrew, 'The heritage film and British cinema' in *Dissolving Views*, ed. Higson (London: Cassell, 1996), pp. 232–48.

Higson, Andrew, *English Heritage, English Cinema: Costume Drama since 1980* (Oxford: Oxford University Press, 2003).

Higson, Andrew, 'English heritage, English literature, English cinema: selling Jane Austen to movie audiences in the 1990s' in *Janespotting and Beyond*, ed. Eckart Voigts-Virchow (Tübingen: Gunter Narr, 2004), pp. 35–50.

Hill, John, *British Cinema in the 1980s* (Oxford: Oxford University Press, 1999).

Hills, Matt, *Fan Cultures* (London: Routledge, 2002).

Hipsky, Martin A., 'Anglophil(m)ia: Why does America watch Merchant–Ivory movies?', *Journal of Popular Film and Television*, 22:3, 1994, pp. 98–107.

Hoare, Sarajane, 'Actors' tweeds' [fashion tie-in with *Maurice*], *Vogue* (UK), November 1987, pp. 270–5.

Hollinghurst, Alan, 'Suppressive nostalgia' [review: *Maurice*], *Times Literary Supplement*, 6–12 November 1987, p. 1225.

Internet Movie Database [website], message boards on *Maurice*: www.imdb.com/title/tt0093512/board [28 March 2011].

Jameson, Fredric, 'Post-modernism, or the cultural logic of late capitalism', *New Left Review*, 146, 1984, pp. 53–92.

Jancovich, Mark, 'Genre and the audience: genre classifications and cultural distinctions in the mediation of *The Silence of the Lambs*' in *Hollywood Spectatorship*, ed. Melvyn Stokes and Richard Maltby (London: British Film Institute, 2001), pp. 33–45.

Jarman, Derek, 'Freedom fighter for a vision of the truth', *Sunday Times*, 17 January 1988, p. C9.

Jenkins, Henry, *Textual Poachers: Television Fans and Participatory Culture* (London: Routledge, 1992).

Jenkins, Henry, 'Reception theory and audience research: the mystery of the vampire's kiss' in *Reinventing Film Studies*, ed. Christine Gledhill and Linda Williams (London: Arnold, 2000), pp. 165–82.

K., David, 'Re-seeing *Maurice*', *Nightcharm* [online gay magazine], undated, www.nightcharm.com/features/maurice [10 April 2007].

Kerr, Sarah, 'Janet Maslin: Why can't the *New York Times* movie critic tell us what she really thinks?', *Slate* [online magazine], 5 June 1999, www.slate.com/id/29811/ [30 June 2006].

Kerr, Paul, 'Classic serials: to be continued', *Screen*, 23.1, 1982, pp. 6–19.

King, Justine, 'Crossing thresholds: the contemporary British woman's film' in *Dissolving Views*, ed. Andrew Higson (London: Cassell, 1996), pp. 216–31. Revised and updated as Justine Ashby, '"It's been emotional": reassessing the contemporary British woman's film' in *British Women's Cinema*, ed. Melanie Bell and Melanie Williams (Abingdon: Routledge, 2010), pp. 153–69.

Kuhn, Annette, *An Everyday Magic: Cinema and Cultural Memory* (London: I. B. Tauris, 2002).

Kureishi, Hanif, 'England, bloody England', *Guardian*, 15 January 1988, p. 19.

Lacey, Joanne, 'Seeing through happiness: Hollywood musicals and the construction of the American dream in Liverpool in the 1950s', *Journal of Popular British Cinema*, 2, 1999, pp. 54–65.

Landy, Marcia (ed.), *The Historical Film: History and Memory in Media* (New Brunswick, NJ: Rutgers University Press, 2001).

Light, Alison, 'Englishness' [letter], *Sight & Sound*, 1:3, July 1991, p. 63.

Lovell, Alan, 'The British cinema: the known cinema?' in *The British Cinema Book*, 1st edn, ed. Robert Murphy (London: British Film Institute, 1997), pp. 235–43.

Luckett, Moya, 'Image and nation in 1990s British cinema' in *British Cinema of the 90s*, ed. Robert Murphy (London: British Film Institute, 2000), pp. 88–99.

Lynch, Deidre (ed.), *Janeites: Jane Austen's Disciples and Devotees* (Princeton: Princeton University Press, 2000).

Lyttle, John, 'Knights in white flannel', *City Limits*, 29 March–5 April 1990, pp. 18–20.

McKechnie, Kara, 'Taking liberties with the monarch: the royal bio-pic in the 1990s' in *British Historical Cinema*, ed. Claire Monk and Amy Sargeant (London: Routledge, 2002), pp. 217–36.

Mantel, Hilary, 'Tasteful repro' [review: *Maurice*], *Spectator*, 21 November 1987, pp. 87–8.

Mayne, Judith, *Cinema and Spectatorship* (London: Routledge, 1993).

Medhurst, Andy, 'Dressing the part', *Sight & Sound*, 6:6, June 1996. Republished in *Film/Literature/Heritage*, ed. Ginette Vincendeau (London: British Film Institute, 2001), pp. 11–14.

Monk, Claire, *Sex, Politics and the Past: Merchant Ivory, the Heritage Film and its Critics in 1980s and 1990s Britain*, MA dissertation, British Film Institute/Birkbeck, University of London, 1994.

Monk, Claire, 'The British "heritage film" and its critics', *Critical Survey*, 7:2, 1995, pp. 116–24.

Monk, Claire, 'The heritage film and gendered spectatorship', *Close Up: The Electronic Journal of British Cinema*, 1, 1997 [Sheffield Hallam University: available at www.shu.ac.uk/services/lc/closeup].

Monk, Claire, 'Heritage films and the British cinema audience in the 1990s', *Journal of Popular British Cinema*, 2, 1999, pp. 22–38.

Monk, Claire, 'Underbelly UK: the 1990s underclass film, masculinity, and the ideologies of "new" Britain' in *British Cinema, Past and Present*, ed. Justine Ashby and Andrew Higson (London: Routledge, 2000), pp. 274–87.

Monk, Claire, 'Sexuality and heritage', *Sight & Sound*, 5:10, October 1995. Republished as 'Sexuality and heritage' in *Film/Literature/Heritage*, ed. Ginette Vincendeau (London: British Film Institute, 2001), pp. 6–11.

Monk, Claire, '*Sense and Sensibility*' [review], *Sight & Sound*, 6:3, March 1996. Republished in *Film/Literature/Heritage*, ed. Ginette Vincendeau (London: British Film Institute, 2001), pp. 179–82.

Monk, Claire, 'Projecting a "New Britain"', *Cineaste*, 26:4, Fall 2001, pp. 34–7 and p. 42.

Monk, Claire, 'The British heritage-film debate revisited' in *British Historical Cinema*, ed. Claire Monk and Amy Sargeant (London: Routledge, 2002), pp. 176–98.

Monk, Claire and Amy Sargeant (eds), *British Historical Cinema: The History, Heritage and Costume Film* (London: Routledge, 2002).

Montgomery-Massingberd, Hugh, '*A Handful of Dust*' [review], *Daily Telegraph*, 9 June 1988, p. 10.

Mulvey, Laura, 'Visual pleasure and narrative cinema', *Screen*, 16:3, 1975, pp. 6–18. Reprinted in Sue Thornham (ed.), *Feminist Film Theory: A Reader* (Edinburgh: Edinburgh University Press, 1999) pp. 58–69.

Murphy, Robert, *Realism and Tinsel: Cinema and Society in Britain, 1939–1949* (London: Routledge, 1989).

National Trust Magazine Membership Survey, 1993 (provided by the National Trust).

National Trust Membership by Region, 30 May 1997 (provided by the National Trust).

Nichols, Bill, 'Form wars: the political unconscious of formalist theory' in *Classical Hollywood Narrative: The Paradigm Wars*, ed. Jane Gaines (Durham, NC: Duke University Press), pp. 49–78.

Office of National Statistics, 'Achievement at GCE A Level or equivalent: by gender, 1975/76 to 1997/98', *Social Trends 30* (Norwich: HMSO, 2000).

Office of National Statistics, 'Population of working age: by highest qualification' [at Spring 2001], *Regional Trends 36* (Norwich: HMSO, 2001).

Office of National Statistics, *The National Statistics Socio-Economic Classification User Manual*, Version No. 1 (Norwich: HMSO, 2002).

Office of National Statistics website: www.statistics.gov.uk/ [various dates].

Parker, Alan, *Making Movies: Cartoons by Alan Parker* (London: British Film Institute, 1998).

Peachment, Chris, '*A Passage to India*' [film review], reprinted in Tom Milne (ed.), *The Time Out Film Guide*, 1st edn (London: Penguin, 1989), p. 449.

Pidduck, Julianne, 'Of windows and country walks: frames of space and movement in 1990s Austen adaptations', *Screen*, 39:4, 1998, pp. 318–400.

Pidduck, Julianne, *Contemporary Costume Film: Space, Place and the Past* (London: British Film Institute, 2004).

Policy Studies Institute (eds Andrew Feist and Robert Hutchison), *Cultural Trends*, 2:6 (London: PSI, 1990).

Policy Studies Institute (eds uncredited), *Cultural Trends*, 3:10 (London: PSI, 1991).

Policy Studies Institute (eds Rachael Dunlop and Jeremy Eckstein), *Cultural Trends*, 6:23 (London: PSI, 1994).

Policy Studies Institute (eds uncredited), *Cultural Trends*, 25:7 (London: PSI, 1995/6).

Powrie, Phil, 'On the threshold between past and present: "alternative heritage"' in *British Cinema, Past and Present*, ed. Justine Ashby and Andrew Higson (London: Routledge, 2000), pp. 316–26.

Public Broadcasting Service (PBS) (USA) website: www.pbs.org; specifically the Masterpiece Theatre archive: www.pbs.org/wgbh/masterpiece/archive/index.html [12 June 2006].

Richards, Jeffrey, *Films and British National Identity: From Dickens to Dad's Army* (Manchester: Manchester University Press, 1997).

Roberts, Andrew, 'They hated the family, revered gay sex and loathed their country . . . we're still paying the price of the Bloomsbury Set' [feature: *Carrington*], *Daily Mail*, 9 June 1995, pp. 20–1.

Rose, Jonathan, *The Intellectual Life of the British Working Classes* (New Haven, CT: Yale University Press, 2001).

Samuel, Raphael, *Theatres of Memory, Volume 1* (London: Verso, 1994).

Samuel, Raphael, 'Dockland Dickens' in *Theatres of Memory, Volume 1*, by Samuel (London: Verso, 1994), pp. 402–5. Previously published in *Patriotism: The Making and Unmaking of British National Identity, Volume 3: National Fictions*, ed. Samuel (London: Routledge, 1989), pp. 275–85.

Sargeant, Amy, 'Making and selling heritage culture: style and authenticity in historical fictions on film and television' in *British Cinema, Past and Present*, ed. Justine Ashby and Andrew Higson (London: Routledge, 2000), pp. 301–15.

Sargeant, Amy, 'The content and the form: invoking "pastness" in three recent retro films' in *British Historical Cinema*, ed. Claire Monk and Amy Sargeant (London: Routledge, 2002), pp. 199–216.

Selfe, Melanie, 'Inflected accounts and irreversible journeys', *Participations*, 5:1, 2008 [www.participations.org].

Soila, Tytti, 'National cinema and notions of quality: the Swedish example', *The European "Heritage" Film: A Workshop Conference*, University of Warwick, 24 June 1995.

Stacey, Jackie, *Star Gazing: Hollywood Cinema and Female Spectatorship* (London: Routledge, 1994).

Stokes, Melvyn, 'Introduction: historical Hollywood spectatorship' in *Hollywood Spectatorship*, ed. Melvyn Stokes and Richard Maltby (London: British Film Institute, 2001), pp. 1–16.

Stokes, Melvyn and Richard Maltby (eds), *Hollywood Spectatorship: Changing Perceptions of Cinema Audiences* (London: British Film Institute, 2001).

Stone, Norman, 'Through a lens darkly', *Sunday Times*, 10 January 1988, pp. C1–C2.

Street, Sarah, *British National Cinema* (London: Routledge, 1997).

Street, Sarah, 'Stepping westward: the distribution of British feature films in America, and the case of *The Private Life of Henry VIII*' in *British Cinema, Past and Present*, ed. Justine Ashby and Andrew Higson (London: Routledge, 2000), pp. 316–26.

Street, Sarah, *Transatlantic Crossings: British Feature Films in the USA* (New York: Continuum, 2002).

Taylor, Helen, *Scarlett's Women: Gone With the Wind and its Female Fans* (London: Virago, 1989).

Time Out Readership Survey 97, 1997 (provided by *Time Out* magazine's advertising department).

Turner, Graeme, *British Cultural Studies: An Introduction*, 2nd edn (London: Routledge, 1996).

UK Film Council (authors Sean Perkins, David Steele and Jim Barratt), *Films in the UK 2002: Statistical Yearbook* (London: UKFC Research and Statistics Unit, 2003).

UK Film Council (authors Sean Perkins, Edmond Ng and David Steele), *RSU Statistical Yearbook 2005/06* (London: UKFC Research and Statistics Unit, 2006).

Up My Street website: www.upmystreet.com (for access to CACI Acorn neighbourhood profiles) [12–16 November 2002 and 10 August 2006].

Usher, Shaun, 'A breath-taking view . . .!' [review: *A Room with a View*], *Daily Mail*, 11 April 1986, p. 28.

Usher, Shaun, 'The gentle English conquering America' [feature: *A Room with a View*], *Daily Mail*, 14 July 1986, p. 7.

Vincendeau, Ginette (ed.), *Film/Literature/Heritage: A Sight & Sound Reader* (London: British Film Institute, 2001).

Voigts-Virchow, Eckart (ed.), *Janespotting and Beyond: British Heritage Retrovisions Since the Mid-1990s* (Tübingen: Gunter Narr, 2004).

Voigts-Virchow, Eckart, '"Corset wars": an introduction to syncretic heritage film culture since the mid-1990s' in *Janespotting and Beyond*, ed. Voigts-Virchow (Tübingen: Gunter Narr, 2004), pp. 9–31.

Watts, Janet, 'Three's company' [profile of Merchant, Ivory and Jhabvala], *Observer Magazine*, 17 June 1979, pp. 61–5.

Waugh, Thomas, *The Fruit Machine: Twenty Years of Writings on Gay Cinema* (Durham, NC: Duke University Press, 2000).

Williams, Raymond, *The Country and the City* (London: Chatto & Windus, 1973).

Wollen, Tana, 'Over our shoulders: nostalgic screen fictions for the 1980s' in *Enterprise and Heritage*, ed. John Corner and Sylvia Harvey (London: Routledge, 1991), pp. 178–93.

Wright, Patrick, *On Living in an Old Country: The National Past in Contemporary Britain* (London: Verso, 1985).

YouTube [website], user comments on *Maurice* (part 13 of 14): www.youtube.com/watch?v=ufS4-nkdSSM&feature=related [28 March 2011].

Index